ACCESS TO ORIGINS
AFFINES, ANCESTORS, AND ARISTOCRATS

Mary W. Helms

ACCESS

to ORIGINS

AFFINES
ANCESTORS and
ARISTOCRATS

University of Texas Press ⬩ Austin

First University of Texas Press edition, 1998

Requests for permission to reproduce material from this work should be sent
to Permissions, University of Texas Press, Box 7819, Austin, TX 78713-7819.

⊗ The paper used in this publication meets the minimum requirements of
American National Standard for Information Sciences–Permanence of Paper
for Printed Library Materials, ANSI Z39. 48-1984.

LIBRARY OF CONGRESS CATALOGING-IN-PUBLICATION DATA

Helms, Mary W.
    Access to origins :   affines, ancestors, and aristocrats / Mary W. Helms.
        p.   cm.
    Includes bibliographical references and index.
    ISBN 0-292-73119-1 (cloth   :   alk. paper)
        1. Kinship—Philosophy.   2. Mothers-in-law.   3. Fathers-in-law.
    4. Chiefdoms.   5. Aristocracy (Social class)   I. Title.
    GN487.H45   1998
    306.83—dc21   97-45155

We cannot reject plausible forces because we do not see them directly.

STEPHEN J. GOULD,
Jove's Thunderbolts, 1994, P. 12

CONTENTS

List of Figures   ix
Preface   xi

INTRODUCTION
1. The Setting   *3*
2. The House   *14*

PART ONE
3. The Dead   *23*
4. Ancestors   *34*
5. Affines   *55*
6. Origins   *73*

PART TWO
7. Hierarchy   *95*
8. Qualities and Aristocrats   *109*
9. Aristocrats and Affines   *121*

PART THREE
10. Structure and Communitas   *147*
11. Tangible Durability   *164*
12. Concluding Remarks   *174*

Appendix. Geographical
Distribution of Select
Ethnographic Sources   181
Notes   185
References   213
Index   253

FIGURES

1. Contexts of ancestorness and origins.
    A. The house and its emergent house ancestors. *39*
    B. The house and precedent first-principle origins. *39*
2. Affines co-opted as house ancestors. *53*
3. Affinal contexts.
    A. Affines as not-Us. *56*
    B. Others as affines. *56*
4. Affines and the dead.
    A. Affines as liminal category between the house and the dead. *69*
    B. Affines as categorical correlate of the dead. *69*
5. Avenues of affinal authority.
    A. Community leaders as independent high-level affines. *71*
    B. Community leaders as emergent lower-level affines. *71*
6. Hierarchical superiority of affines relative to the house. *100*
7. Hierarchical superiority of aristocrats relative to commoners as influenced by affinity. *123*

8. Ancestor, aristocrat, and commoner ties when aristocrats are defined as affines and as living ancestors. *125*

9. Changes in status of aristocrats and commoners related to roles as wife-givers and wife-providers. *133*

10. Access to origins when commoners are spouse-providers for aristocrats. *134*

11. Wealth items expressive of contexts of Others and origins. *167*

12. Contractual and processual perspectives of Others and origins. *177*

PREFACE

From the literary perspective of scholarship I am inclined to agree that there is only one method of discovery better than reading a book on a subject, and that is by researching and writing one. Putting this thought into practice, *Access to Origins* is the fourth volume in which I have sought to explore implications of the general hypothesis, first presented a number of years ago in *Ancient Panama* (1979), that in human cosmologies geographical distance corresponds with supernatural distance. This idea was initially suggested to me as I pondered the fact that indigenous peoples of pre-Columbian Panama, and especially the elites of the centralized polities or chiefdoms characteristic of the isthmus, tangibly embodied the qualities of the celestial realm in skillfully crafted golden ornaments frequently obtained from neighboring Colombia, a locale situated not celestially "up there" but geographically "out there"—yet apparently evocative, nonetheless, of the qualities associated with the cosmological realm "above."

Intrigued by the theoretical possibilities suggested by investigation of geographically distant or outside locales in terms of cosmography rather than of ecology, as was then the fashion, I sought to further ground the initial hypothesis in a broader, cross-cultural setting. Thus, in *Ulysses' Sail* (1988), using ethnographic data from a wide range of societies, I argued that awareness of geographically distant places, peoples, and things constitutes a valued type of esoteric knowledge often avidly sought and greatly prized as a politically useful resource by politically ambitious persons in both centralized and noncentralized polities. In the succeeding volume, *Craft and the Kingly Ideal* (1993), also broadly cross-cultural in scope, I focused on the qualities accorded tangible goods obtained from cosmographically significant distant locales and on the qualitative nature of their production and acquisition.

In the volume presented here I explore the idea that certain categories of people, especially affines (in-laws), are associated with the cosmographically charged outside world and, therefore, convey distinctive supernaturally informed qualities associated with the wider cosmos. In this volume I also return more directly to chiefdoms to explore implications of the fact that high-status elites or aristocrats very often are structurally related to the general population through marriage, and thus embody the qualities of affines relative to the populace at large.

In pursuing this research I have been informed and encouraged by the work of numerous ethnologists, many of whom are cited as references. To each of these I extend my deep appreciation and most sincere thanks. Unfortunately, it has not been possible to document in the text every source I consulted. The ethnographic and ethnohistoric investigations on which this study is based were conducted over many decades by diverse anthropologists whose published accounts vary greatly with respect to the type of information recorded, the amount of detail provided, and the manner in which material is presented. Some reports contain suggestive or fragmentary information that often was helpful to my thinking but is not sufficiently complete to be meaningful to readers of this volume without extensive explanations that would add many pages to the presentation but provide little additional useful information. Most of these sources are not cited. Some reports contain considerable useful material but present it in a scattered fashion or in a manner of reporting that would also require considerable lengthy explication to be meaningful. Some but not all of these sources are cited. Fortunately some reports not only contain reasonably complete information on some aspect of the study but also recount it in sufficiently clear and concise form to be useful to readers as examples and illustrations of the points I wish to make in my analysis. These sources are cited, and select passages are often quoted; they are also listed in the appendix for easier reference. It should be noted, too, that when several sources are cited at the end of ethnographic quotes, the first is the source of the quote; the others refer to additional relevant material either from the same or from comparable settings.

The extensive scope of ethnographic coverage that I have used in the preparation of this study and its predecessors necessitates a broad, qualitative approach to the interpretation of ethnographic data. I support and pursue this type of research because I fully concur with Rubel and Rosman's reaffirmation that "anthropology's goal has always been . . . , and still is to many of us, the understanding of human behavior, both the similarities and the differences across cultures" (1994:341). In pursuit of that end I also agree with the argument (e.g., Vansina 1990:260–262) that even if the methods usually employed in comparative analysis are far from perfect, this approach nonetheless allows us to address fundamental issues in anthropology that are usually not as readily apparent in the study of individual cultures. In addition, as a result of my extensive reading in the ethnographic record, I have become thoroughly convinced that indeed "there are uniformities and common patterns in the customs and institutions of mankind; and if we want to understand them we must take into account the common intellectual and emotional dispositions of mankind" (Fortes 1983:1–2). The following pages assert and examine some of these common dispositions as they inform basic qualitative and structural elements of social and political life, ideology, and cosmology in low-technology societies.

INTRODUCTION

*What does living mean for a
man who belongs to a
traditional culture? Above
all, it means living in
accordance with extrahuman
models, in conformity
with archetypes.*

MIRCEA ELIADE,
Cosmos and History, 1959, P. 95

1

THE SETTING

In spite of their apparent complexities and culturally specific diversities,
the fundamental constructions of human society seem to rest upon relatively few basic premises. These include individual and group identifications of Us and not-Us, or Other, and conceptualizations of spatial/
temporal parameters that contrast the here-and-now with the there-and-
then. Implied in such discriminations, essential to their very recognition,
are assignments of *qualities* of being (characteristics of inherent nature
and worth that define what it means to be Us and not-Us) and recognition of *states* of being as they are associated with the immediacy of the
here-and-now or the distanciation of the there-and-then.

For the members of any given society the attribution of qualities and
states of being to groups of living things, human and nonhuman, identifies who and what they are and defines what roles and positions they
may legitimately fill in the organization and operation of human affairs.
For social scientists interested in understanding human sociality and its
extensions into economic and political activities, ascertaining what defining qualities and states of being are applied to categories of living

things can offer major insights into the workings of human social life (Béteille 1977; Goldman 1970: chap. 1).

In this study I intend to apply this approach to an investigation of some of the circumstances that may have facilitated social inequality and political hierarchy in human affairs and led to the development of the type of centralized polities broadly referred to as "chiefdoms." (Chiefdoms can be loosely described as hierarchical forms of nonindustrial social and political organization that operate under the rubrics of kinship and in which formal leadership is legitimately monopolized by members of one or more select families or "houses," who thereby constitute a political-ideological aristocracy and a social elite relative to the general population.)[1]

Western anthropologists have thoughtfully considered the nature of such societies, and much is now understood about the dynamics of their operation. Yet many social scientists, whose own culture (responsive to its own historical contingencies) currently inculcates an idealized and "naturalized" view of the utopian Enlightenment assumptions of "equality," "freedom," and "independence" in human nature and human affairs and discourages expressions of any sort of nobility among individuals or groups, find the willing acceptance of a legitimately recognized social elite or political aristocracy almost perverse (see Flanagan and Rayner 1988:1–5; Flanagan 1989:261; Marcus 1992:295–298; D'Andrade 1995). Considered from this perspective, in which hierarchy is confused with power and submission could never be voluntary, chiefdoms often appear to be rife with oppositions and tensions not only among members of the aristocracy but also between members of the hierarchically ordered social sectors of aristocrats and commoners. How could it be otherwise? How could any population willingly tolerate an aristocracy for any length of time and why would any people regret the loss of their elite or feel frighteningly vulnerable if that should occur?

There is no denying that restrictions, competitions, factionings, and oppositions (other than external warfare per se) are common in the social and political life of chiefdoms, particularly those that are more complexly organized (Anderson 1994b:28–52). Most of these, however, express maneuverings for power and authority within the aristocracy. Tensions between aristocrats and other members of society as a condition of hierarchy may be significantly tempered in many polities because (or to the extent that) it is understood at some point that groups or categories of human beings and other, related types of living things must be accorded differentiating qualities in order to be identified and that it is right, proper (meaning legitimizing), and beneficial to do so. In other words (and casting the matter in the form of a working hypothesis), when, or to the extent that, commoners accept social elites as politically legitimate aristocrats, they do so because of their "willingness to acknowledge that in certain aspects of social life some individuals or groups are *more important* than others, in whatever terms this importance might be framed," as Petersen has put it (1993:3; Peebles and Kus 1977:431).

This point can be expanded and elucidated by recognition that, when elites are accepted as legitimate aristocrats,[2] it is because commoners regard and accept them as *qualitatively different types of beings* from themselves, and vice-versa. Indeed, it is their distinctive differentiating qualities that mark the aristocracy as both inherently and legitimately fit for the job—fit, that is, to lead a populace unified in the wish that the polity be strong and victorious, that food be plentiful, that death and destruction stay away, and that animals and women be fertile (Gluckman 1965:293). Consequently, the differentiating qualities of aristocrats relative to commoners must be more fully comprehended by scholars if we are to better understand not only how but also why chiefdoms come into being and how they operate. In other words, as Irving Goldman has argued, although we know a great deal about what aristocrats *do,* we must better understand what aristocrats *are,* because what they are lies at the heart of any understanding of why they can act as they do (1970: 4; see also Becker 1975:42–43).

As the chapter epigram by Eliade indicates, the models used to define proper human behavior in traditional societies are archetypes referencing extrahuman prototypes. Gurevich elaborates:

> the deeds of men from time immemorial were examples for posterity. Only such traditional behaviour had a moral strength. . . . A standard of human conduct was attributed to the prime men, gods, cultural heroes. Repetition of the actions going back to the heavenly archetypus connected the people with the god and gave reality to them and their conduct. Every kind of human activity—productive, social, family and even the intimate and personal—received meaning and sanction from participation in the sacral arts and observance of ritual established at "the beginning of time."
> (1969:49–50)

One of the most important archetypes defining qualitative characteristics attributed to aristocrats in centralized polities is well noted, if less well understood, in the scholarly literature: aristocrats are known to be closely associated with ancestors. More specifically, the qualities of seniority or of being "first," often expressed by concepts of primogeniture, relate aristocrats as a group to ancestral founders and creators of social order and customs, and this association with cosmological origins legitimizes their primacy and their aristocratic positions.

Yet it is insufficient to recognize a close association of aristocrats with ancestors. Aristocrats must be understood as qualitatively ancestral themselves. That is to say, we must recognize that aristocrats as a group, and especially as a ruling sector, are frequently believed by the commoner population to be literally imbued with ancestral qualities and to be distinguished as a social collectivity by *living* ancestorship that places them in a qualitatively different state or condition of being relative to commoners.

As living ancestors, aristocrats are, by definition, no longer associated solely with the cosmological here-and-now of conventional life even though they are physically alive in this time and place. Instead they reach beyond the immediate and ordinary to be contained within the more distant or more encompassing realms of the cosmological there-and-then. It follows, then, that to understand aristocracies and the nature of hierarchical and centralized polities, such as chiefdoms, we must extend the context of our investigations to include not just the polity per se or even neighboring groups but the entire cosmos within which it is centered and contained. Similarly, if aristocrats are to be regarded as qualitatively distinct living ancestors, it would be advisable to investigate the nature of ancestors in order to better understand the nature of aristocrats. It would be appropriate, too, to consider whether there are other categories of persons or other beings that are also routinely accorded an identification as living ancestor in either centralized or noncentralized societies, for the roles and characteristics accorded such groups might provide additional insights into the origins of aristocratic groups and the manner in which aristocrats evidence their exceptional status.

Groups qualitatively identified as living ancestors constitute a type of societal Other relative to the identifying unit, the societal Us. But societal Others who serve as living ancestors are also cosmological Others related to the spatial/temporal there-and-then. As such, they link the societal Us, situated in the here-and-now, with that wider, more distanced cosmological realm. Socio-cosmological Others can serve this function because of their distinctive ambiguous or liminal nature; that is, while such Others, with their own existence and being, are perceived to be qualitatively different and distinct from Us, they are also sufficiently like Us to be significantly involved with Our nature, Our space and time, and Our affairs.

Why should such ties and relationships be important for Us? Why should social-cum-cosmological Others, as living ancestors indicative of more distant time and space, be necessary in Our lives and bound to Us (Giddens 1984:181)? The reason ultimately lies in the human capacity for self-awareness, especially in the ability to "know" that birth and death exist and to seek answers to simple but profound questions of how and why. The realizations of birth and of existence are most fundamental. Cosmologies can waffle the reality of death, to some extent even deny it and turn death into a celebration of life (hence ancestors). But the reality of birth, of origins, of coming into being is the one great truth that cannot be contested and thus is recognized as truly true.

As numerous studies have documented, in nonindustrial polities, centralized and noncentralized, the life of the world (that is, the cosmos) and of all beings in the world/cosmos is believed to have been created by cosmological powers and energized by cosmological dynamics expressed in a general consubstantiality of life (Goldman 1975:22).[3] In such a system nothing is thought to be self-founding (Goodrich 1990: 283). It is believed that people per se and societies per se cannot exist or have identity, cannot live and reproduce, cannot achieve any worthwhile accomplishments by themselves but only with the assistance of, and by virtue of, the energizing vitalities of cosmological powers or beings. Consequently, a fundamental distinction is drawn in traditional cosmologies between ordinary humans and other types of cosmological beings; the latter are considered active sources of creational and energizing powers while the former are merely the created products and the recipients of that energy. In addition, only those activities that are perceived as socially beneficial and as conducted with the aid and assistance of cosmological powers are accorded social and political legitimacy in human society, and only those activities bring honor to the persons who pursue them. Contacts with the wider cosmos are therefore believed to be absolutely essential for both personal and social survival, reproduction, and esteem.

Any society's conceptual model of the universe also identifies its component parts, the nature of its organization, and the mechanisms of its functioning in terms appropriate to and comprehensible within the ordering and functioning of the earthly society. For nonindustrial societies with limited technologies the fundamental resources available for the definition, organization, and operation of earthly society are people, other animate beings of the natural world, the natural processes of life (birth, reproduction, aging, death), and the relationships among groups and individuals. Consequently, the conceptual models that inform the populace about the nature of the cosmos are also animate, personalized, often anthropomorphized, generative, and relational in form and content (cf. Horton 1979:251). Not only are society and cosmos thought to share common modes of identification, organization, and functioning but, because of those parallels, it also becomes possible, on an operational level, for particular social groups or categories of persons in the immediate earthly realm to assume concurrent identities, roles, and statuses within the broader cosmological realm, thereby directly linking and relating encapsulated society with encapsulating cosmos.

Cosmological contacts can be achieved by many means, including formal ceremony, artistic creativity, long-distance acquisitional trade, hunting, and physical and spiritual travel. Thus religious specialists, many types of skilled artists and artisans, traveler/traders, and hunters can activate links with the wider cosmos and by so doing stand as cosmological Others at least during the performance of their specific duties or abilities (Helms 1988, 1993). But other members of society may fill this role, too. Firstborns may provide cosmological connections by the quality of primacy attributed to their birth since their arrival heralds for their parents, as a reproductive couple, the initiation of connections with the fertile universe that hopefully will yield additional children. Elders create such linkages with their increasing closeness to death and imminent passage into the other realm as, occasionally, do lastborns because of the immediacy of their arrival from that place. Finally, and perhaps foremost, are affines, permanent outsiders who constitute the quintessential Other for the quintessential Us.

Affinal groups (including what is sometimes identified as the "other" moiety) are frequently associated not just with the cosmological outside in general but more specifically with access to ancestral eras or ancestral beings whose continued presence and intercession is expressed most significantly in the fruitful unrolling of the generations in legitimated marriages. Indeed, affines themselves may be identified as living representatives of ancestral beings, most notably during rituals and ceremonies, such as mortuary rites, when the existence and presence of ancestors and contact with the ancestral realm are most directly experienced (see Chapter 5).

Because affines as cosmological Others are related to the outside cosmological realm, association with affinal groups also holds potential for
social inequality and hierarchy (assuming that hierarchy, the ranked relationship of parts to the whole, "posit[s] an ontological order with a
source outside human relations" [Myers 1986:17]; see Chapter 7). Any
group identified as cosmological Other must be, by definition, different
from Us. In cosmological contexts "different" refers both to moral contrast, that is, Others are either better than or worse than we are, and to
inherent supernatural power that is greater than ours. Relationships
with such a group, again by definition, will have to recognize and ac-
commodate these qualitative differences in the relative statuses and roles
accorded the parties involved. In other words, the relationships between
home group and affinal group as cosmological Other can never be
inherently equal (though they may be deliberately moved toward this
plane by social custom and ceremony); they will always contain an element of inferiority/superiority based on the inherent hierarchical qualities accorded to all things, beings, and conditions of the wider cosmos
(Bean 1977; Turner 1977:54; Dumont 1982;[4] Viveiros de Castro 1986:
86–87; see Chapter 7).

What significance does recognition of affinal groups as living ancestors and of affinal relationships as inherently unequal and potentially
hierarchical hold for an understanding of aristocratic qualities and
aristocratic-commoner relationships in centralized polities? First, in social structural terms, aristocrats very often establish actual or formal
affinal ties with commoners and, second, in centralized polities, as in
noncentralized ones, kin-based (including affinal) relationships constitute "not merely a logical apparatus consisting of complicated rules for
terminology and marriage; [they are] instead a way of apprehending and
ordering the world, replete with implications for the evolution and organization of political life" (Lindholm 1986:337). In other words, the
hierarchically and politically superior role of aristocrats becomes much
more understandable and acceptable to the populace when (from the
commoners' point of view) aristocrats are viewed as affinal outsiders
who are qualitatively defined as inherently superior living ancestors. For
the scholar, understanding the implications of aristocrats as affines can
explain a good deal about the institutionalized right accorded such
groups not only to appropriate or coordinate a portion of other people's
labor and resources in the name of the general good but to be thought
to "deserve" to do so (Godelier 1986:188).

Yet there is more to this scenario. Identification of certain categories of persons as ancestrally related, recognition of a fundamental hierarchical principle inherent in the nature of the universe, and the essential need to effect contact with the vitalizing powers of the wider cosmos all address another basic premise underlying social life in many nonindustrial settings. In kin-based societies where physical force or coercion per se is not normally condoned as a legitimizing principle for political authority (as distinct from its role in effecting political power), the ultimate source of such authority is perceived to exist in conditions of cosmological origins. Consequently, those persons or social groups who can evidence the most privileged access to contexts of cosmological origins will be most likely to be accorded political legitimacy and political authority.[5]

If we judge from the ethnographic literature, cosmological origins will be identified with places or events situated some distance away in space/time. Given that the cosmos surrounds the earthly center in all directions and dimensions, such places or events may be located at celestially, chthonically, or cosmographically distant venues. Though removed from the here-and-now of life in the immediate society, places and conditions of cosmological origins must be contacted by the living population, whose society takes its very form and meaning from its relationship to its beginnings (Goodrich 1990:280–282). The ethnographic literature documents diverse means of accessing contexts or conditions of origins and of giving tangible form to such connections. As was mentioned above, these include (in addition to formal religious ceremonies at times of birth, initiation, marriage, and death) long-distance acquisitional trade and travel, creative artistry of all sorts, warfare, hunting, and (the focus of this work) connections with particular groups or categories of people, such as affines, elders, firstborns, and ancestors, who are believed to have special access to spatially/temporally distant origins by virtue of their identification as sociological/cosmological Others.

The legitimizing power contained in a concept of cosmological origins or beginnings is logically very simple: not only is the fact that things and beings exist the one great sacred truth that cannot be denied or contested but those things and beings that came into existence first hold ultimate primacy. Before existence there was nothing, only the cosmic void, only zero. Nothing can precede zero, and no power can exceed the potency of the original procreative forces that first created, named, and ordered the elements of the world, life forms, and human societies (cf. Goodrich 1990:280–282). The fact of this coming into being and the puissance of the original creative process and of its first products cannot be disputed. Since these are the ultimate undebatable truths, they also constitute and confer the ultimate legitimacy. Therefore, whatever person, group, or other social collectivity can evidence the most direct or effective contact with this original and most powerful primacy of being and becoming cannot be legitimately superseded by any greater force. This tenet lies at the heart of politics in kin-based society. Fundamentally it is in an effort to demonstrate precedence in effecting access to cosmological origins that politically influential persons and groups compete with each other so vigorously, so relentlessly, and in so many diverse ideological and "materialistic" ways, even to the death if necessary (cf. Allen 1981:105–106; Petersen 1993).

It is in an effort to demonstrate such legitimizing precedence that politically influential persons or groups also require the tangible presence of origins-related personages, such as affinal groups, as guests or observers at those public events (e.g., mortuary feasts, formal initiations, or political installations) when the validity of their claim to authority is publicly addressed. These presences do not simply represent "social" validations. At such times, as later chapters will discuss in more detail, the presence of living sociological Others becomes transformed into the presence of living cosmological Others who embody the legitimating witness of original creators (Kan 1989:186–187; Helms 1993: 184–185).

Looking at political life from this perspective entails viewing societies "externally," looking at how political elements claim or obtain their legitimacy by reference to contexts of origins that are situated spatially/ temporally outside or beyond the immediate living society. Petersen has suggested that hierarchically organized societies may appear most strongly or conspicuously so with reference to external or foreign audiences—other communities or populations—toward whom people may employ an exaggerated ideology of commitment to an organized hierarchy that does not necessarily function as effectively within their daily lives (1993:6, 16; see also Sahlins 1965; Poyer 1993). I further suggest that connections with cosmologically defined origins-related outside entities, including other kin groups or even other polities, are essential not only to the formal outward expression of hierarchy but also to its manifestations, however uneven, within society and that the dynamics of internal social inequality and political jockeying are expressed most vividly in reference to such contexts, too.

These, then, are the issues that will be further examined in this study. Following a further setting of the scene in Chapter 2, Part One will explore in more detail the development of the concept of ancestors, affines as cosmological Others, and the nature of cosmological origins particularly (though not exclusively) as evidenced in noncentralized societies. These themes will generate insights that will be useful, in Parts Two and Three, in exploring the qualities that are associated with the concept of aristocracy in hierarchical societies and in considering how the structural ties that relate politically dominant aristocrats with commoners in centralized polities are in keeping with such qualitative characteristics. Ultimately I argue that, to understand the development of an aristocracy and the interaction of aristocrats and commoners within any society, concepts concerning the nature of ancestors, affines, and the structure of the cosmos must be added to the investigation, for such concepts are prior to and fundamental to the "celebration" (Petersen 1993:2) of hierarchy and the consequent political centralization characteristic of chiefdoms.

Such concepts should not be regarded as mystifications or after-the-fact constructions intended to shield otherwise unpalatable political actions but, as this study will describe in some detail, as fundamental to the political process itself. The basic problem is to account for the manner in which differential access to cosmological origins becomes institutionalized and significantly monopolized by an aristocracy. To accomplish that goal we must move beyond (but not ignore) the economy and even beyond society proper and embark upon wider cosmological waters that "stretch" social systems across time and space (Giddens 1984:181).

Consideration of cosmology in cultural process in kin-based societies involves the assumption that "the society has to be thought of as including the dead, the relations with them being constitutive of it and offering the global framework within which not only all the detail of ritual and festive exchanges, but also what there is of social organization proper make sense" (Dumont 1982:230).[6] It is also within this broader context of meaning that material processes of life and the particulars of historical events are given their significance and thus their social and political force (cf. Sahlins 1976). That is to say, in order to understand the political economy of chiefdoms we must first understand the political ideology of hierarchy.[7] Some of the material and historical particulars that concretely reveal the qualities of aristocrats and structurally relate aristocrats and commoners into hierarchically organized centralized polities will be briefly discussed in Part Three, especially those conditions leading to the emergence or earlier development of chiefdoms when particular emphasis is given to establishing legitimate authority by tangible and intangible expressions of political ideology evidencing access to cosmological origins (Lindholm 1986:340; Brumfiel 1994:11; Hastorf 1990:148; Berreman 1978:236 nn. 11, 13; cf. Anderson 1994a: 75–76).

It should be reiterated that just as considering processual elements of cosmology does not mean focusing solely on the mystical or the completely immaterial, so emphasizing concepts of origins is not an exercise in the merely aged or in things benighted. On the contrary, concepts of origins contain tremendous authenticity, motivating power, and legitimacy. As Stephen Jay Gould has noted, in the history of ideas our culture prefers to abide by a model of inevitable progress that excoriates the past merely for being old (1991:16). In our contemporary world the pragmatic here-and-now is thought to be where the action really is and where the emphasis presumably should properly lie. But the particular historical experience of Western industrial culture should not be automatically universalized (Tambiah 1979:362). For nonindustrial societies, as dozens of books, journal articles, and monographs have documented, the old, or better said, the prior, is not irrelevant and the past is not over; both are still actively bound into society and recognized as part of the environment of the present, both constitute a driving force for the present, and actions undertaken within the present cannot be adequately understood without them.

For Lugbara, the "home" and the "outside" together form a conceptualization of the totality of human experience.

JOHN MIDDLETON,
Ritual and Ambiguity in Lugbara Society, 1977, P. 76

2

THE HOUSE

Consideration of affines, ancestors, and, eventually, aristocrats as comparable sociological-cum-cosmological Others offering (among other things) legitimizing access to cosmological origins requires that we recognize an entity identifiable as Us to serve as the center of reference in the discussion of outside Others. Given that this study is multicultural in design and that a wide range of social and political organizations will be referenced, the entity defined as Us must be generic in type rather than culture specific.

The traditional anthropological concepts of "society" or "culture" are too broad and all-inclusive to serve this purpose since, as commonly used, they would be expected to incorporate categories of beings, such as affines, ancestors, and aristocracies, that I wish to define as Others, not as Us. In other words, terms like "society," "culture," or even "social system" easily carry assumptions of what Giddens has called "endogenous" or "unfolding models" in which it is presumed that "the main structural features of a society, governing both stability and change, are internal to that society" (1984:163, 164). Like Giddens, I prefer a more "open" approach in which the focal unit identifying Us is fundamentally interrelated with, influenced by, and ultimately dependent upon various "outside" collectivities, especially those that also encode vital spatial and temporal dimensions and attributes (Giddens 1979:224).

There is, however, another concept that admirably suits my purposes: the "house." This term (not to be confused with "household" since the two need not coincide) is increasingly encountered in the literature, sometimes as a useful analytical tool for investigators and often as a direct translation for distinct native terms and concepts referencing fundamental units of group association and personal identification. The concept of the house can also be applied to (though it is not limited to) virtually any type of kinship-defined social organization, whether based on sibling ties, lineal or bilateral descent principles, or cognatic networks, and has been accorded a range of connotations that, when considered overall, fits the generalized corporate role required of the focal sociological/cosmological entity (Us) in this discussion.

The concept of the house as a general social unit was directly discussed by Lévi-Strauss in his identification of so-called "house societies." In Lévi-Strauss's purview, the concept of the house refers not to buildings per se but to a bounded social entity, a corporate body, or a core group of persons related or incorporated by various forms of real or fictive ties of kinship or alliance and possessing an estate or domain consisting of material and immaterial (including supernaturally derived) wealth or "honours" (as in the familiar sense of "noble house") that is perpetuated over time by transmission of its name, wealth, and titles down the generations (Lévi-Strauss 1982:174–187, 1987:150–152). In substantive terms, the material form of the house as dwelling—that is, as a symbolically laden architectural and artistic unit, together with the people it "contains"—may become a "veritable microcosm reflecting in its smallest details an image of the universe and of the whole system of social relations" (Lévi-Strauss 1987:156).[1] Something of the idea of the house as a total "community" is also found in the complex domestic unit, the *oikía*, discussed by Aristotle as "the minimal segment from which the supra-category of the *pólis* is elaborated" (Weissleder 1978:190). In Aristotle's world, the *oikía* as distinct social entity was a household composed of both kin and nonkin (free persons and slaves or semislaves) and a political form created by diverse bonds of authority and responsibility between master-husband-father and slaves, wife, and children (Weissleder 1978; Aristotle 1995:chap. 3, 12–13).

Consideration of the house as a fundamental entity identifying an Us has also been the focus of a major study of Neolithic Europe by Hodder (1990). Hodder's development of the concept of the house as the "domus" (home) and as central to both social and symbolic life in the Neolithic of the Near East and of Europe introduces perspectives that relate the house more directly and explicitly to my interests. In addition to pondering the changes in both social form and ideation associated with, or even preceding, the "domestication" of various elements of the wild or of the natural world (including plants, animals, individuality, and death), Hodder discusses the general idea of the household or domus as a metaphor for the domestication of society. The house as always was a safe haven, a place of warmth and security, and the focus of early life. It now also becomes the main unit and the center of domestic production. Consequently the hearth is emphasized, the physical dwelling itself may be aesthetically decorated, and the dead may be interred near or in the house.[2] In essence, the "matter and ideal" of the house becomes linked to the "matter and ideal" of social reproduction.

As such, the house in Hodder's terms becomes "a conceptual unit opposed to the wild, the dangerous and the unsocial" (1990:38, 39; see also Gurevich 1969:43), the "wild" having been conceptually constructed at an early stage of cultural development as a separate domain and as the Other in order to oppose concepts of the "cultural" and the home (Hodder 1990:288). In addition, "the domus provided a way of thinking about the control of the wild and thus for the larger oppositions between culture and nature, social and unsocial" (39, 45). Some of these oppositions will be included in later discussions of the relationship of the house to the outside as represented or encapsulated in concepts of animals, the dead (especially ancestors), and affinal groups. Hodder pursues a somewhat parallel course by discussing the relationship of the domus to the "agrios," a term he employs to describe the wild as the realm of animals, hunting and fighting, acquisition of raw materials, and death (69, 84–85), and the relationship of the domus to the "foris," the enclosure against or boundary with the outside (the forest, the foreign; 130).

Following particularly upon Lévi-Strauss's formulation, numerous other ethnographers discussing all regions of the world have further refined and analytically elaborated the idea of the house or the domus as a corporate entity with specific political, economic, social, or ideological features (Carsten and Hugh-Jones 1995). A brief review of some of their findings highlights many of the salient features of the concept of the house in cross-cultural perspective.[3] The house has been described in the broadest and most all-inclusive terms as an enduring structural and spatial economic, sociopolitical, and symbolic entity or corporate group:

> The Kwak'wala term *'na'mima* (one kind) . . . anglicized as "numaym," refers to the basic social group in traditional Kwakiutl society. . . . It was a social entity that owned one or more plank houses in a winter village, and several seasonal sites where it had the right to harvest certain resources. It had its own tradition of origin, identifying its first ancestor and its rights to its resource sites, hereditary names, and ceremonial privileges. The numaym consisted of a head chief, lesser chiefs, and commoners, together with their families. (Jonaitis 1991:86 regarding the northwest coast of North America)

Since boundaries of the house can effectively separate those who are "in" from those who are "out" (Bloch 1992:70), it has also been defined as conceptually delineating the "truly human" and the "Us" as qualitatively distinct from "Others" or "Them": "People who are 'not-other' are first and foremost members of the same 'house' . . . " (Valeri 1994:6); "[with respect to consanguinity and marriage] 'house' is a container, and 'inside' vis-à-vis the non-consanguineous 'outside' world" (Headley 1987:210).[4] Similarly, "throughout all Lugbara thought . . . runs the basic differentiation between the two spheres of the 'home' (*aku*) and the 'outside' (*amve*). The former pertains to the social, moral, predictable, controllable, to authority, to men, the lineage dead; the latter pertains to the asocial, amoral, unpredictable, uncontrollable, to power without authority, to women, and the world of spirits" (Middleton 1977:76).

In economic terms, the house is sometimes referenced as a unit with respect to resource access and allocation (including trade) and food production (Jonaitis 1991:86; Vansina 1990:75, 100; Horton 1983:51) and possibly, as Hodder has argued, may be correlated particularly with domestication or other forms of delayed yields on labor or with the development of sedentary lifestyles (Gulbrandsen 1991:96–97; Barnard and Woodburn 1988:28–30; Myers 1986:257, 260). The house may also act as a unit in political and military affairs (Gregor 1977:60; Cohen and Comaroff 1976:97–98; Brown 1964:335); indeed it may appear specifically as the establishment of a politically influential person (Hugh-Jones 1979:36; Goldman 1975:65). In equatorial Africa "the basic level of social organization was that of the House, the establishment of a big man. Often it lasted beyond its founder's death and was taken over by another big man among its members" (Vansina 1990:74–75). The house has also been graphically described as a "container" for political-ideological, supernatural, and informational resources (Goldman 1975:64; Giddens 1984:261–262). Among the Tsimshian, "the matrilineage is imaged as a house, which is a container motif, like the box containing preserved food and/or wealth" (Seguin 1986b:483). "The Tsimshian local matriclan, which was the functioning feast group, was a 'waab' (house). A house is symbolically a box, a container. Persons were not 'in a "waab",' they *were* the 'waab' " (ibid.).

Finally, the house has been perceived as a corporate unity in various expressions of political ideology. It may appear as an enduring historical/mythical entity: "The 'Annals' [of the Cakchiquels] is, in reality, a history of the Xahil family, in the same way that the Popol Vuh is, ultimately, a history of the Cavek family of the Quiché. In both cases, family history and 'national history' are merged to some extent . . . and extend back to semimythical events to give both families (and the respective polities that they helped to lead) the legitimacy of ancient lineage, all the way back to the legendary times of the fantastic Toltecs" (Hill 1991:286). The house, both as physical structure and as a "congregation" of believers, also becomes a ritual center and functions as an ideological unit. "The term [*fada*, 'house'] designates both a group and a dwelling, but the socially significant dwelling is not an everyday domicile. The unity of a group is materially embodied in its 'cult house' (*fadlisa*) a named place of worship where ancestral sacra are kept and where house members reunite for ritual purposes" (Traube 1989:326–327 regarding the Mambai of east Indonesia). In like fashion, "grand funerals and *nulang* [rites involving bones] are the largest events in the life of the longhouse" among the Berawan of Borneo (Metcalf 1982:21; Fortes 1945:208; Cunningham 1964).

Such events are especially crucial in the context of the house because they extend the experiences of the house beyond the immediacy of the here-and-now, strictly defined, into the wider space-time of the outside supernatural realm.[5] Since, in low-technology, nonindustrial societies, the idiom of kinship underlies the organization and operation of virtually all basic relationships and activities, it is obvious that the house's extensions into the there-and-then should be derived from, assume some aspect of, or be expressed in terms of the kinship idiom or at least be relational in a social-ideological sense. Consequently, in the primarily temporal dimension of the outside cosmological realm, the house's extensions into the there-and-then involve relationships with the human dead and the ancestors (see note 7). "Situated below the smokehole, the fireplace was the house's link with the outside, and especially with the immaterial land of the dead" (Kan 1989:112–113 regarding the Kwakiutl).[6] Similarly, marriage, which effects a primarily spatial kinship-idiomed relationship by creating affines, extends the house outward toward a cosmographical expression of the there-and-then inhabited by other categories of living beings. "Tsimshian saw symbolic associations between fathers, foreigners, animals, and supernaturals" (Seguin 1986b: 488). This association "allowed the Tsimshian to maintain reciprocal relations with supernaturals and animals in their own world through the feasts and payments made to the father's side" (489).[7]

Considered overall, the house may be regarded generically as a fundamental social, political, ideological, and moral domain that in many ways functions structurally and organizationally as a distinctive entity defining, protecting, and sustaining its members, both as a group and in the aggregate. The house may be taken to represent in various ways home, the inside, the Us, and the here-and-now. As such, the concept of the house serves quite adequately and appropriately as a focus or pivotal starting point for further discussion linking the house, whatever its ethnographic characteristics in any given culture, with the cosmological outside and with expressions of the Other, including affines and ancestors. In this perspective (and as the chapter epigram succinctly states), the house, though distinct as a sociopolitical or even economic unit, is not truly independent and self-sustaining. Far from it. As its numerous ceremonial responsibilities make clear, the house exists and is perpetuated in the here-and-now only because it is linked in space and time to outside agencies representing the there-and-then. It is from these crucial sources that means are derived for the generational continuation of the life of the house, for the solace and success of its members as they pursue their various interests, and, by the ultimate authority invested in origins and beginnings, for the legitimate authority of its leadership.

PART ONE

*Why do we die? Stone doesn't
die. Earth doesn't die. Trees do
die but only after a long long
time. Why do we die?*

WAYÃPÍ MOURNER QUOTED IN
ALAN CAMPBELL,
To Square with Genesis, 1989, P. 81

3

THE DEAD

Awareness of the "reality" of death stands second only to awareness of
the reality of being in human philosophies. Similarly, the proposition
that the dead may still live must be one of the most comforting or most
terrifying insights of human eschatology. It has also been one of the most
influential in terms of affecting events in the world of the physically living, not only with respect to ordinary everyday affairs but also, and
most notably, when the political and ideological leadership of the polity
and the power (fertility) essential for reproduction of the social order
and of the house are linked to belief in the superordinate authority and
energizing powers of the dead.

Obviously the acquisition of such benefits necessitates belief that the
dead comprise a distinct cosmological entity experientially situated outside the house and constituting a spatial/temporal category of Other in
relation to the house and that linkages and communications can be effected between the tangible world of the physically living and the intangible realm of the dead. Such ethnological truisms would hardly bear re-
peating were it not that the secular Western world is so firmly convinced

that no such conjunctions exist between the living and the dead in the "real" world of experience. For the industrial West, death, often conceived of as "the final malfunctioning of the body as machine" (Metcalf 1982:46), is a dreadful concept; a pollution, a final event to be approached with apprehension, and a subject to be consciously avoided and repressed as much as possible by the living (Lévi-Strauss 1993:50; Judkins 1973:4–5). In light of such cultural "baggage," it seems appropriate to reiterate the strength of belief in the absolute existence of the dead as Other and the immediacy of the often (though by no means always) positive sociopolitical significance accorded to the dead and to life-death articulations in the vast majority of nonindustrial, non-Western societies, where such beliefs are accepted as part of life without serious question.[1]

The creation of the dead as Other is often expressed in very tangible terms, most directly in the transformations that occur at the cessation of physical life with the loss of signs of physical viability and the decay and decomposition of the flesh and blood of the human form (Hertz 1960a:43–46). Otherness may then be accorded a new physical identity evidenced by the strength and durability of the hard, dry bones that contrast strongly in appearance with the physical forms of the living (Kan 1989:111). The Otherness of the dead, meaning the "fact" that the dead continue their own existence separate and distinct from that of the physically living, may be further recognized sociologically by according some sort of identification to the deceased to keep memory—and thus existence—alive (Mbiti 1969:25–26; Fortune 1935:9). Distinctive humanlike lifestyles may be attributed to the world of the dead, too. Familial and village social relations, complete with marriages and births, friendships and rivalries, may be thought to exist (Maranda 1967:91; Keesing 1982:103; Goody 1962:73, 89); subsistence needs may be met with familiar types of activity (Goodale and Koss 1967:178); taxes may even still be paid by ghostly residents to ghostly colonial district officers (Fortune 1935:9–10).

The dead can also be recognized as Other because they can "return" to the living in the guise of otherwise ordinary members of the house or when house members disguise their current identity under masks and costumes and, by songs and dances, literally bring the dead into the present (Connerton 1989:69). Lévi-Strauss also offers a fascinating interpretation of the role of children as incarnations and personifications of the dead, given that children are incompletely incorporated into society and still share the Otherness that characterizes the dead relative to the living (1993:49–51).[2] Indeed, the Otherness of the dead is generated or granted by any and all of the diverse means of communication by which the other world may be contacted since such conversing, by definition, assumes that there is something out there to be communicated with. Such interactions are by no means limited to formal "ritual" settings or official ceremonials, where distinctive and limiting behaviors may mark the "Otherness" of the occasion (Bloch 1974; Leach 1979c), but may be a very real part of "normal" everyday life, too. For example, the Sora of eastern India converse with the dead frequently, on a weekly or even daily basis. "In dialogues between living and dead, speakers persuade, cajole, tease, remind, deceive, plead with each other. Dialogues represent a mutual quest for awareness about the other person's state of mind" (Vitebsky 1993:5, 6). Similarly, "a substantial proportion of the conversations that take place in a Kwaio settlement are not between living humans but between the living and the dead" (Keesing 1982:112): a neighbor "carr[ies] on a lengthy conversation with his oldest son, whose skull overlooks the clearing"; "a woman sits in a corner of the house whispering to a dead relative; a man addresses a clump of trees" (33, 113). McKellin notes that the participation of the physically dead in the society of the physically living among the Managalase of Papua New Guinea is so constant in both daily and ritual affairs that "the two groups might well be conceived as moieties" (1985:181).

Achievement of the final conditions and of the state of being that identify the deceased as truly dead often necessitates complex transitional processes culturally constructed to evidence that the Otherness of the dead takes the form of being "like us but different." This transformation frequently entails recognition that the passage or conjunction between the living and the dead constitutes not a sharp break but a continuum. On the side of the physically living, the continuum can be expressed by liminal conditions of being dead-while-alive in which the incumbent is seen to inhabit both worlds simultaneously or to be moving by degrees from the world of the physically living and the socially engaged to that of the truly dead or of the immortally alive.[3] The natural process of becoming sick and dying may be described in such terms. "The Pygmies express various degrees of illness by saying that someone is hot, with fever, ill, dead, completely or absolutely dead, and, finally, dead for ever" (Turnbull 1961:34). Indeed, the idea is not as foreign to our own world as we might initially think:

> . . . the Bororo do not share our conception of the relation between life and death. Someone said to me one day, of a woman who was lying in a high fever in the corner of her hut: "She's dead"—meaning that they had given up her case as hopeless. And, after all, this is not so different from our army's way of lumping together dead and wounded under the single heading of "casualties." As far as immediate effectiveness goes, they are indeed one and the same, even if, from the wounded man's point of view, there is an undeniable advantage in not being among the dead. (Lévi-Strauss 1964:222–223)[4]

The Western practice of institutionalizing the decrepit elderly also consigns such persons to a category of dead-while-still-alive. Similarly, in the nonindustrial world, old age, often involving people who are so elderly that if they are not dead it is thought they ought to be (McKellin 1985:182; Metcalf 1982:66),[5] constitutes another of the liminal conditions "mythologized as a border of life and death" and conveying "a sense of special power, derived from having traversed so much of life and moved beyond its immediate struggles" as well as "being closer to . . . death and therefore more knowledgeable about it than others" (Lifton 1979:89; Counts and Counts 1985:16–17, 22; see also note 6). In the traditional Celtic world of rural Ireland, when the farm and the homestead were turned over to a married son and heir as head of household, the parental couple moved out of the large common or family room into the "west room."[6] Here, in a small chamber explicitly identified with sacrality and family history, the old people relinquished their adult status and, amid heirlooms and photographs of relatives already deceased, became specifically identified with the forces of the dead, "going down with the sun," as one countryman put it (Arensberg 1968:184; Kammeyer 1976:215–216).

Delirium or loss of consciousness, whether caused by drunkenness, shamanic accidents, serious illness, or grave wounds, is also often interpreted as being "dead" or as a state of being that bridges life and death (Viveiros de Castro 1986:196; Keesing 1982:111, 145). "The aged person, after all, is approaching the ancestors; if he is in delirium in the last stages before death, it is thought that he is already holding conversations with them" (Barnes 1974:162, 200). Yet a person does not have to become physically dead or even ill or unconscious to be regarded as socially deceased. Unsuccessful individuals who lack ambition and fail to engage in the activities or accomplish the goals considered indicative of a socially responsible and contributive adult can be considered "dead" for all practical purposes.[7] On a more temporary basis, the socially secluded or socially excluded condition of mourners following a death may also constitute a liminal position situated between life and death (van Gennep 1960:147).

Finally, persons who have died physically may move slowly and only by degrees from the here-and-now of the living into the distanciated world of the "truly dead," being thought to be still vital or quick-while-dead as mortuary rites move through their several stages, during which, for example, the corpse or the shade may still be periodically fed (Metcalf 1976:86–87; Kan 1989:182; Harris 1982:46). This graduated condition may continue as the dead undertakes a lengthy passage to another land (Metcalf 1976:82–84, 1982:66, 215–223). At the end of that journey, however, the theme of continuity is always replaced with alterity. No matter how "like" Us they may be thought to be, ultimately the dead are not-Us. Indeed, "death is where the conceptual determination of alterity takes place" (Viveiros de Castro 1986:4). The dead are the Other, and no matter how close their proximity or how consistent their communication with the living, the proper and ultimate domain of the dead-as-Other is the outside, a locale conceptually and sometimes cosmographically situated beyond the domestic order (Glazier 1984:138) whence death, no matter how firm the defenses of the living, ultimately "comes in from the wilderness" (Bloch and Parry 1982:11) and inevitably invades the house.

The invasion of death, however, is not necessarily an unmitigated disaster. To be sure, the warm security of the day-to-day presence of kith and kin will be periodically shaken as particular individuals depart for the beyond, but the long-term viability of the living is often perceived to depend on the role played by the dead, directly or indirectly, in perpetuating the flow of energies that activate the universe and thus the life of the house. In traditional cosmologies death comes in from the wilderness, but so does fertility and life.

One of the major sources of this most necessary and beneficial gift of the dead is the bones of the deceased (particularly the skull and long bones), which in general are believed to be the seat of life.[8] As such they may contain or enhance the powers of plant growth (Szemiński 1993:294; see also note 10), assist human fertility (Bloch and Parry 1982:23), increase hunting skills and aid warriors (Scheffler 1965:187–188), or protect the house against evil and danger and supervise the moral behavior of its people (Fortune 1935:1; Dalton 1996:406–407). "The skull of the dead was used to become a successful hunter, warrior or shaman" among the Nootka (Wike 1967:100), while "the Arapesh have a well-integrated pattern of chewing the bone of a dead male ancestor with a little ginger, as protective, hunting or gardening magic" (Mead 1938:178, 1940:432–433; Guddemi 1992:306).

Bones convey these energies because they are strong, dry, hard, and relatively imperishable. In addition to being metaphorically and sometimes even literally indicative of perpetuity,[9] bones, because they are durable, can be kept as heirlooms or sacra for generations. Bones thus prefigure the concept of temporal ancestors and may also prefigure the value accorded a variety of other durable and ideologically potent tangible goods, such as metal objects (Traube 1980:99), shells (Foster 1990:441), seeds, and various types of politically indispensable goods acquired through long-distance trade.[10] All such lasting items are also associated with outside realms and can constitute heirlooms (McKinnon 1991:96–97), relics (Morphy 1991:79; Lepowsky 1989:204–205; Brown 1981:86–93), or regalia, and all can be understood as variations and elaborations on the ancient and enduring practice of acquiring and maintaining the bones of the human dead.

Yet not just anyone's bones will do. Among the Arapesh, "whether the bones are taken at all and how many are taken, is a direct expression of the esteem in which a man's personality is held, sometimes tempered a little by filial affection" (Mead 1940:432). The bones of children, most women, and young or ineffectual men are not useful, but the bones of a man "who has been a successful yam planter, a successful hunter, a feast maker, strong in leadership and speechmaking" contain powerful magic (433).[11] Elsewhere it is the bones and skulls of initiated men and sometimes esteemed women who have held high status or given birth that constitute sacra and are accorded ritual significance (Weiner 1982:57–58). On Vanatinai (Sudest Island, Melanesia), it is the bones of long-dead and particularly successful warriors, lovers, or traders that are secretly dug up as relics (Lepowsky 1989:204–205, 207; Kanowski 1987:89–90).

The fact that only the bones of certain types or categories of people are often believed to convey energizing potencies indicates that the category of "the dead" may be further refined to differentiate between those dead whose earthly presence, qualitatively speaking, was in some manner lacking and those whose earthly existence was qualitatively noteworthy for its economic, social, or political influence and "productivity."[12] Only the latter's enduring remains can further benefit the living, and only the latter have the necessary qualitative potential to become truly ancestral and thus to provide the living with personalized access to origins (see Chapter 4).

Distinctive treatment of another type of bones bespeaks links with animals, a category of Others that conceptually may well have preceded the idea of ancestors (see Chapter 4). From the perspective of the house, in contrast to the intangible or nonviable nature of human dead, animal bones are associated with a category of Other that is usually still physically living, although its place of habitation is in the same geographical (cosmographical) outside realm of the cosmos that may be associated with spirits or shades of the human dead, too, since the latter frequently (though not invariably) are believed to dwell likewise in natural places beyond the homestead, in bush areas or forests, hilltops, or water sources (Glazier 1984:138; MacGaffey 1986:54–55; Bloch and Parry 1982:23), or in a transitional zone between domus and bush (Turner 1971:103; Munn 1986:33). Remains of the human dead may also be brought in from the outside, as when headhunters bring back to their homes the severed heads of the enemy, a most efficacious type of relic that enhances fertility and will be "fed" and kept warm by the fire as honored guests (McKinley 1976:114).[13] Far more frequently, however, it is the flesh and bones of game animals that are brought to the domus to feed the living. Here, again, bones may signify a great deal, for animal bones figure prominently in the regeneration of animal life and thus serve to preserve game as food for people, provided they are properly treated. As Ingold has noted, with respect to circumboreal hunter/ pastoralists, "Much of the ritual surrounding the treatment of slaughtered beasts, particularly concerning the careful preservation of bones and other inedible parts, and their deposition in the correct medium and in the precise order that they occur in the skeleton, is designed to assist the reconstitution of the animals from the pieces into which they have been broken for the purposes of consumption, thus ensuring the regeneration of that on which human life depends" (1987:246–247; Kan 1989:50).

The regenerative power attributed to animal bones is paralleled by the not uncommon belief that the buried human body or the souls of at least some human beings may be reconstituted as game (Iteanu 1985: 97, 98; Service 1978:212–213; Karim 1981:45, 79). "Many shamans say that *all* game animals, including game birds and certain fish, are transformed [human] souls" (Reichel-Dolmatoff 1985:121, 1986:69– 70, regarding the Tukano of the Colombian Amazon). The Bororo "do think, seemingly, that every tapir, and every wild pig, and every alligator, and possibly every member of some other family of animals, shelters the shade of one or another of their departed tribesmen . . ." (Karsten 1968:484; Melatti 1979:61). This concept helps to identify animals as another category of Other that is "like us but different" (Berger 1985: 275–277; Ingold 1988; Reichel-Dolmatoff 1986:73–74). It is in accord with common beliefs that animals in their life forms or habits are actually transformed humans or that there is no strict dividing line between humans and animals as "persons" (Willis 1990:6–7; Ingold 1987:247–248).[14] For the Kogi of northern Colombia, "the animals are considered essentially as beings endowed with all the characteristics of man excepting only his outward appearance. The Kogi believe that the animals talk, think, have 'souls' and live an ordered life just as humans do . . . . The animals are . . . simply beings who live apart and who man should treat . . . [the same as] he would treat any neighbouring human family in his own society" (Reichel-Dolmatoff, quoted in Schrimpff 1989:75–76).[15]

In short, by accounting for the fate of human bodies and souls and attending to the proper disposal of animal bones, humans and animals can be interrelated in a reciprocal process of mutual regeneration (Sanday 1986:114–115; Kan 1989:50; Karsten 1968:chap. 9). Indeed, animal bones and human souls and bodily remains, as regenerative sources, may be more or less conceptually interchangeable when game is perceived as essentially anthropomorphic. The same may hold for plant life, too: "There is in contemporary Andean society a Quechua word (*mallki*) that means both 'divine ancestors' and 'new plants'. The logic of this concept . . . expresses, among other things, the ideal of respectful burial of human remains or the bones of a sacrificial offering such as a llama. The idea is that that which is recommitted to the earth will be the source of new life" (Szemiński 1993:294; cf. Karim 1981; Vitebsky 1993:31).[16] Similarly, "the fertility of the crops and the prosperity of the village are closely associated with the dead, whose life-substance is conceived of as forming a continuous cycle of reproduction, passing from men to cereals sown, and thence back through grain eaten, or through the flesh of animals that have eaten it, to man again" (Hutton, quoted in Woodward and Russell 1989:13, regarding the Naga).

There is yet another category of residents in addition to human dead and animals inhabiting the temporal/spatial outside realm that can be referenced one way or another by the dead of the house. Like human dead and animals, affines are also "like Us but different," "persons" who are not-Us but are conjoined with Us and live much as We do. One way to reference affines by means of the dead is rather indirect, referring to procreation rather than death per se. It lies in terminological distinctions that distinguish between kin and affines through such circumlocutions as "relatives of the bone" and "relatives of the flesh," alluding to widespread beliefs that each of the parents contributes one of the several components necessary for the developing fetus (see note 8; Lévi-Strauss 1969a:472). This belief has relevance within the context of death in that the durability of bone and the perishability of flesh and blood at the physical death of an individual can emphasize the endurance of the house against the impermanence of affinal ties to Others. "Only upon death does the adult Dobuan finally shed all unwelcome obligations and attachments to those outside the matrilineage (that is, affines, or those resulting from marriage). Interment in his or her lineage's burial mound secures entrance into an ideal community of enates, a descent group with hermetically sealed boundaries in which 'the generations succeed each other without the unpleasant necessity of exchange'" (Foster 1990:432).[17]

Death not only offers a certain freedom from affines but death and affines also share a certain common conceptual ground in that, as Bloch and Parry comment, "the final triumph over death is also a triumph over the necessity for affines and over the world of sexual reproduction which they represent" (1982:21). Stated otherwise, the inability to sustain physical life forever and the unsuitability (immorality) of social self-reproduction necessitate the twin evils of death and affines, both of which can now be said to "come in from the wilderness." It is not surprising, then, to find that the conduct of mortuary rites often provides a major setting where fundamental contrasts between affines as Others and house members as Us and between affines and the dead as related categories of Other versus the living Us are emphasized and tangibly reiterated.

Macintyre provides a very explicit example from Tubetube, where both the corpse of the house member and the surviving spouse no longer have a place with the living kin group (lineage, or *susu*): "Just as the body of the deceased is gradually transformed from a *susu* member to an ancestor, from a rotting corpse in the village to a basket of bones in a remote ancestral cave, so the widow/widower is transformed from an affine within the hamlet to a marriageable person outside the village.... The rites that today structure the mortuary sequence still reflect the dual problem that besets the *susu*: the removal of the dead person from the realm of the living and the removal of the spouse from the hamlet"

(Macintyre 1989:134). Through such rites the integrity of the lineage is symbolically reconstructed at death with numerous metaphors expressing "closure, exclusion, and severance of social links beyond the hamlet," and the bereaved spouse becomes "the archetypal 'stranger,' utterly isolated, all links to the hamlet having been severed by death" (135). In sum, "the gradual transformation of the deceased from corpse within the village to ancestor in the cave is still implicit in all the ceremonies that focus on the widow. The metaphorical relationship between the widow and the corpse remains central in all the rituals, and the widow . . . is the focus for all negative connotations of death" (137–138).[18]

In this example from Tubetube the dead ultimately prove to be the more endurable expression of Other; the whitened bones in the mortuary cave "testified to the lineage's control over its own regeneration and continuity, for the bones were believed to have been formed by *susu* breastmilk. The flesh and blood, now vanished, were produced by foods and 'paternal substance,' their disintegration proclaiming the ephemeral nature of the affinal relation" (Macintyre 1989:138).[19] The Araweté of Brazil provide an intriguing variation on this theme in which the affinal context is treated much differently in imagery relating the dead, the affinal, Us, and—a new outside element—the enemy when they imagine the reception of their dead in the land of the gods (the Maï). Initially the gods are portrayed as acting like Us while the human dead, when they reach the village of the Maï, are portrayed as strangers and enemies and treated as We would treat an enemy who threatens Us from the outside. Yet the living also refer to the gods by affinal terms and regard them as affines relative to living humans. The reaction of the Maï to the human dead as enemy thus becomes a variation on the theme of affines as enemy Others.[20] Ultimately the human dead are believed to marry the Maï, thereby creating a bridge by which the living and the gods may become allies (Viveiros de Castro 1986:63, 90, 211, 215–217).

For the Araweté, as Viveiros de Castro notes, the conquest of death does not lead to the avoidance of Others; rather, "others do exist in Araweté eternity; furthermore, it is precisely there that they are found. Affinity has been transported to the heavens, or rather, to the relations between heaven and earth. Death permits the great cosmological chasm to be bridged" (1986:216). Raising the sociological/cosmological distinction between Us and Others to truly universal proportions, the Araweté affirm that "what is pertinent are the kinship relations between the living and the dead, and the affinal relations between the living and divinities" (216). For the Araweté, "the transformation into divinity that benefits the dead is not intended to ancestralize them, but rather, to affinalize the gods" (236).

Animals and affines, deities and the dead. When considered not just from the perspective of individual ethnographic studies but as a set of phenomena suitable as prototypes for a more broadly applicable general model, all are seen to be identifiable as categories of Other vis-à-vis the house. All are in some fashion "like Us but different," all are situated in spatial/temporal cosmological realms outside or beyond the here-and-now of the house, and all to varying degrees are conceptually inter-related, even interchangeable, from the perspective of the house. It is to certain of these interrelationships and interchangeabilities among animals, affines, deities, and the dead that I now turn in more detail.

Primitive society was a formal organization for the apotheosis of man.

ERNEST BECKER,
Escape from Evil, 1975, P. 16

4

ANCESTORS

In the beginning were animals, ancestors, and other people. In world-views based upon the consubstantiality of life, the qualities attributed to the cosmos must be tangibly or intangibly expressed in "life-forms," some of which, though they constitute expressions of the Other relative to Us, must be comprehended as significantly like Us if they are to be conceptually useful as "extensions" of the here-and-now into the spatial/ temporal there-and-then, which is what any cosmology is basically about from the purview of the house. The nature of the cosmological linkages provided for the house by animals, ancestral dead, and other people, including affines, fundamentally rests on the belief, often expressed in myths, that all three categories of being are simply different forms or manifestations of a common quality of "personness" shared not only with each other but also with members of the house. The specific character of these connections, however, will also reflect particular expressions of the quality of being that sets animals, ancestral dead, and other people independently apart from the house as respective Others. They will also express the mutually interchangeable or interrelatable qualities of Otherness that all three categories share among themselves given that they all are situated spatially/temporally outside or beyond the environs of the house.

A variety of activities, including (though not limited to) hunting, marriage, and mortuary rites, constitute the major means of "connecting" the house with animals, other people, and the dead. The significance and effectiveness of these conjuncting endeavors are heightened, however, by the qualitative interrelatedness that is believed to associate qualities of animals with qualities of the dead and with qualities of other people in the social cosmology of the house. In other words, affines created by marriage ties can ultimately connect the house with its ancestral dead or the presence of other people as guests at mortuary feasts can assist in the creation of house ancestors or proper conduct of mortuary rites can allow the dead to metamorphose into animals or abstinence from marital relations can assist the hunter's success. The interrelationship among categories of Other that is most pertinent for this study is that which connects the ancestral dead of the house to other people, specifically to its affines. Development of this theme requires that we review the roles of both ancestors and affines as spatial/temporal Others. This chapter will discuss ancestors in this context; the following chapter will discuss affines.

The term "ancestor" has been used rather freely in anthropology. Often it has simply been a gloss for "the dead." As "the dead" in cross-cultural terms can include a wide range of ghosts, shades, and spirit beings, it is advisable to apply the term "ancestor" with greater specificity. It is also appropriate to consider how or where categories or contexts of ancestor are cosmographically or structurally situated relative to the house since the creation and recognition of ancestors is associated primarily and directly with "the familial domain of social life" (Fortes 1976:3); indeed, it may serve to distinguish or identify a given house as socially distinct from other houses.

In general the concept of ancestor, as used here, will refer either to rather distant beings related to the house in a context of original or prior origins (see Chapter 6) or to specific named dead of the house who are remembered as having achieved exceptional socially significant goals while still physically alive.[1] The nature of such accomplishment, of course, can vary tremendously in its particulars. Successful parenthood often establishes the necessary criteria for an honored (remembered) ancestral status even if the deceased has failed in other respects (Fortes 1976:9; Uchendu 1976:293; Taylor and Aragon 1991:42). Similarly, "a man who was strong when he was alive—a man who killed, who talked strongly, who was an important priest—when he dies, his shade will be strong . . ." (Keesing 1982:108, 109–110, regarding the Kwaio, Solomon Islands). Alternatively, conscientious maintenance of the highest moral standards may be required (Uchendu 1976:292) or exceptional understanding of tradition and knowledge (Reichel-Dolmatoff 1987:11–12; Lindstrom 1990) or the good fortune of having been a firstborn (Pomponio 1992:91, 76) or a good provider of the family's material needs (Goody 1962:201, 177–178) or outstanding success as an acquirer and "manager" of corporate resources and foreign affairs for the kin group (Scheffler 1965:185–186, 247). Ancestors also include those persons who have died a "good" death and had a proper funeral or whose remains have been properly interred or otherwise appropriately disposed of (Battaglia 1990:66–71; Uchendu 1976:293–295; Goody 1962:52, 223, 383). Those who die under less fortunate circumstances or who failed to succeed in their lifetimes often will not be so honored and will not constitute ancestors (Anderson 1994a:68; Colson 1960:383–384).

The conditions that are conducive to ancestorship may apply to most deceased adults of a given society or to relatively few. The length of time a deceased individual is remembered and honored also varies greatly cross-culturally. More consistent is the effort and intent to transform the quality of being of the honorably deceased from that of an *individual* member of living society to that of an ancestral *person* or archetype associated with qualitatively distinctive sociological/cosmological roles (Weeks 1979:70; Eliade 1959a:46–47). In other words, the unique idiosyncrasies and peculiarities of mortal existence are often extinguished so that only those qualities and attributes associated with the "standard" or "ideal" role of ancestor will be remembered or newly applied. "What seems to have been of primary importance was not so much the indication of *who* (the individual) but of *what* (the person) was represented" (Weeks 1979:71; Endicott 1979:111–112, 128; Jackson 1977:293–294; Battaglia 1990:10).[2]

Decorating the corpse is one way to achieve the new ancestral identity. On Sabarl Island (part of the Louisiade Archipelago near New Guinea), the deceased is washed, shaved, dressed in his or her best clothes, and anointed with coconut oil. Shell chokers and necklaces are tied round the neck, the face is painted with black and white designs, a stone ax blade is placed under the head, and the mouth covered with various forms of shell and paper currency. "Thus the body is made into an effigy of the social person—an artifact, displaying the accoutrements of status and youthful beauty. This project visually equates the dead person with an ancestral ideal . . ." (Battaglia 1990:163; Goody 1962:71). Carving wooden ancestral figures replete with elements indicating high rank rather than indicating the individual's physical features is another way of expressing societal and ideological, instead of individual, identity (Taylor and Aragon 1991:73). Ultimately, as a result of such transformative manipulations, ancestors of a house, considered en masse as a distinctive "kind" of collective being, come to represent certain basic qualities or embody a "repertory of rules" (Valeri 1990:160) in terms of which they are then related back to the house, perhaps as benevolent guardians and bountiful providers, perhaps as stern, moralistic, and potentially vengeful juridical presences.

In anthropological thinking the most familiar ancestral context or realm probably emphasizes the temporal dimension of ancestral being over the spatial, understandably so given that the concept of ancestorness would appear by definition to be inherently temporal. The spatial location of ancestors may appear more problematical, especially since in Western societies the dead traditionally have been believed to go to a locale "up above" or "down below" rather than to a setting somewhere "out there" (Miller 1955). The ethnographic literature indicates, however, that the spatial location of ancestors is as important as the temporal and that ancestorlike beings may be situated on either or both of the horizontal (geographical) and vertical (celestial/chthonic) cosmological axes. Since these distinctions are significant for the argument relating affines to ancestors and, eventually, both to aristocrats, it is necessary to distinguish more closely among the various spatial and temporal ancestral settings.

Let us begin with intangible beings associated with past time relative to the house.[3] In contrast to the more usual perspective in which the living are viewed as descendants of ancestors, I prefer to consider this "type" of ancestral classification as a processually "emergent" form in which ancestors, though distinct from the physically living membership of the house in terms of state of being, have "grown out of" the living membership of the house as a temporal elaboration of that house; "the lineage consists of two groups, those who are at present living in this world and an ever increasing group dwelling in the under-world" (Winter 1956:18 regarding the Amba of Uganda). This imagery also sees ancestors extending the house into the temporal realm as a closed or "pure" entity that does not require alliance with other people or other orders of being to maintain its spiritual viability or its moral propriety; that is, it postulates a "domestication" of death in which "death . . . is brought inwards" (Hodder 1970:292) so that the living and the dead of the house, as Us and related Other, constitute a self-contained ideological, juridical, and legitimizing moral order (Rowlands 1985:51–52; Bloch 1982:211; Strathern 1982:38).

This self-containment may be paralleled by imagery of parent-child relationships (Uchendu 1976:284) or by an emphasis on the ideological value and ritual role of sibling ties over affinal relations given that the latter implies the intrusion of outsiders (Howell 1992:131).[4] In extreme "emergent" ancestral contexts the house, wishing to be entirely self-contained, may take full responsibility for the preparation of the corpse and related funeral activities, preventing living Others (such as affines) from assisting with the washing and decorating of the remains of the deceased; "this desire of the lineage to turn in on itself and abrogate all relations with outsiders emerges as a central feature of the symbolism of Dobuan mortuary practice" (Bloch and Parry 1982:29, 30; Vitebsky 1993:22). In addition, house ancestors of the "emergent" type, who generally were notable achievers when physically alive, are characteristically perceived as juridical and authoritative in nature, requiring perpetual service and obedience in return for providing the wherewithal (health, wealth, children) for the "good life" and likely to cause misfortune if the living do not satisfactorily meet their ritual obligations (Uchendu 1976:206; Goody 1962:430; Keesing 1975:60; Fortes 1976: 14–15, 1983:22, 30; Kerner 1976:207–208).

In contrast with "emergent" ancestral settings, in which ancestors are still directly linked to the house from which they derived (Fig. 1a), another category of ancestors references cosmological first principles or conditions of first creation; that is to say, it identifies the concept of ancestor with questions of primordial source and originations (Keesing 1971:165; Lévi-Strauss 1966:236). In this context ancestral beings are conceptualized not as emerging from the house but as *preceding* the house—that is, as existing or originating separate from the house and as "coming to" the house from a cosmological setting that was originally somewhere outside it, implying a spatial component as basic to the identification (Fig. 1b). "First principle" ancestors (as we may call them) may be perceived as originally having been immigrants from another land or may be regarded as still situated at very distant cosmographical locales, perhaps above the firmament or beneath the sea or at the eastern or western horizons. Sometimes first-principle or creator ancestors are ob-

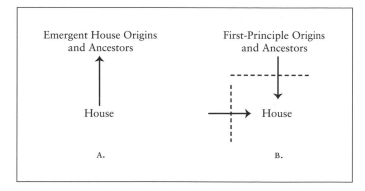

FIGURE 1   Contexts of ancestorness and origins.
A. The house and its emergent house ancestors.
B. The house and precedent first-principle origins.

jectified or made accessible at specified locales on the cultural landscape of the earth (Gudeman 1986:92; Evens 1984:327–328; Endicott 1979: 124; Myers 1986:126, 240–243; Goldman 1963:184, 254).

Not infrequently houses combine aspects of both contexts of ancestorness. In some cases this involves acknowledging both a relatively short-lived ancestral existence for the recently dead, many of whom then gradually fade into oblivion, and the existence of more mythologized ancestral first-principle creators who are unrelated to the immediate, personalized dead of the house (Winter 1956:212; Kan 1989:68–69, 184). Alternatively, certain of the dead of the house, especially those of very high rank, over time may become remembered as a separate body of ancestors ultimately apotheosized as a "collective immortality" or as first-principle deities (Uchendu 1976:293–295; Taylor and Aragon 1991:175). It is noteworthy that creator or first-principle ancestors characteristically are less concerned with juridical matters and associated more with concepts of house origins and destiny (Kan 1989:68–69, 123).

The cosmological context that associates the condition of first-principle or creator ancestorness with a strong spatial as well as a temporal dimension of spatial/temporal distance also permits the identification of distinctive tangible beings as personifications of the principles involved. Like the creational process they represent, such tangible personifications of the Other are initially situated outside the house and are then brought into closer contact with it through relational imagery that (in contrast to that of emergent house ancestors) is usually distinctly "contractual" rather than "processual" (emergent) in form.[5] The general world of nature, including animals and other people, situated cosmographically beyond the house provides the theater for many of these conceptualizations, as when the Bette and Mullu Kurumba, South Indian hunter-gatherer-horticultural groups, metaphorically recognize the forest as "ancestors who reciprocate with them and themselves as kin" (Bird-David 1990:192; see also note 5).

Frequently, however, the ancestral creators spatially situated in the world of nature outside the house are defined more specifically in affinal terms. The Tukanoan Desana of the Vaupés region of Colombia provide a case in point. The Tukanoan personify the tapir as a strange and hostile outsider with curious customs, a figure recognized metaphorically as ancestral "father-in-law" in myths and hunting lore. This identification refers to the historical fact that the original Vaupés Tukanoan invaded the region and raided indigenous Arawakans, known to Tukanoans as the Tapir People, for women. These early raids now are "described in the oral literature either as hunting expeditions in which the prey are the female of a certain species or as chance encounters between men . . . , the Tukanoans, and beings . . . [who are] the 'others', the animallike inhabitants of the forest" (Reichel-Dolmatoff 1985:113). Since it was the Tapir People who first provided the Tukanoans with wives, they "became their fathers-in-law and their ancestors," a relationship that is perpetuated in the imagery and symbolism still accorded the "affinal" tapir (111, 115, 131). Comparable metaphors and symbolism identify deer as "mothers-in-law" to the first Vaupés Tukanoans, for the daughters of the Tapir were Deer. "In ancient times both [tapir and deer] were, as the Desana say, . . . our-transformer-people-women" (131). In short, when speaking of their initial contacts with other people, glossed as animals, from whom the first Tukanoans obtained wives, "the Indians will use the term . . . ancestors to designate their maternal origins" (135). "What might appear to be totemic animals are the remnants and reminiscences of former inhabitants with whom, in earlier times, there was considerable intercourse. These people became transformed, in the eyes of the newcomers, from beasts of the forest into wife-givers and, eventually, into allies and thus into a category of lineage founders" (139).

The Chambri of New Guinea also assert that most of their ancestors were of foreign origin, although they were recognized as other people, not as animals. "Virtually all of the patriclans were founded by men whose ancestors originated elsewhere" and whose association with

Chambri brought powerful secret names and ritual objects and techniques that allow living Chambri to establish identity with their ancestors (Errington and Gewertz 1986:99, 100). In comparable fashion, the Manambu recognize a category of "totemic ancestors" who are associated with particular kin groups on the basis of myths describing their transfer from other groups via matrifiliation, fosterage, or co-residence. These original outsiders are specified by secret names and the "ancestral affines and matrikin are . . . recognized as totemic ancestors of particular subclans." Ownership of a corpus of such named totemic ancestors gives a group its independent identity as a marriage unit (Harrison 1990:57, 67).

The affinal nature of original, first-principle or creator ancestral relationships involving outside Others, either other people or especially animals-cum-other-people, probably derives from the view, encountered particularly among hunter-gatherers and part-time horticultural groups, that human beings and animal beings originally shared a common "personness." This unity not only underlies beliefs that the souls of human dead may be reconstituted as game animals (see Chapter 3) but also implies that animals and humans share a common mythical ancestry, that "in the beginning people and animals were not distinct but all lived together in a single village led by the elephant . . . ," as the !Kung origin myth puts it (Lee, quoted in Kent 1989:12). Although this primordial commonality is eventually broken and people and animals go their separate ways, belief in their original shared consubstantiality is referenced in numerous tales that relate how humans and animals once could intermarry, how animals could be human affines, and how human-animal offspring (descendants) sprang from such unions. These mythical offspring of animal-human relations may be accorded superior spiritual status as original culture heroes (another kind of creator ancestor) who first taught humans vital customs, skills, and knowledge.[6]

The definitive characteristic expressed in such tales—that animals, like human affines, are like-Us-but-different—continues to be expressed in widespread beliefs that a certain consubstantiality is still shared between the humans of the house and the animal beings of the outside world: "[In the perspective of] all hunter-gatherers (if not all mankind) . . . animals are both the same as man and they are other than man. . . . Their otherness derives from their distinctive anatomies, their polytypic heterogeneity, their lack of sapience, symboling and language, and their innocence of the incest taboo and its resultant social patterns. Yet they are also man, in their basic anatomical plan, their basic behavioural repertoire (eating, sleeping, mating, fleeing or attacking) and their shared basic patterns of sentience" (Guenther 1988:195–196). This similarity can also include recognition of animals as sharing essential spiritual features, such as souls, with humans (Kent 1989:12–13, 16). On the other hand, in spite of shared "personness," animals as ancestors originally existed in realms outside the living house and in times prior to the living house and thereby constitute an original Other relative to the living Us (Kent 1989:11). "The key creation myth, and the exemplar of Bushman cosmology, is the myth of double creation . . . it pronounces the present order of existence to be a reversal of primal time—an earlier time when animals were human and humans animals. . . . Animality was an intrinsic component of the ontological condition of the beings of the 'first race,' the forebears of Bushman society and culture" (Guenther 1988:193, 195–196).

Animality continues to be identified with the Other in the context of "other people," including affinally related relatives who are also separate from the house. The New Guinea Karam explicitly regard the cassowary, the primary forest game representing the undomesticated wild, as metaphorical sister (who marries out of the natal group) and as cross-cousin (father's sister's child whose name you should not say) and their descendants, people who, though connected to the house by lateral ties, also stand outside it in significant respects (Bulmer 1967; see Chapter 5). The Karam apply equally interesting ideas to dogs, which constitute wild forest animals that are admitted to human settlement as tamed animals but who remain "uncivilized" and do a lot of damage around human habitations. "Myth and folklore assign to dogs their own society, analogous to human society, and in one myth men stole women married to dogs and made them their own wives. Both in myth and in reality domestic dogs are the adopted children of their owners, adoptees of a special class for which there is a human parallel, taken as foundlings from distant places and unrelated people" (19). In Bulmer's view, "cassowaries and dogs are quasi-humans, cassowaries the metaphorical cognates of men and dogs the distant potential affines and adopted children . . ." (20).

In further contrast to "emergent" house ancestors, spatially situated "affinal" ancestors referencing first-principle origins characteristically appear as bountiful or nurturing beings, rather than as juridical in nature, in their disposition towards house members. For South India hunter-gatherer-horticulturalists the "forest as ancestor" is basically generous and benevolent (Bird-David 1990:192; Myers 1986:22, 220). Among the BaKongo of Zaire (whose houses are organized matrilineally), individuals may appeal to their ancestral fathers for blessings for success rather than to the dead of their own matrilineage, whose powers to affect well-being lie essentially in potential for withholding it (MacGaffey 1986:83, 84, 67). This generally helpful and benevolent attitude is comparable to that expected of physically living human affines and lateral relatives. It is noteworthy, too, that during mortuary rites among houses recognizing spatial or "affinal" ancestors, and in contrast to the more extreme expressions of emergent house ancestorness mentioned above, critical roles are frequently assigned to living outsiders, including affines, in the preparation of the corpse and other necessary activities (see Chapter 5).

In many, probably most, cultural settings conceptualizations of ancestors combine, in various ways and to varying degrees, the temporal and the spatial dimensions of ancestorness to recognize emergent house ancestors and first-principle or "affinal" ancestors. The Kwaio, for example, identify both founding ancestors of the patrilineal house and ancestors related to the house through in-marrying women (Keesing 1971: 144–153, 1982:36, 63, 84, 109 n. 7). Similarly, the Chamba recognize "mythological" origins of matriclans relating to animal transformations or other natural phenomena ("many matriclan ancestresses were animals") and "legendary" histories of patriclans referring, among other things, to clan (house) founders and "incarnated members" (Fardon 1988:299–300, 170–171, 176, 1990:31, 32).[7] The hunting and gathering Nayaka of South India recognize family relations with the first settlers in the area, on the one hand, and metaphorically regard the forest as "parent" on the other. In festivals they refer to themselves as "children" and address "spirits of local forefathers" and "the local forest" as "big father" and "big mother," respectively (Bird-David 1990:192).

The many examples, particularly from Africa, in which lineage ancestors or "souls" are contrasted with nature spirits, water spirits, or spirits of the bush may express this duality, too, depending on how "ancestor" and "nature" or spirits of nature are conceptualized: "named ancestors, who are the founders of kinship groups, are never identified as nature spirits. However, ghosts, distant ancestors, and the dead of non-relatives can be considered as nature spirits" (Anderson and Kreamer 1989:43; Rowlands 1985:52). "The Gola of Liberia recall that the founders of their ancestral homeland entered into an agreement with its original occupants, who were water spirits. These spirits agreed to drive away monsters and guarantee the fertility of the land, if the

Gola would enter into marriages with them. The spirit spouses of the founders subsequently became ancestral tutelaries" (Anderson and Kreamer 1989:44, based on d'Azevedo; Goody 1962:355 n. 9; Bloch and Parry 1982:11–12; Middleton 1982:141).

Complementarities between ancestor elements of the spatial and the temporal cosmological domains may also reflect the cultural contexts in which the two originally developed and initially came to be interrelated. Consideration of this point encourages a brief, speculative digression concerning the possible sequence of cosmological reconfigurations that may have accompanied major developments in cultural evolution. The discussion will necessarily and prudently be general in scope, my intent being only to suggest how broad cultural strategies historically may have broadly conditioned the various cosmological structurings that are evidenced today in ethnographically known societies and that are the focus of this study in general.

The ethnographic literature suggests that the development of the concept of temporal, emergent house ancestors, whether considered from a historical or structural perspective, probably was a "secondary" development in response to several broad dimensions of cultural change in both social and cosmological "environments." It would appear that in the politically noncentralized and preagricultural hunting, fishing, and gathering world, cosmological conceptualizations associated particularly with nonsedentary hunting and gathering peoples lacking binding group ties (that is, lacking houses and more or less comparable to so-called "immediate-return" societies) would have focused on contacts with Others identified on the spatial or horizontal (geographical) cosmological axis.[8] Presumably the categories of tangible beings "out there" that would have been available for metaphorical identification would have included other people and animals. Of these two, ethnographic analogy suggests particularly close "relationships" and shared "personness" between human beings and animals, particularly animal "masters" or "guardians" of game animals, as people viewed themselves as firmly set within a wider animal world, kin to various wild animals and recognizing animality as an intrinsic component of original beings (Ingold 1987:247–248, 258; Kent 1989:14; James 1990; Guenther 1988: 193; Mundkur 1988).[9]

Among such mobile hunter-gatherers, "other people" as cosmological Others, including potential affines (who do not appear to be directly referenced in the context of origins among immediate-return hunter-gatherers [Glazier 1984:134]), probably also would have been metaphorically subsumed within the wider or more inclusive realm of animal existence. This is suggested ethnographically by parallels drawn between hunting and sexual conquest/spouse attainment (marriage): "There are many stories that tell of how the hunter, captivated by his female quarry, goes off to live with her, so that the animal master becomes his father-in-law. But by the same token, the master is somewhat enamoured of human girls and women, who run the risk of being raped if caught in a lonely spot" (Ingold 1987:251).[10] In such circumstances there also would have been no need to anthropomorphize or personalize the human dead per se. Indeed, Woodburn (1982b:188, 202, 207) describes little interest among immediate-return hunter-gatherers toward using the human dead symbolically in any way, although they may bring illness to society (see note 9). Death was probably felt to affect relationships among the living more than it affected relationships between the living and the dead (Myers 1986:133–134, 117). If contemporary ethnography is taken as guide, the remains of the human dead themselves may have been literally distanced from the living, buried in unmarked graves or left in the bush, their names no longer publicly mentioned, and the household or camp moved away from the place of death (Glazier 1984:133; Woodburn 1982b; Myers 1986:117, 132–134).[11]

Regardless of what particular problems, pressures, or opportunities encouraged or necessitated a gradual reduction in residential mobility (or permitted more settled residence in the first place; Rosenberg 1990; Kelly 1992), increasingly sedentary lifestyles were accompanied by significant changes in social organization that were paralleled by equally significant changes in cosmological construction and emphasis (Hodder 1990; Kent 1989:11). In considering these adjustments it is heuristically useful and probably historically accurate to separate sedentism per se from the development of food production, although perhaps not from resource management (Bishop 1991; Kent 1989; Kelly 1992:49, 52; Eder 1991:249–250; Price and Gebauer 1995:8, 17–18; Hayden 1995: 277–279). Hodder, for example, argues persuasively that "the possibility exists . . . that domestication in the social and symbolic sense occurred prior to domestication in the economic sense. Indeed . . . the agricultural revolution may have been an epiphenomenon of deeper changes" (1990:31; Woodburn 1988:57).[12]

Some of these "deeper changes" would have occurred in more complexly organized "delayed-return" societies, including foraging, fishing, and part-time farming groups characterized by limited logistical mobility or "settling down."[13] Such societies, with at least seasonally fixed settlements, allowed for greater delineation of the house as an ongoing sociological, ideological, demographic unit whose corporate well-being increasingly preempted and absorbed the fortunes of the individual (Hodder 1990:32–33, 38, 294; Barnard and Woodburn 1988:28–31; Woodburn 1988:34; Johnson and Earle 1987:195; Rousseau 1985: 41–42).[14] Concurrently the relative emphasis accorded the several categories of spatially situated cosmological Others may have shifted either to deemphasize, relatively speaking, identity and connections between people and animals or to enlarge the field of spatial Others by increasing identification between the house (Us) and other people (Rousseau 1985:42).

To be sure, the identity accorded to Others in more residentially mobile hunting-gathering or fishing societies postulates a strong personalistic context even for animal Others (Philippi 1985). In more sedentary conditions, however, the Otherness not of anthropomorphized animals but of humanized other people is accorded equal or even primary referential authority as the house and its growing relational and contractual community, including its affinal connections, are projected onto the cosmological stage (Harrison 1990:46–47). Now access to animals (and other naturalistic forms) as cosmological Other would more likely be conceptualized metaphorically as variations on the theme of other people as Others rather than vice-versa (Mundkur 1988:142).[15]

The cosmological imagery of the contemporary Manambu of Papua New Guinea, villagers whose economy is based on fishing and exploitation of sago palm with secondary interest in hunting and limited swidden agriculture (Harrison 1990:13–14), is suggestive of this postulated emphasis on other people rather (or more) than on animals as primary form for metaphors of Other in societies where the house has become important:[16]

> A time came when all the totemic beings emerged from their settlements and created the world. Some fashioned the mountains, lakes, and river. Others issued forth in the form of the winds, animals, plants and birds. . . . The totemic ancestral spirits, they say, are men and women too; but their faces . . . are hidden because these beings do not show themselves to living people in their true forms. They are only visible as animal and plant species, as rivers, mountains, ritual sacra, and so on. . . . There are two separate orders of existence: the everyday world of sense experience, in which living human beings exist, and a second, concealed world, in which

all things exist in their real forms, which are human forms. (Harrison 1990:45, 46; see also Chesser 1975:118)[17]

Often, however, in more settled foraging and limited farming societies, where in sociological terms affinity is a primary means for relating the house to other people, the cosmological relationship with Others is also expressed through themes entailing contractual arrangements with other people, especially themes of affinity and the acquisition of spouses. Consider again the Manambu, where relationships with "totemic ancestors" involve affinal Others as well as the totemic beings of the house itself. In this case the secret names of totemic ancestors are essential to a kin group's magical and ritual powers and are the basis of spells. To be effective, however, a spell must contain the secret names not only of a totemic ancestor of the house but also those of that ancestor's father, mother, and mother's brother. More specifically, "the magic has full efficacy only by the presence in the spell of the names of those four beings: two belonging to the subclan which owns the spell and two belonging to a subclan with which it exchanges women. Just as a subclan cannot create human life itself, but only by a marriage with another group, so it acquires magical powers only through a kind of onomastic exogamy, an exchange of magic names with its marriageables . . . all of a subclan's spells are frozen records of mythical alliance relationships" (Harrison 1990:57). Indeed, in the world of the Manambu, where natural phenomenon of all sorts are also personalized as totemic ancestors and, in ritual contexts, addressed by kin terms, the phenomenal world of plants, animals, and landscape also constitutes "the visible form of a vast, invisible connubium that forms the timeless pattern after which living people must marry" (58).[18] Such imagery very nicely complements Leach's discussion of concepts of creational beginnings based on affinality: "for men who thought in these terms, 'the beginning' would be the creation of contraries, that is to say the creation of male and female not as brother and sister but as husband and wife" (1979b:226). Leach also notes the absence of cosmological temporality in such perspective: "Time has no 'depth' to it, all past is equally past; it is simply the opposite of now" (223).

In the cosmological structuring posited for nonagricultural (or only partially agricultural) sedentary peoples, the role of the human dead as Other also presumably became more closely associated with other people than with animals.[19] The fate of the human dead now may have affected broader questions concerning the emergence, transformation, or reincarnation of human life as expressed in the fecundity of marital relations; concepts that may be expressed sociologically by the names accorded new members of the house (Lopes da Silva 1989; Harrison 1990:552–559; Leach 1979b). With the elaboration of the concept of the house, distinctive mortuary rites would have addressed the "experience of social community," too (Judkins 1973:83). Remains of the human dead (at least the most honored dead), identified perhaps rather ephemerally as a collectivity of "generic" dead of the house, would likely be buried in closer association with the house, perhaps by interment beneath the floor of the dwelling itself (Plog 1990:189; Melatti 1979:49; Hodder 1990:33; Glazier 1984; Woodburn 1982b:206; Binford 1968).[20]

Full-time resource production (agriculture and the domestication of animals), occurring within an already complexly conceptualized symbolic and cosmological world (Hodder 1990:36), was accompanied by yet another major cosmological restructuring, one in which the temporal dimension of cosmological space and time came to be more fully developed. Provisioning of staples by domestication demands more direct and sustained responsibility by members of the house for the care and tending of plants as they develop over a period of time from planting through germination to harvest (and even beyond for storable resources) or of domestic animals as they grow from birth to useful maturity. These roles, entailing responsibility for the processes (spiritual as well as material) as well as the conditions of growth, stand in distinct contrast with hunting and gathering to the extent that foraging is based on spatial acquisition of resources as already "mature" products involving, in some situations, a certain amount of resource management but far less human responsibility overall for the processes of their production.[21]

Presumably paralleling increased and temporally sustained responsibility for processes of resource production was a growing sense of the importance of temporal durability and of the political-ideological responsibility, as "process manager," of the house, already established as a corporate sociological and ideological entity by sedentism per se (Hodder 1990:292, 296; Price 1995:140–143). Concurrently, there was an elaboration of the importance of senior persons—firstborns and house elders—as social persona incorporating cosmological qualities of temporality and duration and holding spiritual responsibility for proper process in production (see Chapter 6). It is to be expected, too, that temporality would also be increasingly recognized in cosmological structurings. This is not to say that spatial referents for the Other would be lost. For one thing, the domestication process was extremely long and slow, and the identification accorded to other people and animals as major cosmological Others certainly continued throughout much of that process, just as hunting and gathering continued as important subsistence practices (Bird-David 1992, 1990). But the spatial or cosmographical dimension was no longer the sole or dominant referent for delineating contacts with the beyond.

Conceptual development of the temporal cosmological axis required or permitted significant additions to and reconfigurations of the world of Others. For one thing, categories of temporal Others, strictly defined, have no inherent physical or tangible referents to assist conceptual development. In contrast to the existence of other life-forms on the spatial plane, there are no visible entities "out there" in the strictly temporal realm to be defined and elaborated into cosmological formats, no physically living personifications to parallel the diverse populations of birds, beasts, and homo sapiens that exist, quite independent of cosmological identification (but as potential raw material for cosmological structurings), in the spatial, geographical distances beyond the house. Conceptual development of the temporal cosmological axis required, therefore, that personifications of temporal Others be created in their entirety from nontemporal prototypes.

The already existing and available possibilities for cosmological Otherness would have included the original spatially situated Others—animals of the wild and other people—as well as the human dead. Of these, the definitive characteristics of animals and of other people as Others would have been long established conceptually and presumably complexly developed, allowing relatively little intellectual flexibility for elaboration into the newly emerging temporal cosmological context. The human dead, however, held far more potential.[22] In a cosmos focused on readily available and readily visible spatially defined metaphors and tangibilities (other people, animals), the dead of the house, inherently invisible and intangible after the disposal of the physical remains, presumably were relatively undeveloped as a conceptual category. They were also inherently temporal in quality if what was heretofore seen as direct and fairly immediate transformational processes from physical viability to pure "soul" or to other life-forms or to nothing could be prolonged and elaborated to include concepts of duration and of durability *for the dead themselves*.

In other words, as the temporal cosmological axis developed the fate of the dead of the house (or at least those who were the most memorable, the most deserving) was not to be returned, in soul form, to the pool of life that regenerated other physical life-forms (e.g., animals) or to reappear, perhaps after a period of existence as a spirit, as a reincarnated human member of the house or to pass into oblivion. Instead the distinguished dead of the house remained viable or "alive" (though physically deceased) as a temporal category of "house ancestors," a distinct classification of intangible but personalized Other that could express concepts pertinent to duration in general and to the continuity of the house in particular as its deceased members, though changed from their physical state of being, nonetheless remained linked to the living in temporal terms.

This cosmological reconfiguration required that several qualitative images be developed. For one thing, the creation of temporal house ancestors from decomposing corpses necessitated that the traditional imagery of death as marked by physical decomposition and concepts of pollution be countered with images that defined death as an emergent process of moral and existential purification—a concept implying both continuation of connections with the still impure but aspiring living members of the house and continued (durable) life in an ideal state of existence, even the attainment of immortality as the ultimate expression of temporality (Lifton 1979:97; Hertz 1960a; Watson 1982:178–182). In addition, some means of material representation was required to make temporal ancestors manifest, make them "real," and to assist the transformation of the inert dead into viable ancestral beings (Fortes 1976:7; Lifton 1979:95; Lévi-Strauss 1962:237).

Elaboration of mortuary rites, including burial in more lasting and elaborate shrines, tombs, or cemeteries and interment of select artifacts, clothes, and ornaments appropriate to the new ancestral social persona, provided one means to accomplish these changes of state and of being, as did elaboration of concepts regarding reincarnation, naming, or other means of extending remembrance among living house members.[23] But an even better way to express tangibly the ongoing relation of the human dead with the house, this new temporal durability made manifest by emergent house ancestors, was to cleanse (purify) and keep (by secondary burial) the most enduring portions of the physical remains of the dead themselves—long bones and skulls (Plog 1990:188–189; Hodder 1990:40, 245–246).

Bones of the dead considered as relics, as a type of power-filled "wealth" or "treasure," give tangible evidence of the "truth" of the existence of ancestors since the bones that are kept are, by definition, special; they are not just the bones of the generic dead (Metcalf 1982:19–20). The bones of those unfortunates who do not die "at the correct time, in the correct place, and in the correct manner" (Middleton 1982:142) or who die physically without having achieved the successes in this life by which ancestor qualifications can be met in the "other" world, will not be preserved. Such individuals will still "truly and completely" die; neither their bones nor their names will be remembered, and they will sink into anonymity and thus oblivion (Metcalf 1982:243; Middleton 1982:141–147). Preservation of the bones of those who do deserve to be remembered, however, helps to create that memory and thus tangibly evidences the reality of house ancestors. Such bones could also assist in the production of life. Since the general context in which the elaboration of the temporal cosmological axis emerged involved recognition of temporal duration expressed in processes of resource production, what better way to assist and ensure this production than to tap, through ritual, the processual fertility inherent in the bones of the ancestral dead (see Chapter 3)?

From a broadly sociological perspective sedentism, combined with highly successful resource production or management, provides thresholds for demographic growth and increasing social and political complexity, structural clarification, and social distancing, paralleled on the cosmological plane by increasing elaboration of the temporal cosmological axis. As the past acquires depth, temporal duration becomes structurally extended. Ancestral genealogies grow and ramify as emergent ancestors' links with the house become quantitatively more diversified (Evans-Pritchard 1940:104–110). They also become more qualitatively differentiated, too, as connections between the living and the ancestral via seniority and primogeniture become valued more, especially for political purposes, than connections between "lesser" living members of the house and "lesser" ancestors (Dillehay 1992). In contrast, the spatial cosmological axis and the categories of Others that for so long had tangibly identified this axis and linked it with the house continue to be recognized, but with varying importance and significance relative to the growing ideological strength and legitimizing power of the temporal domain.

In relatively sedentary and increasingly hierarchical and centralized hunting and gathering societies (like those on the northwest coast of

North America), where subsistence was based on increasingly successful management of extremely abundant wild resources, animals and temporal ancestors became closely linked conceptually (Goldman 1975). In many agricultural societies, as reliance on food production grew, game animals gradually declined in subsistence value but often continued to be accorded important ritual significance as "natural" or "earth" manifestations of the managerial aspects of supernatural power. Various large, predatory nongame animals also continued to manifest first-principle ancestral beings and power (Fortes 1945:142–143, 145; Mundkur 1988).[24] A somewhat different cosmological fate, however, befell other people, especially affines, as cosmological Other.

Affines, still essential for the social reproduction of the house, increasingly have their role as cosmological Other co-opted by the need to legitimize the expanding temporal cosmological axis, particularly as this expansion comes to support both the processual (temporal) and the managerial or contractual (spatial) aspects of the political life of the house or polity.[25] This cosmological "power play" can be seen, for example, in beliefs that relegate the temporary, noxiously decomposable, flesh-and-blood components of the human body to spatial affines and the purifiable, processually potent and enduring bones to temporal house ancestors. By positing such ontological contrasts (also evidenced among the living in increasing gender inequalities), the power of affines as spatial cosmological Others that had developed as the corporateness of the house increasingly emphasized the management of "other people" is reduced in significance relative to temporal potencies.

On the other hand, and most important, the "support" of affines, both as tangible Others and *as an established, previously existing, or logically prior category of Other identifying a type of first-principle ancestral origins,* remains essential to enhance the legitimacy of the much newer concept of temporal house ancestors (see Chapter 6).[26] Similarly, the "support" of affines as representatives of the spatial or managerial aspect of the cosmological order becomes an essential political complement to the temporal process-oriented political-ideological order espoused by political authorities of the house. In short, affines remain indispensable as Other not only for the social reproduction of the house but also for its political-ideological and cosmological legitimation and thus its political viability. These social, political, and ideological dependencies can be most succinctly expressed and activated if aspects of affinity are related to aspects of emergent house ancestorness. Therefore,

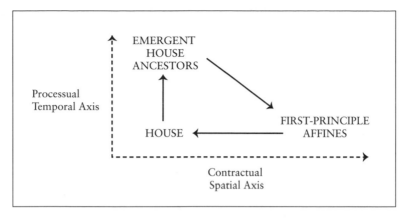

FIGURE 2   Affines co-opted as house ancestors.

in a move that neatly combines cosmological co-optation with the need to affirm the temporally based political legitimacy and ancestry of the house, affinity becomes directly linked, conceptually, to house ancestry, and living affines as legitimizing Others become identified as tangible representations of *both* original first-principle origins and emergent house ancestors in politically significant ritual contexts of the house (Fig. 2 and Chapter 6).

The pinnacle of the appropriation of the Otherness of spatial affinity to support the Otherness of temporal house ancestors is achieved in politically centralized hierarchical societies where this cosmological co-optation is used to legitimize increasingly complex political affairs. In chiefdoms, for example, where not only are deceased aristocrats identified with emergent ancestors but physically viable aristocrats are also apotheosized as tangible living ancestors (Chapter 8), it is essential that this hubris be "witnessed" and legitimized by affines and affinity, as discussed in later chapters. In a broader sense, the conjoining of elements of the spatial and the temporal cosmological domains also encourages and legitimizes the amassing of tangible evidence of the social and especially political (re)productive success of the house and the polity, both in the quantitative idiom of "abundance" generally expressed in size of family and in bountiful resource production at home and in the aggressive acquisition of qualitatively valued wealth items (often by marriage payments and through long-distance trade) from spatially distant or outside realms (Helms 1993). Ultimately the combined wealth of fields, flocks, and foreign affairs, of the processual and the managerial or con-tractual, the quantitative and the qualitative aspects of power stands as evidence of the exemplary, ancestor-patterned abilities of the leadership of the house or polity to access both temporal and spatial cosmological sources of social reproduction and political legitimation.[27]

*. . . for men divide themselves
into two groups in order that
they may impart life to one
another, that they may
intermarry, compete with one
another, make offerings to one
another, and do to one another
whatever is required by their
theory of prosperity.*

ARTHUR M. HOCART,
Kings and Councillors, 1970, P. 290

5

AFFINES

Because the house views itself as embedded within an encircling and qualitatively definitive cosmic setting, the house can never be complete unto itself. Like it or not, its continued existence as a political, social, and ideological entity is held hostage by the moral and political necessity of recognizing and forming attachments with cosmological Others, especially those who represent, embody, and activate principles or conditions of cosmological origins and related legitimacies. Among the several categories of universally recognized cosmological Others are affines, nonmembers of the house who constitute a category of other people that stands in close structural proximity with the house and who are linked to the house by distinctive metaphorical and sociological relationships.

In fact, affines constitute a distinctive category of Other expressly created by the house to assist in its immediate social and ideological reproduction. In so doing the house may be guided by either of two general cosmological perspectives. On the one hand, the house may consider the need for affines as something of a necessary evil forced upon it by the inability to legitimately (morally) achieve self-perpetuation and reproduc-

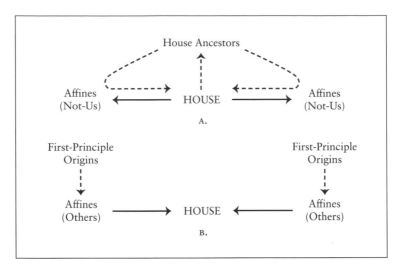

FIGURE 3   Affinal contexts.
            A. Affines as not-Us.
            B. Others as affines.

tion within itself (Taylor and Aragon 1991:116). Instead, the house is forced, reluctantly, to extend itself outward by attaching affinal groups from other houses that, while they are not-Us, are only "slightly" Other. (For example, the house may prefer marriages into previously allied affinal groups or with a distant range of consanguineal "cousins.") Such affinal groups, as relatively "close" spatial/temporal Others, may serve essentially as indirect conduit for creative ancestral energies that are inherent in, but directly forbidden to, the house per se (Errington 1987; Bloch 1992:4–6, chap. 5; Bozzoli de Wille 1975:8; see Fig. 3a). On the other hand, the house may envision the need for affines as constituting more of a positive good, as a means to end disputes or to open the house to greater benefits, including social reproduction, from a cosmos inherently more powerful and creative than itself (Chernela 1993:26, 54–55, 73). Affines in this scenario are viewed very distinctly as "outside Others" who directly channel creative powers deriving from original, first-principle origins independent of and prior to the house (Lévi-Strauss 1966:236; Lopes da Silva 1989; Harrison 1990; see Fig. 3b).[1]

In either case, living affines constitute spatial/temporal Others. They do so not only by virtue of their structural position vis-à-vis the house, as Lévi-Strauss (1969a:114) and Sahlins (1976:24–25, 29) would have it, but also because of their association with particular qualities widely deemed to be generally characteristic of cosmological Others who effect contact with cosmological origins. It is the combination of both structural positioning and a distinctive qualitative state of being relative to that structure that confers legitimating authority upon living affinal groups and conditions the roles of individual spouses, in-laws, and lateral relatives of the house. The nature of affinal qualities will be considered in this chapter. Structural matters relating to affines will be introduced here and more thoroughly explored in later chapters.

It should be clear by now that the term and concept of "affines" is used in this study to identify a social category clearly distinct from the consanguineal group composing the house. In Sahlins's words, "Taken as a whole, the domain of kinship is composed of two 'kinds' of people, own relatives and affinal" (1976:29). There has been considerable uncertainty in much traditional anthropological analysis, however, regarding the "kinship" status of affines and affinity, for " 'kin' or 'kinship' is sometimes opposed to affinity and sometimes taken as embracing it" (Dumont 1983:74). Some anthropologists, including Dumont, have cautioned against the automatic inclusion of affines within certain consanguineal kinship categories in formal analyses, viewing this practice as a "customary and peculiar vocabulary" of anthropologists (14, 22) that reflects a distinctly Western perspective: "with us modern Westerners, affinity is subordinated to consanguinity, for my brother-in-law, an affine, becomes an uncle, a consanguineal relative, for my children. In other words, affinity is ephemeral, it merges into consanguinity for the next generation. As values are by definition conceived as permanent, durable, I may say that affinity is inferior to consanguinity, or *undervalued in relation to it*" (Dumont 1983:vii, 32–33; Appell 1976a:147).

Dumont's statement was made to facilitate discussion of South Indian kinship systems in which affinity, in contrast, "is transmitted from generation to generation, is thus permanent or durable, and so has *equal status* with consanguinity or a value equal to it" (1983:72). I believe the implications of his comments should be considered more carefully; therefore, in this study, for heuristic purposes I accord affinity separate status and distinctive value from consanguineal kinship, especially as the latter applies to relations among members of the house. It must be understood, too, if affinity is accorded this distinctive identity, that affinity is applicable not only for ego's generation but also across generations to include "lateral" relatives who originally stood outside the consanguineal membership of the house—that is to say, to patrilateral relatives of matrilineal houses (e.g., relatives of ego's father and mother's father) and matrilateral relatives of patrilineal houses (e.g., relatives of ego's mother and father's mother; Goody 1959:67; Keesing 1968:59–60, 63, 64).[2] I would also agree with Dumont's contention that "the concept of affinity should be extended so as to include not only immediate, individual relationships (affines in the ordinary sense) but also the people who inherit such a relationship from their parents, those who share it as siblings of the individual affines, etc. . . . ." (1983:73).[3]

Recognition of affines as a kinship category distinct from consanguines and indications of "the inherent antithesis between kinship bonds and affinal relations" (Fortes 1962a:2) are also readily evidenced ethnographically in situations where individuals or groups stand as consanguineal relatives in some contexts but as affines in others. In these cases affinal identity is not only recognized as clearly distinctive from the consanguineal (e.g., Levi-Strauss 1987:166; Vitebsky 1993:184) but also frequently accorded priority for reasons that we shall examine later (Fortes 1962a:2). "Where agnatic and affinal or matrilateral ties coincide, the latter are held to take precedence" (Comaroff and Comaroff 1981:37 regarding endogamy among the Tswana Tshidi; La Fontaine 1962:94). Similarly, " . . . if the premiss of most marriages is this 'friendship' with people who are at the borderline of otherness and non-otherness, the actual contracting of marriage implies stressing otherness, since it means starting the process of alliance constitution all over again" (Valeri 1994:10 regarding the Huaulu of eastern Indonesia; Cohen and Comaroff 1976:98). Speaking of the Giriama of Kenya, Parkin further explains that

> while affines are always likely also to be kin, and kin to become affines . . . , there is another sense in which affines remain distinct from each other and recognise that they are each a party to an alliance between two clans. This is the aspect of affinity which, then, stresses differences between clans, and marks clans out as marriageable groups. As if fearing the confusion of affinity and therefore clanship that might occur if all affines were regarded as no more than blood relatives, funerals are great occasions at which alliances based on marriage between clans are highlighted. (Parkin 1991:103; Lévi-Strauss 1987:165–166; Chowning 1989:99)

Affines are also identified as a distinctive category or "type" of being, specifically as Others, in the numerous and often explicit ethnographic references to affines, or potential affines, as foreigners, outsiders, opposites, enemies, strangers, or sojourners.[4] "The major social distinction made by the Hua is between their consanguines, . . . ('one skin') and their affines, . . . ('heavy or difficult people'). Relations of distrust exist mainly between affines because, like other New Guinea Highland people, wives often come from groups with whom the husband's group does not enjoy a secure and stable relationship" (Sanday 1986:67; Errington 1987:420). "Men from other villages and tribes can become linked to one's home village through trade and feast invitations, but above all through marriage to resident women. 'Foreign' men are, in other words, a sort of prototypical brother-in-law" (Howard 1991:64 regarding the Waiwai of Brazil). " . . . the old Tupinamba Indians called both brothers-in-law and enemies by the same word, tobajara, which etymologically means to be face to face with, to be opposite" (Huxley 1995:242, 253, regarding the Urubu, also of Brazil).

Barnard and Woodburn have argued that, with respect to the development of corporate households (i.e., houses) and other social and political attributes of "delayed-return" societies, "not enough attention has been paid to the way in which binding relationships are developed between close kin and affines" (1988:29). They stress that such relationships involve, among other things, a form of "ideological elaboration" in which "people are believed to be involved mystically in other people and such involvement, intentional or unintentional, affects their health or welfare. The power to bless or to curse someone, the power to bewitch them, and the power to contaminate them through pollution are all examples of such elaborations" (ibid.). This important insight can be taken further, for these ideological elaborations not only affect relationships between affines and the house but also identify the major qualities characteristic of affines as a sociological category that can relate the house to greater cosmological legitimations (Leach 1979a:166; Valeri 1994:6, 8). In this context affines and relations of affinity constitute an interface between the house and the encompassing cosmos, and as a result affines are accorded a certain liminal status that may place them in a potentially ambiguous, and thus ideologically very powerful, position as cosmological Others vis-à-vis the house.[5]

The most fundamental roles and contexts that the house assigns to affines and lateral affinal groups (a father's natal house in a matrilineal society or a mother's natal house in a patrilineal society) concern the maintenance of life-sustaining and life-renewing connections with cosmological origins and a striving toward ideal conditions of humanness by members of the house. Both of these can be realized to a significant degree by the familiar role affines play in the social reproduction of the house. The attainment of adult status by house members as manifested by the taking of spouses (and thus the establishment of associations with affinal groups) and the production of offspring constitutes achievement of a human ideal aspired to by all house members. This attainment has significance, however, not only in sociological but also cosmological terms, for affinal alliances constitute successful connections with agents of cosmological potency. As such, relationships with affines contain expectations and responsibilities comparable to at least some of those associated with other political-ideological specialists associated with the house, including house elders, firstborns, priests and shamans, and even skilled artisans (see Chapter 11). In the performance of their roles all these persons reach outward, beyond the domain of the house proper, to contact elements of the all-encompassing cosmos and acquire or control aspects of that powerful realm for the ultimate good of the house or the polity (Helms 1993; see also Chapter 6). Affines provide a comparable service.

Affines benefit the house not only by contributing to its social reproduction but also by taking major roles in house ritual and ceremony (to be discussed below) and by influencing the behavior and well-being of individual house members to maintain a proper striving toward social and ideological proprieties and ideals. In other words, by virtue of the inherent qualities of origins-related Otherness that imbues them by definition with cosmological potency and authority, affines (including lateral relatives) have the capability to assist or to punish members of the house, and their relationships with the house are often guided accordingly.

Usually affines are viewed as a generous source of life and general prosperity for the house. Gifts and services proffered by a suitor or a spouse as evidence of capabilities as a provider (e.g., in "brideservice" societies) may constitute tangible means of establishing this role (Collier 1988:24–27). Affinal kin may also pay particular attention to the children born into the house by a spouse they have provided, offering nurturance, teaching magical knowledge and useful powers, and ceremonially enhancing the child's vitality and eventual fertility (Dalton 1996: 402–403 regarding the Rawa of Papua New Guinea). By the same token, among the Toba Batak and the Kedang of Indonesia, "should the wife-takers be childless, suffer long illness, deaths in the family, or fires, they may turn to their [wife-givers] for help..." (Barnes 1974:248). For the Batak, the wife-giver is "a sort of stand-in for God to his daughter's children" (249). Conversely, however, if a Toba Batak sister's son does not visit his mother's brother or opposes him and fails to respect his authority, the latter may curse him and bring illness, even death, to the miscreant (249–250; Lévi-Strauss 1969a:305) just as, among the New Guinea Rawa, "a bride's parents are supposed to have the capability to make her children sick and die, and men endeavor to assuage their wives' parents' anger by bringing them gifts of food . . ." (Dalton 1996: 400). Similarly, among the Gisu, where "the mother's brother, as in many African societies with patrilineal lineages, is the source of help and affection for his sister's son" and where "a mother's brother should make the gift of a cow to his sister's son at the latter's initiation and at his marriage," that same mother's brother "also has mystical power over his sister's son and his curse is feared" (La Fontaine 1975:84, 85; Gough 1971:102; Winter 1956:91, 183; Schapera 1950:145).[6]

There may be several ways to understand the dual nature of house-affine relationships. The mysterious cosmic powers that affines are privy to are generally believed to contain both good and evil aspects, and affines, constituting a liminal category of persons in their own right, can have access to both sides of the cosmic coin. But the matter can be approached somewhat differently if, in the purview of the house, the close relationships among its members are expected, at least ideally, to properly entail positive, morally acceptable behavior. In this case, when evil or immoral things, such as illness and death, do occur, the cause can only be sought in an external source, such as affines who, though sufficiently like Us to provide spouses, are also by definition not-Us or Others. If We represent cosmological good, it follows that the Other must, again by definition, represent or have access to the darker side of existence (Bloch 1973:78). So it is that witchcraft by in-laws explains many deaths among the Mehinaku of Brazil, who at the best of times regard affines with "covert antagonism" (Gregor 1977:285, 286; Maybury-Lewis 1974:274, 308, 291), and accusations of sorcery fall heavily upon affines in Dobu, where "one marries into a village of enemies, witches and sorcerers . . ." (Fortune, quoted in Bloch and Parry 1982:27; Robinson 1962:153; Weiner 1976:65; Weiner 1992:116, 127), while fears of magically induced sanctions convince Wape (New Guinea) men to give much of the wealth they have acquired as wage laborers to their matrilateral relatives, especially mothers' brothers (Mitchell 1978:11).

Cosmological involvement for good or for evil may be forthcoming not only from living affines but also from the dead of affinal groups. "It is in their role as affines that the maternal ancestors make a sister's child ill" in some South African patrilineal groups (Ngubane 1981:85), while among the BaKongo of Zaire, organized into matrilineal houses, paternal ancestors can visit sickness and death upon those who upset them. But a member of a house also appeals to paternal ancestors for blessings for success: "The children are entitled to receive gifts and blessings from their deceased father . . . if therefore anyone finds that he is not succeeding, he goes to his father's [clan], first to the living, and then to those who have died and are buried" (Laman, quoted in MacGaffey 1986:84; Radcliffe-Brown 1952:26–27; Richards 1950:237).[7] Similarly, garden magic passed down from father to son among matrilineal Trobrianders is particularly reliable, and "in the most powerful spell of Trobriand garden magic, . . . the magician invokes the aid of his father, his father's father and his mother's father." Likewise, ". . . it is a woman's father and other members of his subclan who, to a very great extent, insure her fertility and procreation, and magically protect her progeny. Now we see the role of the paternal ancestors in magically insuring the fertility of the gardens" (Robinson 1962:148–149; Sider 1967:101).

It must be emphasized that the power of affines either to effect well-being or to create disaster for the house springs from belief in the power of an outside ancestral order in general to sustain proper social and moral behavior within the house (Rowlands 1985:58). When some or even all of this spiritual authority is attributed to the spatial cosmological axis, to affines or to affinal ancestors, it is frequently contraposed to the jural authority of the corporate house and its own emergent ancestors (Barnes 1974:251–252). In such circumstances affines and affinal laterals are usually viewed as essentially benevolent in character and intent, and their amiable ministrations contrast significantly with the tensions and dissensions that may arise from competitions among members of the house. "The principle that agnates compete and challenge each other's status, while marriageables are interdependent and support one another [in disputes over ceremonial rights] expresses itself in Avatip social organization in many different forms" (Harrison 1990:58). "Close agnation is held to be fraught with rivalry and competition; matrilateral ties are recognized as supportive and privileged" (Comaroff and Comaroff 1981:32, 37, regarding the Tshidi; Cohen and Comaroff 1976:96–98).[8] A brief vignette from Karavar, a matrilineal society in Melanesia, nicely captures the essence of this point. Thinking of the good things of life, especially during the season when the prevailing winds switch direction, an anthropologist's cook rhapsodized about how, at such times, "the whole world is lovely and fresh. The islands seem to just float on top of the water; women go slipping through the woods thinking of their husbands or lovers. Such is the time a man thinks of his father and all the things his father has given him." "No one," the anthropologist notes, "talks about a mother's brother that way" (Errington 1974:52).

In addition to their inherent abilities to succor or to curse, to offer assistance or to destroy, affines and lateral relatives, being cosmological Others, are also frequently viewed as reliable repositories of ritual knowledge and as sources of ritual authority. This role is expressed metaphorically among the matrilineal Crow by interpreting the relationship between an individual's supernatural patron (acquired through vision quest) and the seeker or protégé "as that of a father and his child" (Lowie 1979:287). Comparable relationships exist between members of the house and living affinal groups in many other societies. Among certain Nuba tribes of the Sudan (Africa), for example, where different intermarrying clans stand in affinal relationship one to another, "the clans hang together, as it were, by two hinges; one is biological necessity—clans depend on each other for marriage and thus for the continuity of the species; the other is spiritual necessity—the knowledge that the welfare of each clan depends on supernatural help in the possession of the other" (Nadel 1947:207). In comparable fashion, MacGaffey explains how, among the BaKongo of Zaire, members of affinal clans linked to the matrilineal house through patrifiliation could be entrusted with the house's traditions and insignia and exercised ritual supervision as priests of the house (MacGaffey 1986:26, 99, 151).[9] The Manambu of New Guinea appear to have pursued a similar practice in which "every subclan allows all its magical and ritual specialisations to be learned and carried out by its male allies, most especially by its sisters' sons. . . . Rights to know myths are transmitted between subclans from wife-givers to wife-takers" (Harrison 1990:127, 128). More specifically (and anticipating political themes to be explored in later chapters),

> it can happen that . . . the leader of a small, declining subclan, has no subclan-agnates able or willing to inherit his knowledge. He therefore has to teach the whole of this lore to a sister's husband or sister's son, or bestow a wife on an orator specifically to teach him. The subclan's esoterica thereby pass entirely into the hands of its allies, and when this happens the subclan becomes dependent politically on these outsiders. The subclan becomes dependent on them for defending it in debates; for eventually returning its mythology to it; and for keeping this lore secret from groups—including their own subclans—which would use it against the subclan in debates. (130)[10]

Affinal-like roles as cosmological Others and ritual authorities relative to the house are also found in so-called dialectical societies where the contrast between Us and Others is formalized in "dual organizations" or moieties (Maybury-Lewis 1989a; Almagor 1989:143–144). To recognize this parallel, however, it is necessary to move from the usual interpretation of dual social organization as comprising two comparable social sectors interacting in complementary reciprocal relationships to a more centered perspective in which, at a given time or for a given occasion, one of the moieties as focal sector is seen to constitute Us while the other moiety becomes the cosmological Other.[11] This perspective is especially apparent in exogamous dual organizations, when the relationship between the two units may be expected to be conditioned to greater or lesser degree by the qualities of "affines" and "house" that identify the intermarrying halves from the position of each, respectively (Crocker 1979:283, 284; Maybury-Lewis 1979:230, 234; Kan 1989:24).

Indeed, the opposite half may be quite explicitly identified as outsiders or as "Other" in the eyes of members of the focal or "house" moiety (Maybury-Lewis 1974:167, 239, 244, 1979:230–232).[12] Members of the "Other" half may be perceived as differing in kind from the house moiety with respect to supernatural connections (Crocker 1979:285, 1969); or the opposite moiety, especially as affinal Other, may be recognized as holding some degree of ritual authority relative to the house moiety such that (stated more conventionally) "neither moiety can carry out the ritual without the assistance of the other" (Hocart 1970:263; Hertz 1960b:95–96).[13] Thus "the Bororo can never ceremonially represent the totems belonging to their own clan but must enable members of groups in the opposite moiety to personify these" (Crocker 1969: 54–55; the opposite moiety is the affinal moiety), just as among the Cahuilla of southern California, mortuary rites required the presence of members of both moieties since the ritual knowledge "owned" by the "Other" moiety was necessary to complement the ritual knowledge "owned" by the moiety of the "house" (Bean 1972:85).

The Cahuilla are far from unique in this respect. In fact, the ultimate expression of the role of affines as tangible cosmological Others familiarly involved with and deeply knowledgeable about the mysteries of the spatial/temporal beyond may be found in the ritual roles frequently assigned to affines in mortuary rites.[14] Now the same potent affines whose powers as life-givers provide children for the house, whose blessings may bring success and well-being for the house, or whose curses may open the way for misfortune and pain for members of the house shoulder the responsibility for removing death from the house and for safely escorting the deceased to a final disposition in that Other realm whose boundaries may be safely broached by living affines as well as by the dead. Affines may also protect the mourners of the house, temporarily vulnerable in their grief and in the existential disorder created by the intrusion of death into their lives, from too close involvement with the activities and things of death lest they, too, slip irretrievably across the now-opened border between physical life and whatever fate lies beyond.

Actual ritual details vary considerably, but common to many mortuary rites is an official division of duties between the house (or moiety) of the deceased and some category of Others, often (although not inevitably) involving affinal/lateral relatives (or members of the Other moiety). In some instances one group, frequently the members of the house, mourn the dead while the other, frequently affinal relatives (especially wife-givers), undertake arrangements necessary for proper disposal of the remains such as dressing the corpse and preparing the funeral pyre or digging the grave and burying the deceased.[15] In other cases it is affines and lateral relatives who publicly mourn the dead while members of the house, trying to remain emotionally controlled, prepare the mortuary feasts (Campbell 1989:49–50, 52–53; Thune 1989:163–164; Grinker 1990:114; Foster 1990:442). In their intermediate status as "like Us but different" relative to the house, affines may also assist in the removal of death-associated pollution from the living mourners of the house (Keesing 1982:89) or from the spouse of the deceased, who is often considered to be most vulnerably immersed in the content of the death itself (Jackson 1977:277); they may also protect the living from harmful contact with a still-unsettled ghost (Jackson 1977:290–292), prepare the way for future communications between the living and the dead (Pauwels 1985:136), and assist the mourners' return to normal life (Macintyre 1989:136; see also Damon and Wagner 1989; Kan 1989).

Regardless of the particulars, in their role as the most benevolent of Others, affines facilitate the "proper" conduct of mortuary rites that will achieve the transformation of the deceased (provided he or she was also a "good" person and endured a "good" death) into a new life as a spirit, possibly an ancestral being. "Affines are necessary for a proper funeral and the subsequent transformation of the dead into ancestors" (Howell 1991:231 regarding the Lio of eastern Indonesia; Pauwels 1985:137); affines "have the power to guarantee the existence of a person's spirit after death" (Patterson 1981:217 regarding North Ambryn). By so doing, however, affines and laterals not only are active agents in rites of separation that move a member of the house from one state of being to another but, while engaged in events situated on the critical cosmological threshold between two worlds, may also themselves be seen as occupying a liminal position between states of life and death: "in him the living unite with the dead, and he is the necessary hyphen" (MacGaffey 1986:66–67, 70, regarding the patrilateral relative who officiates at ancestor cults among the BaKongo).

This situational liminality reflects the equally liminal position affines and lateral relatives hold more permanently as persons perpetually situated between the house and the spatial/temporal "distances" of the cosmological beyond. Stationed at such a crucial junction between the here and the there, affines and laterals represent conditions or principles of transformation which "form the ground and mechanism" of cosmological and sociopolitical contrasts (T. Turner 1977:68).[16] This structural positioning betwixt and between is informed by qualitative characteristics peculiar to positions and conditions of liminality and generally contained under the rubric of "communitas." Certain applications of these qualitative characteristics have been briefly reviewed above, including the potent capacity of affines either to curse or to assist and their roles as repositories for ritual knowledge and as agents of transformation in mortuary rituals. But the content—the communitas—of the broader, underlying context that qualifies affines and laterals for such activities needs to be examined more closely.

The concept of communitas, closely associated with the work of Victor Turner, refers to a condition or situation stressing a shared, egalitarian, generic sentiment of common identity, a type of communion that supersedes or stands in contrast to more structured conditions where role and status differences divide a population (V. Turner 1969:96–97, 111, 1977:46–47; Berger 1967:54). In Turner's interpretation, communitas is "anti-structure" ("communitas emerges where social structure is not"; 1969:126) and is identified, in part, as a condition or attitude frequently expressed by groups that are jurally weak or unrepresented, such as low-status groups that exist in the interstices of society proper, structurally marginal groups that accept a permanent institutionalized state of liminality as professional strangers or transients (such as mendicants; Turner 1969:106–111, 128). However, Turner also associates communitas with ritual or mystical "magico-religious" power (108, 114, 128) and in this context relates communitas to initiates undergoing "coming of age" rites and to laterality: "matrilaterality in patrilineal systems [and] patrilaterality in matrilineal systems" (125, 113).

With respect to the latter, Turner contrasts the characteristics of the patrilineage among the Tallensi ("property, office, political allegiance, exclusiveness, . . . particularistic and segmenting interests. It is the 'structural' link par excellence") with those associated with matrilateral ties: "spiritual characteristics, mutual interests and concerns, and collaterality . . . it does not serve material interests. In brief, matrilaterality represents . . . the notion of communitas" (114, 115–118). He also examines, with particular reference to the Nuer, the "sacred and 'affectional' aspects" of the relationship between the mother's brother and the sister's son in patrilineal societies in which, "as numerous scholars have shown, the mother's brother, who has weak jural authority over his nephew, nevertheless may have a close personal tie of friendship with him, may give him sanctuary from paternal harshness and, very often, has mystical powers of blessing and cursing over him" (119). Turner also examines the role of patrilateral links among the matrilineal Ashanti, emphasizing the "structurally inferior" nature of father-son ties but noting that "the symbols with which [this tie] is associated build up into a picture of formidable communitas value" (121–126).

In the perspective of this study I follow Turner in proposing that affines and laterals, as a category of persons contrasted with the house, are associated with, identified by, and qualitatively embody the condition of communitas, which overtly and explicitly contrasts with the potentially more divisive, competitive, or conflictive structural relationships that exist within the corporate organization of the house.[17] In so doing, however, I move away from a major point of Turner's interpretation of communitas in that I do not identify affines and laterals as jurally weak or "submerged" or in some manner "dispossessed" or marginal relative to the house (1969:114, 125, 118). Instead I view them (as Turner also does) as standing cosmologically ("spiritually" in Turner's terms) beyond the house, and for this reason as imbued with the mystical or ritual potency that underwrites the capacity for aid, benevolence, and protection—that is, the communitas—that affines and laterals can render to members of the house either individually or collectively.

In the particular context of mortuary services, affinal communitas is further associated both with the condition of liminality affecting affines who are positioned between the realm of the physically living and the realm of the dead (see also Turner 1969:100) and with principles of transformation that affect changes in states of being for house members. These transformational principles replicate higher-order first-principle origins (T. Turner 1977:68) that order the "rebirths" of spirits or ancestors into the intangible world of the there-and-then just as they order the physical births of infants (again through the mediation of affines) into the here-and-now and the "rebirths" of initiates into adulthood during rites of passage, where actual or categorical affines or lateral relatives again frequently play important roles.[18] According to Bloch, persons who have moved through liminal rites of passage (such as initiated young people) do not just return to new structural positions in society (e.g., as adults) but advance to such positions permanently transformed as social persons because they have been permanently imbued with the transcendental outside qualities that defined their transformational experience, qualities that are essentially expressive of the shared experience of communitas (Turner 1969:103). In addition, the enduring experience of communitas that parallels the structural shift from one state of being ("child") to another ("adult") and that does not dissipate with the return to "normal" life imbues initiated adults of the house with the spiritual authority, ideological power, and mystical unity that legitimizes the jural authority of adults and elders (Bloch 1992:5–6).

Guided by this insight that qualitative characteristics originating in realms and experiences outside the house or polity can inform structural positions within the house or polity (Bloch 1992:15–16; Turner 1969: 177),[19] it can be argued that, in comparable fashion, affines and laterals are empowered to perform their ministrative and transformational or mediating functions during mortuary and other rites of passage (see Chapter 6), as well as to constitute legitimate life-giving spouses and parents for members of the house, because they, too, embody "outside" principles of communitas. But because they are also permanent outsiders, communitas-imbued affines and laterals not only mediate between the house and the outside but also achieve a distinctive structural shift relative to the house within the higher and prior cosmological realm that encompasses them both.

The structural position held by a house's affines as communitas-embodying Others is comparable both to the position of initiated house adults, whom they marry, and to the position assigned by the house to other categories of outside beings, particularly the dead (Fig. 4).[20] It is really because they hold a structural position comparable to that of the dead and because they embody the same transcendent communitas that imbues the collective world of the dead that affines are authorized to

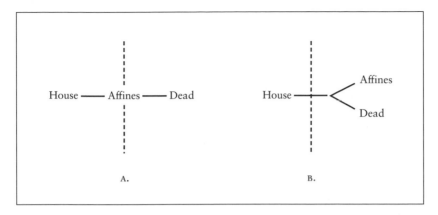

FIGURE 4   Affines and the dead.
            A. Affines as liminal category between the house and the dead.
            B. Affines as categorical correlate of the dead.

guide and direct the transformational journeys of newly deceased house
members, aid and assist (or if necessary curse) the living members of the
house, serve as repositories of ritual knowledge and authority, and provide new reproductive life for the house. Included within and diagnostic of this structural and qualitative transcendency are the additional
facts that affines stand apart from or escape the jural controls of the
house, just as the dead do, and that affines may provide access to contexts of cosmological origins by embodying the dead of the house in tangible form—that is, by becoming living ancestors, as Chapter 6 will discuss in more detail.[21]

Within the context of communitas, affinal groups not only exist outside the jural authority of the house but also "precede" the house by
their association with death and the dead and by providing members of
the house with spouses. In other words, affines reflect the reality of death
as an already established and ongoing condition (relative to the physically living house) that constantly necessitates the continued creation of
new life for the house, and affines reflect the need for the exogamic
house to recognize the presence of already existing other persons in its
wider socio-cosmological "environment" in order to achieve its social
reproduction. In addition, by virtue of standing beyond the jural authority of the house, representing contexts of cosmological precedence
relative to the house and embodying qualities of communitas which, by
definition, can override the divisiveness of the house in the name of a

shared humanity, affines may also achieve political as well as ideological influence over the house (Turner 1969:103, 104, 117). By so doing, affines are simply expressing on a higher structural level the position of initiated adults within the lower-level structuration of the house. That is to say, affines : house :: initiated adults : noninitiates.

To be properly developed, the topic of affinal authority must include consideration of the qualitative inequality and structural hierarchy implicit in conditions of cosmological Otherness, to be discussed at greater length in Part Two. Nonetheless, it seems appropriate to conclude this general consideration of affines by noting several situations in which the qualitative value of affines or laterals is related to higher-level political-ideological authorities superordinate to the house.

An intriguing paper by Barnes (1979) documents with comparative linguistics how, in Austronesian vocabularies, the root term for "affine" (wife-giver) is also found not only in terms glossed as "ancestor," "grandparent," "forefathers," and "god," but also in terms for "lord," "master," and "owner" of something. Barnes notes that the underlying principle relative to all these contexts is spiritual authority and suggests that these diverse uses for root constructions express symbolic equivalence as "sources = life-givers = divinity." Turning to the ethnographic repertoire, Victor Turner examines the role of Nuer leopard-skin priests as categorical mothers' brothers to the patrilineages under their charge.[22] Leopard-skin priests, who are politically unaligned, are also mystically related to the earth and its fertility, seek to preserve the peace, provide mediating functions among the lineages, and represent the larger community. Considered all together, in Turner's view the leopard-skin priest, in a generalized role of mother's brother, places the advantages of affinal/lateral communitas at the service of society at large (1969:119–120; Forde 1950:309, 314–316, 329–330; see Fig. 5a). An equally striking example is furnished by Schlegel's discussion of the political system of the matrilineal Hopi. She emphasizes the burden assumed by those who undertake positions of authority:

> . . . for they bear the responsibility for maintaining the spiritual well-being of the community and can be blamed if they fail. It is significant that the village chief and the other ceremonial-political leaders were thought of as paternal, being ceremonially addressed by the term for *father*, for in Hopi thinking this connotes nurturance rather than patriarchy . . . . The leaders, holders of high office, were considered to be fathers who took on the burden of protecting their children from spiritual danger and who,

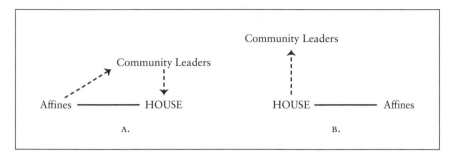

FIGURE 5   Avenues of affinal authority.
            A. Community leaders as independent high-level affines.
            B. Community leaders as emergent lower-level affines.

through their intercession, brought the blessings of abundance and harmony to their children. (1992:390)

"Fathers" as affinally defined community (suprahouse) leaders are also encountered among the Kayapó of Brazil, where the affinal relationship between in-marrying men and their fathers-in-law is generalized and projected from the level of the extended family to the level of the community as a whole (Turner 1984:357). In this example the political context of the affinal relationship provides authority for resident fathers-in-law and, by virtue of matrilocal residence, positions affinal newcomers (daughters' husbands) in a subordinate position within the house. At the higher, supra-house level the authority of fathers-in-law is expressed in key ritual functions where, as communitywide leaders, they epitomize the communitas of "beauty" in their ceremonial performances. Beauty for the Kayapó is an outside-related phenomenon representing "an *external* perspective upon the social whole, that is, a view of it as related to something above and outside itself" (359).[23] The representation of beauty by community authorities, however, ultimately is also affinally related because a married man (initially himself a subordinate affinal) must wait until he has acquired sons-in-law of his own before he can attain complete social maturity and political identity. In other words, the basis for supra-house authority based on communitas-related beauty flows into the community through the idiom of junior-generation affinal relatives of the house before it "emerges" from the house and is extended over the wider community by former sons-in-law who now serve as generalized, communitas-related fathers-in-law for all (see also Viveiros de Castro 1986:117–118; Fig. 5b).

Finally, we may note that a son-in-law may achieve a position of authority by more direct means than the Kayapó allow if the residential unit with which he becomes affiliated has strong credentials that he can co-opt to support his political ambition. Among the !Kung, for example, according to Richard Lee, marriage to a member of a family "owning" a water hole (*n!ore*)

> is the most frequent route to leadership positions among the !Kung. It usually involves an energetic, capable man from another water hole marrying a woman of the *n!ore*-owning group. The best example of this kind of leader is =Toma n!wa, one of Lorna Marshall's main informants at /Gausha. . . . He married !U, a woman of the *n!ore*-owning sibling group and became the leader of the/Gausha camp, while !U's older brother Gao went to live in the Dobe area. . . . Another example of a leader who married in is =Toma//gwe at Dobe, who married //Koka of the *n!ore*-owning group and settled at Dobe to raise a family that by the 1970s had grown to consist of a group of four married children and their spouses and eight grandchildren. =Tome//gwe is considered gruff and unreasonable by other !Kung, but his large family plus his connections to the owner group validates his leadership role. (1981:91)

Lee further indicates, however, that such marriages are not the only route to leadership. Seniority in a large family and especially seniority in a long line of water-hole owners, as well as personal qualities, may also contribute to leadership. This is not surprising. Like affinity, "ownership" of an important territorial site and qualities associated with seniority provide evidence of access to cosmological origins. Since this condition lies at the heart of so much political structuring and manipulation in both centralized and noncentralized polities and holds particular significance for the development of political centralization, it will be discussed more thoroughly in the following chapter.

6 |

ORIGINS

The cosmological environment beyond the house seems to be well oc-
cupied. Other people and especially affines, house ancestors, anonymous
dead, and animals have all been encountered in the several dimensions
of the spatial/temporal there-and-then. Their existence, whether tangible
or intangible, confirms the reality of the cosmological realm for the living members of the house. In addition, affines and other people, ancestors and other dead, and animal-persons can be perceived as temporally/
spatially preceding (that is, existing before) the physically living members of the house who, as they grow from infancy to initiated adulthood,
only gradually develop an awareness of the existence of a wider world
already populated with these Others. Cosmological Others that preexist
the house also share, with other types of cosmological "resources," a
fundamental association with sources and conditions of cosmological
origins, and it is in terms of origins or beginnings that cosmology has its
greatest significance for the house, both philosophically and by way of
affecting the activities of its members.

The concept of origins relates to the concept of creativity, the idea and the process of bringing things into being, of molding order out of chaos and bringing substance out of the void, of shaping and forming, of directing energy to productive activity, of producing and sustaining life. For members of the house, the dynamics of cosmological origins stand as archetypes for the diverse "economic," "social," and "political" activities undertaken in the cause and in the course of (re)creating its social and political reproduction. Reference to cosmological beginnings validates this activity and, in addition, legitimizes the authority of the persons who conduct or direct these affairs. Consequently, individuals or groups that aspire to positions of legitimate leadership and authority must try to establish tangible evidence of having access to cosmological origins by undertaking or directing enterprises in which success is interpreted as evidence of support and validation by supernatural agencies referencing the power of cosmological beginnings. These activities may include (though they are not limited to) hunting, fishing, raiding and warfare, acquisition of resources defined as wealth or treasure, agriculture and pastoralism, and all types of skilled artistry.

Access to origins may also be evidenced by establishing associations with outside beings of the cosmological "environment" who embody the potency and authority of origins and with fixed locational settings or situational events that stand firm and immovable in cosmographical space and time and can anchor individuals and groups to firm and unshakable circumstances that supersede the fluid, flexible, shifting, and uncertain world of human interactions in the here-and-now so hazardous to political contenders. In short, aspiring leaders who can publicly evidence success in their energetic "economic," "social," and "political" enterprises (the specific nature of which varies greatly cross-culturally), who establish good relationships with cosmologically defined outside Others, or who appear unshakably connected to geographical places of origins will be accorded positions of leadership and authority. Those who fail in these efforts and enterprises, either relative to other candidates or absolutely, will not be so rewarded.

The cosmological credentials of house or polity leadership or authority are further complicated, however, by the several contexts in which both cosmological origins and the activities, locales, and other beings that reference such origins in cosmological space and time can be expressed. One context involves conditions defined as *relationally prior* to the house while another context of origins refers to times and conditions that came into being *first*, preceding the house in an *absolute* sense (cf. Evens 1984:324). These two contexts of origins can be contrasted on a number of points, but the most significant difference between them lies in the greater legitimacy and authority accruing to first-principle origins relative to prior house origins. It follows, by extrapolation, that the various agents and agencies that identify these distinctive contexts will also vary in their legitimizing potential (see also Chapter 4). To more fully appreciate this very important point, it will be useful to discuss briefly basic characteristics of the two contexts of origins, beginning with prior house origins.

"Prior" is, by definition, a relational or structural term; something can be "prior" only with respect to something else. To speak of prior house origins is, therefore, to speak of the origins of the house not only as an "event" or condition that preceded the current organization of the house but also as a circumstance that remains connected to the contemporary house by spatial/temporal relationships that lead the house back to its beginnings (Sahlins 1965). Recognition of a series of emergent house ancestors is one very common means of relating the living members of the house to prior house origins (Fig. 1a). This can be initially effected in tangible terms by identifying burial sites as distinctive locales with extrahuman significance, setting the stage for the further development of ancestral shrines and tombs that can serve as centers for the observance of house rituals that facilitate communication with emergent house ancestors (Glazier 1984 : 133, 144; Bloch and Parry 1982 : 33; Parkin 1991 : 2; Bloch 1971, 1982 : 213; McAnany 1995 : 102, 160–162). Prior origins may be expressed, too, by according specific recognition to the mythical/historical "first occupants" of the house who initially settled a distinct geographical (cosmographical) "place,"[1] a place from which succeeding generations are believed to have derived or toward which contemporary house organization and especially leadership can be directed.[2] As McKinnon succinctly states, with reference to the population of the Tanimbar Islands, ". . . in maintaining a ritual relation to the land, named houses maintain a permanent relation with the founding ancestors who first settled upon the land and who are thought still to reside upon the land with the other ancestral spirits" (1991 : 103).[3]

Recognition of house ancestors and original founders in association with ancestral places and the originating events that give places their significance are not the only avenues to prior origins. Such beginnings can also be referenced by several categories of physically living house members and sometimes by affines of the house. With respect to the former, initiation rites to signify adulthood and recognition of seniority as a significant ranking relative to age or birth order are perhaps the most common sociological means of relating house members to ancestral forebears and original house founders. For purposes of this essay we need not further pursue initiation, but seniority requires brief consideration primarily to distinguish it from the status of the firstborn, a closely related concept associated with first-principle origins that will be discussed below.

As befits the relational nature of prior house origins, seniority also is a relational concept, for someone can only be senior relative to someone else who is junior. Broadly speaking, persons holding positions of seniority within the house command deference and exercise jural or ritual authority over dependent junior house members. They do so by virtue of the close relationship of the senior party to that which holds even greater priority and authority: the emergent ancestral dead of the house. "The dead exercise authority over the living, and the senior living exercise authority over their own juniors precisely because they are regarded as representatives of the dead" (Middleton 1977:83 regarding the Lugbara). "The elders have lived longer than other people; they have known the people of old who are but names to the younger generation. . . . Again, in ritual matters, since they have seen men who have now become 'ancestors' actually carry out the rites in question, they can speak with authority as to how such ceremonial should and should not be done" (Winter 1956:103 regarding the Bwamba; Kan 1989:78–79). Frequently seniority is phrased in terms of parental-offspring relations with the understanding that parental authority reflects the greater authority of emergent house ancestors. "As a jural minor in your father's lifetime you need the consent, or at least the blessing, of your father and often of your lineage elders in order to undertake anything important for yourself" (Fortes 1960:32 regarding West Africa; Mbiti 1969:197). Seniority may be expressed, too, in relationships among siblings, such as that of elder brother to younger brother (Metraux 1978:50–51, 52; Bloch 1989:138–139; Modjeska 1982:64–65).

In some cases connectedness to prior house origins can also be affirmed by living outside progenitors of the house, most notably by those "closer" or "nearer" forms of affinal relationships in which some of Us are converted into not-Us through marriages with more distant consanguineal groups or with already related lateral groups (see Chapter 5). A connection with prior house origins may be evidenced in the manner in which these affines serve as representatives of the ancestral dead on ritual occasions, which will be discussed later in this chapter.

Before proceeding to this topic, however, the nature of first-principle origins and its representatives must be considered.

In contrast to prior house origins, first-principle origins is not an inherently relational condition.[4] Instead, first-principle origins refers to an original state of being expressing principles of ultimate origins or primary being and involving absolute conditions of existence and communitas whose philosophical significance does not require the presence of the house. As a condition of creativity, first-principle beginnings not only precede the house but exist separately and independently of it such that, if the house is to be included, the condition of first-principle origins must be "brought inward" by some means to effect contact with it (Fig. 1b).

In tangible terms, first-principle origins may be identified with cosmographically significant "places" associated with actions of first-principle creator beings or culture heroes and with autochthonous residents of such locales who are believed to have originally emerged in situ. All manner of natural geographical features may be identified as the settings for first-principle origins. River systems in the Amazon Basin, for example, are frequently implicated in first-principle creations by way of mythical anacondas who travel the length of the river or lie spread along the water course and from whose immense bodies the first people emerge at distinct locales along the waterway.[5] Alternatively, the original human beings may be thought to have emerged from river rapids or may be associated with fish migrations and spawning grounds (Chernela 1988:36–37; Goldman 1963:93–94, 96; Århem 1992:51–52). Mountains and their lakes and caves are also often closely associated with first-principle beginnings, including the emergence of the first humans (Barnes 1974:28; Karsten 1968:329–330, 338; Wilson 1995: chap. 3; Dieterlen 1973:638). The Australian Dreaming, in which each individual's spirit being derives (emerges) from a sacred place in the landscape associated with the creational activities of original culture heroes (Myers 1986:50–51; Taylor 1989:377), may be the best-known example of first-principle origins expressed in cosmographical terms, but similar markings of first-principle origins and of the activities of original culture heroes or first persons are also encoded in the energized stones, lakes, and hills of the Melanesian landscape (Kahn 1990). They can be perpetuated, too, in the construction of sacred cities, such as Benares, a holy place "immune to the ravages of time [that] exists perpetually in the Golden Age of origins . . ." (Bloch and Parry 1982:14).[6]

In the sociological world of the house, first-principle origins are expressed in the unique and exceptional qualities so often attributed to firstborns as "absolutes" (distinct from the conditional identity of seniority relative to those junior), though in fact it is not only firstborns but "the first instance" of many things that connects directly to first-principle origins: "Primacy is universally revered. The firstborn child, the first animal of the season killed, the first fruits of a crop, the first menstruation, the first inhabitants to arrive, the first ancestors—all have special merit and the powers of freshness. The first are the beginnings of a sequence, and are hence the primary sources of power" (Goldman 1975:49; Kopytoff 1987:22; van Gennep 1960:175–178). The birth of the first child, however, is particularly significant in that it heralds the opening of a new portal (the fertility of the new couple) between this world and the fundamental creativity of the cosmos. After that momentous new creative beginning, later children are simply "those [who came] behind" (Pomponio 1992:74).[7] The first, therefore, becomes archetypical in his or her social persona and is set apart from ordinary persons by an inherent sanctity. ". . . among the ancient Hebrews, the first born son was ritually singled out by the law that he belonged to God and had to be redeemed" (Fortes 1974:90).[8] Similarly, for the Mandok of Melanesia, "the firstborn represented above all a key symbol of what it meant to be human" (Pomponio 1992:73).

The firstborn, more than any other child, serves as an instrument of regeneration that aims "to annul past time, to abolish history by a continuous return *in illo tempore,* by the repetition of the cosmogonic act" (Eliade 1959a:81). ". . . the firstborn was not just a trailblazer for younger siblings . . . : he/she symbolically represented the continuation of the essential life forces that sustained life for the entire community" (Pomponio 1992:90). Not surprisingly, given such credentials, the firstborn may hold distinctive ritual offices and responsibilities that tend to express principles of communitas on behalf of the house as a whole more than they relate to structured relationships among house members. Thus firstborns may stand as representative of younger siblings in the performance of ritual duties (Fortes 1960:19; Pomponio 1992:89), bear the responsibility to learn and preserve the esoteric knowledge on which the ritual life of the house depends (Keesing 1982:87–88 n. 7), or stand in a crucial pivotal position between the house and the outside world (Bird-David 1990:192; Viveiros de Castro 1986:149; Pomponio 1992:76–77). In addition, like all embodiments of cosmological powers, firstborns are believed capable of inflicting harm, too, particularly

FIRST-PRINCIPLE ORIGINS	PRIOR HOUSE ORIGINS
Absolute qualitative ideals independent of house	Relational ties to existing house
Original creator deities or culture heroes	House founders
Autochthonous populations	First settlers
Principles of things that are first	Principles of seniority
Others as affines (more distant form of affines)	Affines as not-Us (nearer form of affines)
Natural phenomena and landscape as original creations	Natural phenomena and landscape as related to house origins
Communitas	Structural ties

upon parents, who may view their firstborn with considerable ambivalence given that this child is incontrovertible evidence that their own personal and social prominence will one day be usurped by the next generation. In such settings, firstborns, as exceptionally vital but also exceptionally dangerous beings, may be forced to stand apart from parents and be treated with considerable coldness (Sanday 1986:68; Fortes 1974:84–87). Alternatively, by virtue of their exceptional inherent qualities, firstborns as children may enjoy a special status among their peers, receiving "the most attention, the largest portions of food, and the least amount of informal discipline" (Pomponio 1992:75).

First-principle origins may also be expressed at ceremonies and rituals by affines, especially the more "distant" form of affinity in which marriage is appropriately contracted with Others who initially stand as "strangers," "outsiders," even "enemies." Such affines, as representatives of first-principle origins, generally manifest their own ancestors or the generic dead rather than house ancestors per se. In this they may contrast with the type of affinity in which in-laws are preferably "not-Us" and which may be more closely related to expressions of prior house origins (Fig. 3). This and other contrasts between the two contexts of origins are summarized in the table above.

I argued above that, in both centralized and noncentralized polities, political ideology and political economy are grounded in the fundamental necessity that political leaders evidence access to the legitimizing authority inherent in contexts of cosmological origins. In addition, it may be further suggested that practical efforts to access this legitimacy may encourage political development within the house or the polity. Fundamental to this point is the fact that legitimacy may be derived from either or both contexts of cosmological origins. In other words, if (for example) first-principle origins are already well expressed in the political life of the house or polity, the further extension of authority may require elaborating reference to prior house origins. This might be accomplished by emphasizing connections with geographical places associated with first settlers or founders of the house or polity, by manipulating naming practices and memory events to elaborate lines of descent from house ancestors, or perhaps by diversifying variables of rank and seniority by embellishing house genealogies, as did the Otoro Nuba of Kordofan (Sudan), who bridged the gap usually found between clan origins and living clan members by developing a more detailed genealogy for the chiefly house (Nadel 1947:93). Similarly, the Mbeere of Kenya made necessary jural modifications in land tenure by elaborating genealogies and increasing emphasis on identifying house forebears through reference to formal burial sites (Glazier 1984:133–137, 142). In like fashion, Barnard and Woodburn discuss how ideological elaboration of dominance by elders over increasingly dependent young men and women seems to be a necessary prerequisite when structured kin groups (houses) characteristic of delayed-return social systems are formed from the greater behavioral autonomy characteristic of immediate-return systems: "after the ideological destruction of autonomy, and the establishment of ideological domination, political and economic domination may follow" (1988:28–30).

Alternatively, if prior origins are well established for the house or polity, political growth may require enhancing references to first-principle origins. This may be accomplished by ritually elaborating the number of things or conditions associated with primacy or by increasing recognition of the qualities of first events—the first fruits of harvest, the first wife in a compound, the first entrant into ritual initiation, the first person to acquire a title, the first village to establish a cult house or secret society, and especially firstborns and their numerous first accomplishments (Kopytoff 1987:22; Pomponio 1992:73, 79–83, 112).[9] Enhancing the significance of lines of primogeniture also helps to reference first-principle origins (Valeri 1990:169–170), as do practices that extend the history of the house or polity into the realm of archetypical culture heroes (Metcalf 1982:218–219, 220, 223).

However it is done, to be most effective politically the house or polity must strive to access both contexts of cosmological origins—that is, to exhibit qualitative ideals and communitas associated with first-principal origins and to develop structural and relational ties that attest to relationships with prior house origins. "Just as The Dreaming is the source of the present, so are the older men the source of the younger" (Myers 1986:243 regarding the Pintupi). One way to accomplish this double-faceted task is to link principles of rank and seniority among or within kin groups (houses) to birth order from first-principle creators, as the Eastern Tukanoan do on a grand and cosmic scale:

> The hierarchical basis for the relations among localized descent groups and their proprietary rights to particular locations derives from a charter myth relating the origins of all Eastern Tukanoan groups in the Uaupés. In this myth, a sacred anaconda canoe originates from a primordial Water Door and swims upriver to the region of the Uaupés River. Reaching the headwaters, the anaconda canoe turns round, so that its head faces downriver and its tail upriver. From its body emerge brothers, progenitors of all of the sibs of the Uaupés. The birth order of sibs from the body of the ancestor becomes an order of status fixing the relations among sibs of a single language group. The highest-ranked groups are the first to emerge; they are born of the head of the anaconda. Succeedingly junior brothers emerge later, further upriver. The last, or lowest in rank, are born from the tail of the anaconda. (Chernela 1993:149; see also Goldman 1963:94)[10]

Prior house origins and first-principle origins can also be linked by rituals, as when rainmaking (first principle) ceremonies are held at locations sacred to ancestral founders of the house/polity (Parkin 1991:111) or are conducted by senior men whose rank is strengthened by additional criteria of primacy that allow them access to first-principle places of origin: "The rainmaker is the genealogically senior man of his sub-clan and is given attributes that symbolically mark him off from other men. He is regarded as in a way socially dead after his succession . . . . He manipulates rainstones . . . inside his raingrove ('the vagina of the world'), a place kept secret to all but rainmakers" (Middleton 1977:84–85 regarding the Lugbara; Goldman 1975:169).[11]

Yet many, perhaps most, situations relating both contexts of origins are not as straightforward as these few examples. Indeed, much of the political value accruing to the several origins lies in the great diversity of activities and events by which such connections can be expressed and the political potential contained in the ensuing ambiguities. Kopytoff's statement with reference to Africa very likely has relevance for many other ethnographic settings:

> One could be "first" and "senior" in a variety of ways (through age, achievement, length of residence, precedence in initiation, etc.) and in a variety of contexts (such as the kin group, the settlement, an age-set, a civic society, a cult group, etc.). The multifarious semantics of seniority allowed considerable room for "sliding" from one context to another and for argument as to which context was the cause and which the consequence. Does the seniority of authority—say, in village government—imply the seniority of precedence in its rituals, or does it issue from it? Does precedence in ritual ranking more or less reflect precedence in the chronology of settlement, or does it prove that chronology? The semantic sliding was made all the easier because the common way to express different kinds of seniority in different context was by way of the same kinship terms (such as "father," "mother," or "mother's brother"). (1987:58)

Kopytoff stresses the use of the kinship idiom in expressing origins-related identities, but it should also be reiterated that sociological referents are not the only way of evidencing access to origins, nor are they the only theater in which political manipulations and competitions referencing origins can be played. Successful production or acquisition of various types of material resources, including foodstuffs for public events and durable wealth items or treasure, can attest to connections with places and contexts of origins, too, which is why politically influential persons also work diligently to encourage food production above and beyond domestic needs, conduct long-distance trade, and attract skilled artisans to their courts or compounds (see Helms 1993).

Among sociological expressions of access to origins, however, another very common way to both contact and interrelate first-principle and prior house origins is to invite tangible representatives of one context of origins to participate in ritual occasions heralding some aspect of the other context of origins; hence the virtue and necessity of inviting Others to appear as guests at ceremonial events of the house. Most important for this essay is the presence of affines at such gatherings. We have already noted the important role played by affines as liminal agents of transformation during mortuary rites as they assist in the delicate operation of transferring the deceased from the realm of the living to the realm of the dead. Now we must consider the role of affines at other types of ceremonial events, including the final mortuary feasts that reconstitute the society of the living after the final disposal of the remains of the dead.

The value of affines as guests during these final mortuary events derives from the identification that may be accorded to affines in general as embodiments of the dead of the house or as indicative of archetypical connections between the living and the dead. The Krahó of Brazil express this association somewhat obliquely in linguistic terms. There are "certain similarities between the terms used for affines and the terms used for dead relatives," suggesting that "affinal terms . . . have something in common with terms for the dead," most likely reflecting the sharp attitudinal changes that occur both when a relative dies and when a previously somewhat distant consanguine is transformed into an affine (Melatti 1979:64–65). The Dakota express the association more directly and from a different perspective. Landes describes how Santee Dakota annually took to the warpath in spring and summer to avenge deaths that had occurred within their group (whether by age, illness, suicide, murder, accident, or in war) by killing or scalping Ojibwas, their neighbors, visitors, rivals, enemies, and affines (Landes 1986:239, 248). Although they blamed the Ojibwas for the deaths of their relatives, Ojibwa souls were also required to accompany the souls of the dead Santees in the afterlife. "At the victory dance, indeed, villagers treated an enemy scalp, and sometimes a captive, with the mournful tenderness shown the dead Santee with whom the scalp or captive was identified. . . . [Otherwise stoical warriors] could weep in the victory dance over an enemy scalp which they equated with dead kin" (241, 244, 246). War captives were also treated kindly and with respect: "The captive, identified with deceased Santee, was regarded 'lovingly and sadly,' given fine cloths and food, and sometimes, if the captive were female, was married" (248).[12] The BaKongo of Zaire and their neighbors imply a parallel between affines and the world of the dead in yet another manner. The Kongo believe that the world of the living and the world of the dead are separated by a barrier represented as water, and life is interpreted as a cyclical or oscillating movement between these worlds. But marriage is also conventionally represented as an alliance between two shores separated by water, and the term *nzadi* (large river) can also mean "affine" (MacGaffey 1986:43, 92). Ultimately "both cosmology and marital preference are aspects of a single conceptual scheme, unified by the word *nzadi*. When a woman speaks of her doubts about 'cross-ing *nzadi*,' it is only the anthropologist's problem whether her remark belongs to cosmology or to marriage" (93).

According to Lévi-Strauss, complementary relationships between two aggregations where one represents the dead and the other the living are very common, arguably applicable to all occasions when society is di-vided into two groups (1993:45). Moreover, those who personify the dead in a society of the living must be those "who, one way or another, are incompletely incorporated into the group, who, that is, share the *otherness* which symbolizes the supreme dualism: that of the dead and the living. . . . The festival of the dead is basically the festival of the oth-ers, while the fact of being other is the nearest image we get of death" (49, 50). Lévi-Strauss's comments were made with respect to the roles traditionally accorded to children, foreigners, slaves, and other guests at Christmas.[13] However, for many societies the most obvious "group of others" available for identification with the dead is affines or the "op-posite" moiety, which is also frequently affinal relative to the focal moi-ety. "The Bororo believe that death is caused by a bad spirit, *bope*, best represented by the jaguar. The revenge for a person's death is completed by the killing of a jaguar or harpy eagle, or less often a fox, by a male from the moiety opposite that of the deceased. The hunter becomes the representation of the dead person" (Zarur 1991:35). Similarly, speak-ing of the duties and privileges that members of the opposite moiety per-form for ego and his kin, Crocker notes the importance of those medi-ating services in which a member of the opposite moiety exacts revenge for a person who has been harmed or even killed by a natural agent-cum-spirit force. "This function achieves its social climax in the repre-sentation of deceased Bororo by persons in the other moiety" (1979:262); ". . . the most valued elements of prestige are prestations from the other moiety: invitations to represent a clan spirit, to fulfill critical roles in initiation and funeral ceremonies, and, above all, to represent a dead Bororo" (276). Generally the individual of the opposite moiety who will represent the deceased will be a lateral relative, a member of the dece-dent's father's clan, and ideally a brother-in-law to the deceased (285–286, 287).

Affinal/lateral representations of the dead can become quite graphic. Among matrilineal Normanby Islanders, "at death the deceased's spouse and father are expected to assume a formal mourning demeanor and at-tire. These include wearing old, dirty, dark clothing, refraining from public bathing, avoiding certain desirable foods, . . . and withdrawing from participation in the pleasures of day-to-day social life. To a lesser extent, all of the deceased's affines and all affines of the deceased's matrilineal mates are expected to follow these rules" (Thune 1989:163). The disheveled and unclean spouse of the deceased also "serves to evoke and personify the deceased" by behaving in an extremely helpless, confused, passive, detached, isolated, mindless manner; "the spouse's body is expelled from the deceased's matrilineage by rendering it as close to death in terms of social persona and physical appearance as possible" (166, 167; see also Campbell 1989:57, 52; Hocart 1923). Thune continues, "These restrictions take effect immediately after death . . . . they serve to reinforce the formal opposition between the new, clean, controlled, and competent matrilineal mates of the deceased, whose demeanor no longer identifies them with the deceased, and the mourning affines, who, being physically and structurally like the dead, are set apart from the society of the living" (164–165).

Affinal duties relative to the dead not only serve to separate the dead from the living, physically and existentially, but also can be the means of creating ancestors, as in Tanimbar, where affinal wife-givers provide bracelets, sarongs, and loincloths to dress the body of the deceased so that the departed "can see and speak" in the world of the dead. Most important are the bracelets and necklace brought for daughters of the dead by the principle wife-giver of the house, who represents the family's *original* wife-giver. This jewelry constitutes the "ladder of the dead," meaning it "prefigure[s] his future 'coming-downs' when the living who possess [the jewelry] will appear to him to request his help" (Pauwels 1985:136). By these and other ritual attentions, the affines also constitute substitutes for Ratu, the deity who is the giver and taker of life (also mythologically represented as an affine), and make it possible for "the deceased to become an ancestor and become integrated in the world of the dead" (136). In short, it is by means of such affinal attentions that the ritual world of the house is connected to the existence of the ancestors who provide the pigs and rice necessary for life and for prestations with affines (135–137).

Because they essentially embody the dead, affines or laterals, as ceremonial guests, can also reference one or the other of the contexts of origins as particular social and political conditions of the house require. With respect to prior house origins, where formal principles of rank and seniority structurally relate the house to its beginnings, current affines and laterals may be associated with the original (sometimes mythical) affinal relations by which founding house ancestors established descent groups (Peters 1960:29; Grinker 1990; Reichel-Dolmatoff 1985). In a different rendering of house origins, ancestors of affines, over the course of time, may become incorporated into the ancestral group of the focal house through several generations of lateral connections (Keesing 1971: 148–149; Nadel 1947:93 n. 1). In polygamous settings the several affinal spouses may serve as points of origin of new house segments; "if the lineage later subdivides, it will be along lines of the various 'houses,' each tracing its origin to a particular wife of the original remembered male ancestor" (Ngubane 1981:89 regarding the Zulu; Nadel 1947:93 n. 1). Alternatively, the affinal group that provided the spouse may be seen as the "origin and source of life" for the house: "It seems then that agnatic ties are based on shared blood originally acquired from another group," in this case, the mother's brother's house as wife-givers (Barnes 1974:248, 251, regarding the Kédang).

Regardless of how they are structurally expressed, the significance of affines and affinal relations for prior house origins ultimately rests on the belief that affinal groups reference the qualitative creative powers of absolute, formative, first-principle origins. Among the Kédang, wife-giving mothers' brothers relate "to what must be for the Kédang first principles. The wife-giving group is a source of life; even the terms applied to them draw a comparison to other sources of life like the spring, the house post and so on" (Barnes 1974:251). Consider, too, the Lio of eastern Indonesia, for whom ritual contact with the original human being ("child without parents"), his anonymous wife, and the creativity of the mountaintop on which they came into being (along with plants and animals) can be achieved only through affinal relationships with a house (*keda*) that stands as "symbolic affines" to the community as a whole and in that capacity maintains ritual contact with the original couple (Howell 1991:228–231). "A fully sovereign village is one that has direct communication with the original ancestors of humanity, and through the *keda* symbolically stands in a relationship of wife-giver to the original couple" (240). Expressed on an even grander cosmic scale, "conceptually the Ocean, God, Thunder and Sun are above, and in myth and ritual attitudes toward them parallel those toward affinal relations" (Bozzoli de Wille 1975:9 regarding the Bribri of Costa Rica).

A logical result of such conceptual parallels is to define affines as mediators between supreme, first-principle entities and the house, as do the Iban of Borneo, where the "notion of son-in-law relationships as a means of mediation between gods and men carries over into all aspects of Iban folklore. For example, the male culture heroes often marry the daughters of the gods whom they meet in other realms and from whom they receive special charms or perhaps instruction in important rituals and customs" (McKinley 1976:106). Mythological sons-in-law also permit reverse communications from people to gods to proceed along the same affinal route.

> Beneath the Iban earth is the realm of a powerful and mysterious ruler who can control the growth of forests and command all the animals on earth to do his bidding. He probably is a dragon, or Naga, king, that is, an under-world serpent. He holds many charms and secrets of life giving power in his rich domain beneath the earth. Humans encroach on his domain when they burn swidden fields. So he must be placated with offerings. But these cannot be given directly to him. They are given to his favored son-in-law, Pulang Gana. (107) [14]

Access to universal, first-principle qualities of energy, life, and fertility may also be evidenced in more tangible form when living affines act as curers for house members or as artisans whose creative, origins-related, and origins-derived skills are sought by the house for production (carving, weaving, painting, etc.) of ritual items and ceremonial regalia, for construction and decoration of canoes, dwellings, or house memorials, such as "totem" poles, or for performances of music and dance on ceremonial occasions (Seguin 1986b:488–489; Kan 1989: 152; Maddock 1989:83; Sider 1967:101; Hill 1984:535; Hugh-Jones 1979:133, 150–151; see also Helms 1993: Part I and Chapter 11 below). We have also seen that affines are valued, too, for the benevolence of the communitas that they bring to members of the house, a communitas that, by abjuring the tensions arising from intrahouse structuration, is seen to have its wellsprings in the universality of first-principal origins.

Furthermore, it is because affines not only reference the ancestral dead but also provide access to origins that affines, as ceremonial guests, retain the ultimate authority to legitimize proceedings that they witness. The most potent and important of these affinal/ancestral representations and legitimations are those in which affines-cum-ancestors embody first-principle origins at house or polity gatherings (including initiations, competitions of rank, and political successions) where access to prior house origins is evidenced or celebrated. The power of the legitimation provided by affines on such occasions rests simply but profoundly on the fact that, on a higher level of cosmological structurings, *first-principle origins are perceived to hold ontological priority over prior house ori-*

gins. A parallel argument was advanced in Chapter 4 when I suggested that, in a broad historical and developmental sense, the spatial axis of cosmological relations may have preceded formalization and elaboration of the temporal axis of cosmological relations. Combining these two perspectives, I can now suggest that *affines are particularly potent representatives of cosmological Others and cosmological energies for the house precisely because they can combine the power of precedence held by the spatial (cosmographic) dimension of the Other with the power of precedence accorded first-principle origins.*

When it comes to formal witnessings and legitimations of house rituals and ceremonies, affines are everything, and (judging from the ethnographic record) affines and other moiety guests are everywhere, too. Actual or categorical in-laws or lateral relatives offer varying amounts of support, assistance, and verification at formal debating sessions (Harrison 1990:155); initiations into curing societies (Mitchell 1978:10); ear piercings, naming ceremonies, and ceremonial dances (Seguin 1986b: 488, 493; Maybury-Lewis 1979:237–239; Bamberger 1974:372); first hair cuttings and bestowals of ritual loincloths (Valeri 1994:9); men's society feasts and rank-taking ceremonies (Parkin 1991:208, 210; Blackwood 1981:64; Patterson 1981:192–193, 215); rites of passage into adulthood (Myers 1986:174, 230–233; Hugh-Jones 1979:133, 148–149) and other life-crisis rites (Meggitt 1972:69, 73); ceremonies for firstborns (Pomponio 1992:87–88, 120); ceremonies to identify positional successions (Gray 1953:235–236);[15] first planting or first hunting rituals (Muller 1985:72, 74); ceremonies to validate succession to chiefships (MacGaffey 1986:35, 26); and rituals associated with births and deaths (Rosman and Rubel 1989:215). "A man calls upon his sister's husband . . . to help him carry out a rite and to witness the correctness of his ritual acts, but the reverse occurs as well when a man asks his wife's brother . . . to help him with his ritual affairs" (Harris 1962:71 regarding the Taita of Kenya).

Kan offers a particularly full and explicit account of the role of outside guests, members of the opposite moiety including affines, as legitimating witnesses who also assume the guise of the ancestral dead at the memorial feasts (potlatches) that constitute the final observances of mortuary cycles among the Tlingit of the northwest coast of North America (Kan 1986, 1989:24, 43, 151–163). His analysis provides an excellent summary of the association of affines and laterals with the outside and with ancestors in the context of access to origins.

Kan identifies four categories of potlatch participants—hosts, guests, and the deceased matrikin of hosts and of guests—in the ceremonies that ended the official mourning period and validated the bestowal of the ceremonial regalia, names and titles, and other attributes of the deceased upon his matrilineal descendants (1989:214–218, 272). He notes how, for the members of the house (hosts), the potlatch shifted attention from the recently deceased to remembrance of other ancestral dead of the house, who were believed to be present at the ceremony and were "warmed," "clothed," and "fed" by placing food into the fire and by burning a small portion of the gifts intended for distribution to guests. The rest of the food, however, was served to guests, who represented deceased ancestors. Some, especially the favored food of house ancestors, was "specifically marked as belonging to the dead," put into a type of dish called a "fire dish," and "given to close paternal/affinal relatives of the deceased hosts. The donor announces their names as well as those of the guests who received the dishes" (1986:206). In this fashion, "the opposite moiety served as the channel through which tobacco and food could be sent to the recently deceased and other matrilineal ancestors of the mourners" (1989:152, 186–187). (This custom also directly references first-principle origins in that it is believed to have originated in the ancestral time when the culture hero, Raven, was shaping the world into its present form).[16] Then gifts were distributed; "the name of each deceased member of the hosts' lineage or clan was called out, followed by the name of a particular guest who was to receive the gift. The dead received the noncorporeal essence ('inside') of the gift, and the living its corporeal form ('outside')" (1986:198, 1989:185).[17]

Kan is very clear about the role of outside guests at these mortuary ceremonies. Guests, whose presence was requisite for validation of the hosts' claims to the sacred regalia of their house, served as mediators between the hosts and the hosts' deceased matrikin, but "the guests also acted as representatives or impersonators of their own matrilineal ancestors" whose names they carried, whose regalia they wore, and in whose names they thanked the hosts for their generosity ("It is not really me that reached for this food, it is my departed maternal uncle So-and-so"; 1989:187, 186, 1986:202). Particularly close affinal guests ("fathers" and especially brothers-in-law), who were accorded especially high respect during the potlatch, also served as mediators between the house and more distantly related guests-cum-ancestors and, seemingly in the spirit of providing benevolent assistance (communitas) to the house, could contribute to the wealth amassed for distribution by the house (1986:203).[18] It also appears that, although the ancestral dead of the house and of its affinal guests are interrelated in a single ancestral existence, affinal ancestors are accorded precedence in that they preexist the arrival of house dead and thus can benevolently welcome the newcomers. In the words of the husband of a deceased woman, "She is not dead. Her paternal aunts are holding her on their laps. All her paternal uncles are shaking hands with her" (Swanton, quoted in Kan 1989:134, 154). Kan elaborates on this expression of communitas: "Thus, in the village of the dead, the paternal kin continued to play their usual role of comforters who 'pitied' their 'children'" (1989:134).

For the members of the house who were still physically living, the kindly guidance and support of affinal ancestors was expressed through the ministrations of living affinal/lateral relatives when they dressed the leading hosts of the house in the crest-bearing regalia of the hosts' ancestors. "As each guest lifted the sacred regalia, he or she said, 'It is not really me but my beloved mother that is putting this shirt on you' or 'I am placing this staff in your hand, my brother-in-law, on behalf of/in memory of my maternal uncle So-and-so'" (Kan 1989:187). These words and actions essentially state that it was through the hands of affines—as preexisting Others accessing preexisting first-principle origins, both in tangible living form (that is, on the spatial cosmological axis) and on the temporal ancestral plane—that members of the house in the here-and-now were tangibly connected with their own prior origins.[19]

Persons and groups functioning in affinal roles personify cosmological principles of primary precedence. Consequently, members of the house may have their enterprises sanctified by the ultimate and most irrefutable form of legitimacy: that bestowed by the witness and ratification of affines. But there is another, darker side to this legitimizing power. Should members of the house have reason to question the propriety of actions by outside affinal groups, they may be enjoined somewhat to forebear by virtue of the same principles of cosmological precedence, which can also serve to shield affinal groups from undue criticism. In other words, the cosmologically derived power of affines to sanctify and legitimize the actions of the house may also provide affines with room to maneuver at the possible expense of the house.

The double-edged power of affines to bless or to curse is elaborated most completely in politically centralized societies, where evidence of access to the several contexts of origins is aggressively pursued by competitive aristocrats hungry for legitimation. The general relation of aristocracies to the themes of affines and origins will be examined in later chapters. It may be noted here, however, that from the perspective of this essay, the growth point for the development of centralization is seen to lie in general terms in the tangible here-and-now efforts of politically ambitious persons to connect the more restricted legitimacy of prior house origins with the absolute legitimacy that derives from first-principle origins. In other words, efforts are made to co-opt the validation (legitimation) offered by first-principle origins in the support and elaboration of jural authority deriving from prior house origins and accruing to those who can best evidence relationships with both contexts of origins. As Jonathan Friedman demonstrated some years ago (1975), activities evidencing the combination of these two contexts of cosmological beginnings can become flash points of great political potential.

PART TWO

The heavens themselves, the
planets, and this centre
Observe degree, priority,
and place . . .

WILLIAM SHAKESPEARE,
Troilus and Cressida, 1:3

7

HIERARCHY

Generally speaking, among the several characteristics which I believe to
be most diagnostic of chiefdoms is the fact that chiefdom aristocrats,
considered as a social sector or group, seem to be perceived by the general populace as qualitatively distinct, inherently different, from ordinary common people (Béteille 1977:10; Rousseau 1985:40; see also
Chapter 8 below). If this is so, then two additional queries arise: what
unique features constitute this qualitative distinctiveness and how is this
distinctive aristocratic sector structurally articulated with the rest of society? The basic position that I wish to explore in the following chapters
suggests that aristocrats as a group (and particularly the highest aristocratic statuses) are deemed qualitatively to constitute tangible forms of
"living ancestors" relative to the populace at large and are structurally
positioned as affinal Others relative to the rest of society. If this is so,
then aristocrats should also be viewed as positioned cosmologically as
well as socially outside or beyond commoner society if it is accepted that
affines in general and by definition constitute cosmological Others with
distinctive qualities (including communitas, the right to represent the

ancestral dead, and access to contexts of origins) who are situated socially and cosmologically outside the house.

Before reviewing ethnographic evidence that aristocrats do in fact constitute affinal living ancestors for society proper, it is necessary to address a major point that, on the face of it, would seem to disassociate aristocrats from affines—namely, the structurally hierarchical position enjoyed by aristocrats as the most highly ranked social and political sector of a centralized polity. It is the intent of this chapter to erase this apparent but erroneous contrast between affines and aristocrats by positing that hierarchy is inherent in affinal relations in general. This point will support the further argument that both the superordinant hierarchical position of aristocrats and their legitimacy as political authorities are derived in large measure from their generic identification as society's affines or lateral relatives.

I accept as axiomatic that the potential for inequality and hierarchy is inherent in human society as a basic principle of social order given that hierarchy or the potential for hierarchy may be expressed in many different ways, in greatly varying degrees, and with reference to very basic variables of human existence (Barnes 1985:8; Béteille 1977: chap. 1; Berreman 1981:8; Josephides 1985:1, 218).[1] In many societies, especially those labelled as "egalitarian," hierarchy may be actively disliked, even feared, and great efforts may be expended to reduce or deny (though rarely to obliterate totally) the expression of hierarchy and its attendant qualitative valuations of inequality in major areas of social, economic and political life (Flanagan and Rayner 1988; Mitchell 1988; Flanagan 1989).[2] In other polities hierarchy and "equality" may openly coexist by being expressed in different aspects or "orders" of life, perhaps in seasonal shifts in group size, or in ceremonial as opposed to secular or domestic activities, or in the recognized authority of elders as opposed to the ethos of corporate group equality, or in valuations accorded the division of labor. In such settings, however, the expression of hierarchy and its attendant inequality are frequently limited to select, carefully controlled, and sometimes only temporarily active contexts, most notably those involving ritual and ideology.[3]

In contrast, politically centralized chiefdoms not only explicitly recognize hierarchy but also "celebrate" it and "put hierarchy to use instead of avoiding it," though often not without misgivings (Petersen 1993:1–2). So, too, do the various politically noncentralized but socially ranked societies, sometimes termed "complex tribes" (Hoopes 1988:8–9), that maintain more diffuse expressions of jural authority but recognize social rankings of houses based on various criteria of ideology or "prestige,"[4] as do the many societies that, though they may or may not discourage hierarchy within the polity, recognize it in the differential status and qualitative value accorded to affinal units as "wife-givers" or "wife-takers" relative to the house.

Hierarchy is of interest analytically not only in terms of the manner or degree in which it is or is not denied, tolerated, encouraged, or celebrated but also in terms of the "type" of hierarchy that may be expressed. I refer here not to hierarchical distinctions based on specific personal skills and abilities or on specific social, political, and economic criteria such as age, wealth, gender, or sibling birth order but to typological distinctions rooted in the basic identity of the ranked entities relative to each other (Barnes 1985; Dumont 1982). Hierarchy in the abstract or dictionary sense refers to the orderly ranking of units with the added qualifications that the ranking is regarded as legitimate and that it expresses either quantitative or qualitative difference or contrast. In the quantitative type of hierarchy, the constituent units are regarded as basically *alike in kind,* though they differ in degree with respect to one or more fundamental values, and each is ranked as representing more or less of something relative to the others. In the qualitative type of hierarchy, the constituent units are identified as fundamentally *unlike* (superior or inferior) with respect to one or more crucial qualities and thus are regarded as basically *different in kind,* though ultimately all reference a larger whole or mutual context.

Rosaldo, discussing the ritualized expression of hierarchies based on age and wealth in Zinacantan (Chiapas, Mexico), coined the phrase "inclusive hierarchy" in reference to essentially quantitative rankings based on "greater or lesser units of the same order," such as older and younger brothers or religious officials with the same title. In this ethnographic instance these hierarchies of persons paralleled ritual segments that were also "like in kind, greater and lesser in degree" or "basically the same, yet a little different" (1979:272–273). In like fashion, Crocker, referring to the Bororo, notes that "only items of the same type can be ranked" because ranking in this context is intended to "organize their similarity" (1969:53). Inclusive or quantitative hierarchy is also found in the Wanano ritual ranking described by Chernela (1993) in which the order of ritual precedence accorded localized patrilineal groups or sibs (all of which are structured and organized alike) is based on the order of the emergence of their respective ancestors from the body of the primordial anaconda-creator. Similarly, the clans of the Hopi of Orayvi, also structurally "alike in kind," are ceremonially ranked in order of their first arrival in the village and in terms of the ceremonial possessions each brought with it at that time (Levy 1992:8, 23–25, 30, 156).[5]

In contrast to such inclusive or quantitative hierarchies, the type of hierarchy formed by affines and house and by aristocrats and commoners (as well as by formally defined gender or generational contrasts or by the relation of initiates relative to noninitiates) is composed of constituent units (the affinal group and the house; the aristocracy as a group and the general populace) that are not the same type of "thing" relative to each other. In other words, from the perspective of the house, an affinal group is not just another house but a unit identified as Other that is situated outside the house in a different spatial/temporal setting and that evidences the particular qualities of affinity relative to the house. From the purview of the house, affines and house are thus fundamentally qualitatively different in kind. We shall see that a directly comparable contrast also identifies aristocrats as a group as qualitatively different in kind relative to the populace as a whole. Thus the type of qualitative or "exclusive" hierarchy that ranks house and affines or commoners and aristocrats organizes difference rather than similarity and orders diversity into a larger whole (Appadurai 1986:759; Bloch 1989:138–139).[6]

The qualitative hierarchy that ranks the house and its outside affinal groups is based on the postulate (common to nonindustrial, low-technology societies) that hierarchy and inequality are inherent in the very structure of the cosmos.[7] Generally the cosmic hierarchy is defined in terms of different expressions of supernatural qualities or different quantities of supernatural power contained in the various tangibilities and intangibilities of the heavens, the earth (including the human realm), and the underworld (Bean 1977; Woodward 1989). Some cosmological systems regard this diversity as noncomparable and unrankable (Crocker 1969:50), but in others the qualities of one portion of the cosmos may be accorded higher or lower status relative to the qualities of another, as when the sky, as source of fertility, is held to be superior to the earth, while the underworld, as source of strictly material things, is held to be inferior (Woodward 1989:128–129 regarding the Ao Naga). The cosmos overall is also frequently perceived as composed of broad, hierarchically structured orders or levels such as ancestors, country (landscape), and people (Myers 1986:242 regarding the Pintupi) or as a middle world of human life situated between upper and lower universes in a structuring of "inevitable and inherent inequality" that also supports comparable hierarchical orders among nonhuman life-forms (carnivores, for example, being more powerful than plants) and people ("as power is distributed differentially in the universe, so is its acquisition and use by human beings"; Bean 1977:118, 123–128, regarding native California). In similar fashion, the cosmos may be viewed as composed of the world of mystical powers "above" society, the world of initiated men and ritual that constitutes true society, and the "nonsocial" world of domestic life "beneath" society (Harrison 1985b:417 regarding the Manambu), or it may be perceived as a complex of ranked dualities in which the recognition of things and attributes associated with the East relative to things and attributes associated with the West is mirrored in the duality of human beings with their chiefs and paralleled by animals with their supernatural masters (Chapman 1992:xvii, 277–278, regarding the Tolupan of Honduras).

Regardless of structural particulars, however, what is most important in cosmic orderings is belief in the fundamental principle that "hierarchy is not perceived as a human creation. Instead it is simply the form taken by the transmission of something of extraordinary value that *predates* human relations" (Myers 1986:241, 215, 220; my emphasis).[8] As a result, cosmic hierarchy can also underwrite cosmologically referenced authority in human relations: "the cosmological system thus provides the foundation for a scheme of social differentiation in which moral evaluation is intrinsically embedded" (Kelly 1993:13 regarding the Etoro of New Guinea). This form of cosmological ordering has been elegantly described by Viveiros de Castro with reference to the Araweté of Brazil, whose cosmological model contains three domains (gods/divinized souls/sky; living humans/earth; animals/the dead/forest) that can be simply glossed as supernature, society, and nature. According to Viveiros de Castro, this cosmological structure also exhibits hierarchical oppositions in which "the two modalities of the extrasocial (supernature and nature) are opposed globally to the central term of the triad (society), and encompass it hierarchically" (1986:86). Furthermore, and most important, "the symbolic attributes of the positions linked to alterity encompass hierarchically the material dimensions of authority . . . . the internal (sociological) aspect of leadership is subordinated to those aspects pointing towards the extrasocial" (118).

This observation can be extended and directly applied in general terms to the qualitative and structural relationships and political-ideological authorities that link affinal Others with the house and, by extension, aristocrats with commoners. In brief, given that "extra-

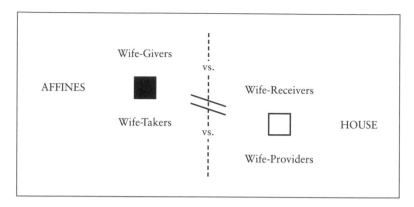

FIGURE 6   Hierarchical superiority of affines relative to the house.

social" Others like affines and aristocrats are, by definition, situated cosmologically as well as sociologically outside the central house and are, therefore, qualitatively different from the house, they must be either better than (superior to) or worse than (inferior to) the house.[9] This qualitative ranking defines, in turn, a fundamental exclusive hierarchical order in which entities (like affines and aristocrats) that reference the cosmological Other for the house (or polity) must be by definition structurally positioned either higher than ("above") or lower than ("below") the house.[10] In some settings this inherent hierarchical ordering between house and Others may be reduced, denied, nullified, or overridden by ritual exchanges so that categories of Others and the house may be idiomatically valued as "equal." In other settings, however, the ranking is recognized, sometimes only tolerated but sometimes celebrated. In these cases the same identification as outside Others that empowers affines with communitas, makes them privy to esoteric understandings, accords them ritual power, and authorizes them to legitimize house proceedings also defines affines as structurally "above," as well as qualitatively superior to, the house (Fig. 6).

In an even more fundamental cosmological sense, such "exclusive" hierarchical ordering recognizes the inherent "higher" structural position of an entity (such as affines) referencing absolute first-principle origins relative to an entity (such as the house) referencing only its own prior origins, for it is the difference in context of origins and the precedence accorded first-principle relative to prior origins that ultimately differentiates conceptually between the unlike units in these "exclusive" hierarchies and structurally gives the one (affines, aristocracies) a higher rank order relative to the other (house, commoners; Harrison 1990:68; McKinnon 1991:280–281).[11] (In contrast, "inclusive" hierarchies may be identified in the fundamental relationship of constituent units that are alike in kind to a single, shared context of origins.)[12]

Although differential access to different forms of cosmological origins may underlie the hierarchical relations between the house and its Others, actual ethnographic expressions of this ranking are likely to be more indirect and to assume a variety of forms, most notably in activities with political significance. Indeed, Miller, discussing the "multifactorial nature of dominance," rightly draws attention to the numerous dimensions that may be manipulated as routes to prestige and power in a given culture and argues that "approaches to dominance centred around the nature of structure and cosmology sometimes tend to over-homogenize the forms of power generated by such cultural constructions." He also notes that "although cosmological orders tend at the most abstract level to present a goal of coherence and totality, when considered in relation to the societies that they orchestrate they may generate often contradictory and heterodox formations" (1989:68).

I have attempted to deal with this situation on the cosmological level by emphasizing the considerable variety that exists even in more abstract or basic cosmological concepts, recognizing diverse categories of Others and separate cosmological axes of space and of time, and identifying several distinctive contexts of cosmological origins and of hierarchy. Conversely, when considering ethnographic particulars, I have sought to find common ground among the almost overwhelming diversity of activities by which people seek achievement, recognition, and especially political influence in the here-and-now by regarding them as alternate means of evincing an individual's or group's ability to establish access to one or another context of cosmological origins by successfully conducting day-to-day operations whose immediate social significance is also cosmologically justifiable. In other words, subsistence activities, reproduction, artistry, trade, and warfare are all ultimately accorded political-ideological significance because abundance, fertility, creativity, acquisition, and victory all signify the presence and support of the supernatural in the life of the house or the polity. In worlds in which it is axiomatic that humans can achieve nothing worthwhile by themselves alone, these enterprises are invaluable as much for that reason as for their more immediate "pragmatic" benefits. "A local lineage that produces a substantial surplus can prepare a feast for the entire community. . . . The capacity to produce a large surplus demonstrates the importance and influence of lineage ancestors with the higher spirits who appear as the source of all prosperity and wealth" (Friedman 1975: 170). "Surplus is represented not as the product of surplus labour, but as the 'work of the gods'" (172, 173).

The tremendous diversity of here-and-now activities that are believed to evidence connections with the supernatural also permits great systemic flexibility and adaptation in the ecologically lived-in world. But many of the choices regarding how to proceed in various enterprises and many of the rewards that are gained or lost in the process are strongly conditioned not only by perceived material results but also, and in my opinion more significantly, by what such events and their outcomes are thought to say about the status of various actors' access to the essential cosmological sources of power, life, and capabilities. In these cosmologically informed worlds, personal abilities and the affairs of houses and polities are not seen to exist sui generis as fortunate concatenations of physical nature and experienced nurture but are interpreted as evidencing connections with cosmologically outside or "higher" sources of being. Consequently, individual and group goals, ambitions, and enterprises become socially (publicly) relevant and acceptable to the extent that they are interpreted as related to "higher" powers, and scholarly investigations of these activities are more completely and accurately understood and evaluated, both in relative cultural terms and cross-culturally, if recognition is accorded to the cosmological contexts that underwrite them.

With that thought in mind, let us return to affines and laterals as categories of Others and the argument that, by virtue of their cosmological placement outside the house and their association with first-principle origins, affines and laterals are accorded a superior qualitative status and elevated hierarchical position relative to the house.[13] The "higher" hierarchical position accorded to affinal groups is recorded in the ethnographic literature in various ways. Often it is expressed in contrasts of spiritual with temporal authority, where "spiritual," generally deemed superior to temporal, is related to first-principle origins and "temporal" refers to prior house origins. For example, Barnes, in his study of Kédang, where authority is associated with status superiority, finds that wife-giving affines, as spiritual authorities, are superior to wife-taking houses while clan elders, who are temporal authorities, are superior to those junior in age. However, since spiritual authority is superior to temporal authority, wife-givers also outrank elders (1974:275–276, 242, 244).

The Kédang are far from unique in this respect. Indeed, probably the most recognizable form of affinally defined exclusive hierarchy is documented as examples of wife-givers standing in a superior and dominating position relative to the house as wife-receivers.[14] "The movement of people and goods between wife-giver and wife-taker, source and issue, is not only conceived as one that moves out and back, but also one that moves down and up" (McKinnon 1991:112 regarding Tanimbar). Similarly, "Gisu believe that no matter how much bride-wealth a man has paid, or how promptly, he is always in his father-in-law's debt for having provided him with a wife and thence the opportunity to beget sons. A father-in-law thus has the right to demand gifts and services from his son-in-law and these must be given. Extreme deference and respect characterize the proper manner of comporting oneself in his presence" (La Fontaine 1975:86, 87).[15] "The feast-giver's wife's father receives a large share of meat, including one of the haunches of the principal sacrificial animal. Wife-takers [of the feast-giver] are required to do much of the manual labor, dance, and sing the praises of the feast-giver. In return they receive minor shares of meat" (Woodward 1989:125–126 regarding the Ao Naga).[16]

Equally well attested to ethnographically are situations in which affinal groups are accorded positions of structural supremacy not as wife-givers but as wife-takers: ". . . when there is a status difference between the 'wife-giving' and 'wife-receiving' [wife-taking, in my phraseology] local descent groups, it is the latter and not the former which rank the higher" (Leach 1961:95, 97, regarding the Lovedu; Ekholm 1978:120; Bloch 1992:72; Liep 1989:232, 233). As Bloch explains (1992:77–78), the rationale offered by wife-providing houses is that if they did not yield up their women to wife-takers, they themselves could not expect to successfully obtain wives from outside. Life must be given if life is to be obtained. When affines stand superior as wife-takers relative to the house as wife-providers, however, the postulated superiority of affinal first-principle origins as a condition underlying exclusive hierarchy would seem to be compromised in that the providers of wives, the source of life and thus the expression of original, first-principle creativity, are accorded lower rather than higher status in the relationship. One solution to this problem lies in recognizing that the concept of first-principle origins can be understood in several senses. In addition or as an alternative to addressing the powers of creation per se, first-principle origins can also be interpreted as acts of controlling or of organizing primordial life-force, of bringing order to heretofore unregulated or chaotic creative energies. Thus, without denying the potency of women of the house as life-givers, wife-takers may claim first-principle hierarchical superiority nonetheless because they are the ones who properly control this basic fecundity.

However, there may be another way to both admit the first-principle potency of life-giving women of the house and allow wife-takers to evidence greater first-principle superiority. This may be accomplished if outside wife-takers provide the wife-providing house with especially valuable and prestigious gifts equal to or even *in excess of* the value accorded the wife (Vansina 1990:103; Ekholm 1977:120; Liep 1989: 232). Such prestations are generally understood anthropologically as intended to maintain the indebtedness or subordination of the wife-providing house (e.g., Vansina 1990:152), but they may also be appropriately interpreted as evincing the superordination of the wife-taking affines. The ability to acquire and accumulate valuable tangible goods constitutes another way of evidencing contact with first-principle origins (Helms 1993; Chapter 11 below), and distribution of such valued goods, as when affinal wife-takers make prestations to their wife-providing houses, expresses the (also first-principle) spirit of communitas especially appropriate for affines, who are expected in general to provide the house with beneficial things that reference first-principle origins. However, since women received from the house as wives can also reference first-principle origins as the primary source of life, it is essential that the valuables given to the house by wife-takers at the very least are equal to and preferably surpass the value of the wives received if the first-principle structural superiority of the affinal wife-takers relative to the house is to be maintained (see further discussion in Chapter 9).

Bridewealth, of course, can also be a factor when affines are wife-givers, but in these circumstances bridewealth, though it may be extensive, does not "outvalue" the wife since the value of these prestige goods is not in competition with the value of a wife's child-bearing ability in terms of attesting to the association of the affinal group with first-principle origins (see, for example, La Fontaine regarding the Gisu, quoted above).[17] In fact, affinal wife-givers, as beneficent sources of well-being for the house (wife-receivers), may generously provide its wife-receivers with more than the means for physical reproduction (spouse) by making additional contributions on specific occasions of select foods and crafted goods that signal the further transferral of life-giving substance to the house (see Van der Kroef [1954:848], quoted below).

In discussing affinal-house relationships as expressive of "exclusive" hierarchy, it is noteworthy that many authors have also commented on the asymmetrical and hierarchical relationship that may exist between moieties or other forms of dual organization, especially if the halves are exogamous.[18] "The relationship between the moieties is most often expressed as one between fathers and sons, rather than between brothers-in-law" (Crocker 1969:54 regarding the matrilineal Bororo). "The relationship of the wife's parents to the daughter's husband, with its connotations of dominance and subordination . . . provides the paradigmatic form of the hierarchical relationship of dominance that is generalized . . . from the [household] level to the level of the community as a whole, through the medium of the moiety structure" (Turner 1984: 343–344 regarding central Brazil).[19]

As several of the ethnographic quotations offered above have shown, the superior or "higher" position of affinal groups relative to the house may be expressed by using idioms that liken the status of affines to that of older generation relative to younger generation either among the living or among house ancestors (Lindholm 1986:340; Vansina 1990: 107; Errington 1987:433; Friedman 1975:175, 176). (When used in this way, "elder" and "younger" are defined as hierarchical disjunctions differing in kind rather than as gradations of like units. See McKinnon [1991:99–101] and Chapter 9 below). Alternatively, affinal-house relations may be compared to the status of men relative to women ("the Wailolong distinguish wife-givers and wife-takers as 'male' and 'female' relatives respectively"; Barnes 1979:19 regarding East Flores islanders) in a general affinal context in which "wife-givers are superior to wife-takers—an inequality which is clearly marked by the ceremonial and spiritual supremacy of givers over takers and by the obligations of service and deference which the takers owe the givers" (ibid.; see also Traube 1989:323; Barraud 1985:123; Ekholm 1978:121). "Men" (wife-giving houses) also may be glossed as superior "brothers and uncles" or "masters" relative to "women" (wife-receiving houses) as inferior "sisters and aunts" in such contexts (McKinnon 1991:115 regarding Tanimbar; see also Chapter 9 below).

Hierarchically defined generational or gender identifications of affinal groups may be joined with equally hierarchically contextualized identifications as conquering strangers, foreigners, or newcomers relative to conquered (by war and by marriage) indigenes. As Ekholm states with respect to Central Africa,

> The relation between super- and subordinate groups is expressed as one between "men" and "women." In one of the Kongo origin myths we are told that Wene (the founder) came with his "men," conquered the indigenous population and married its "women." In fact, most of the ideology of Central African societies is marked by a dualism in which it is imagined that the population consists of two groups, the conquerors and vanquished original inhabitants. The conquerors are "men" and their subjects "women." The women of (the highest) "wife-taking" groups also had the status of "men." (Ekholm 1978:121; see also Sahlins 1976:26)

The combining of affinal relations and conquest to effect hierarchical relations of dominance will be addressed in more detail in later chapters, but it is appropriate to note here that using the idiom of affinity or laterality to relate newcomers to indigenes may also be reversed to emphasize the superiority of earlier settlers as founders (and thus as referencing first-principle beginnings, origins, or sources) relative to newcomers. The agnatic Proto-Nuer and Proto-Dinka provide a case in point in which founder lines, entitled to the most favorable camp locations, are recognized as "mother's brothers of the camp" relative to latecomers, who, as "sister's sons," accept both their "mother's brothers'" political authority and less desirable camp sites (Kelly 1985:218–221).[20] Similarly, in the Kei Archipelago (southeast Moluccas) "feminine" wife-giving houses, being landholders and related to the origins of society, stand superior to "masculine" wife-receiving houses that are identified as inferior foreigners related to the sea (husbands being compared to flotsam; Barraud 1985:123).

Common to all these affinal identifications and positionings is the fundamental "legitimate" preference accorded to first-principle origins or sources and, by hierarchical extension, to things and beings that connote or promote first-principle origins or have temporal precedence in the sense of being primordially "first." "If one [part] cannot be conceptualized as the source of the other [part] there can be no hierarchy, only differentiation and equality" (McKinnon 1991:36, 34). Affines are recognized as such "sources" both by encompassing the qualities of first-principle origins and as a consequence of their role either as beneficent life- (wife-) givers for the house or as superior controllers or "orderers" (wife-takers) of life for themselves. This same identification of affines as first-principle, outside source, or controller of life underlies and informs the frequent and numerous ideological, political, and economic dimensions or expressions of exclusive hierarchical superordinance/subordi-

nance in affinal-house relationships (Comaroff and Comaroff 1981:37–
42; McKinnon 1991:115; Traube 1989:324), just as it informs the
quality of communitas in those same affinal affairs. The hierarchical
nature of affinal-house ties also suggests further comparison with the
shorter-term hierarchical relationship characteristic of rites of passage,
and it is not surprising to find that many of the more formal features of
the hierarchical structuring between affines and house readily conform
to the "generic features" postulated by Turner as characterizing a "very
large class of social and cultural structures" dealing with social transi-
tions and their rituals.[21]

Both the origins-related potency of affines and the hierarchical positioning of their first-principle or "primordial" status relative to the
house are well expressed by Barraud with reference to Tanebar-Evav islanders (southeast Moluccas):

> Marriage exchanges are the expressions of *haratut* [social] values. The
> wife-giver is superior to the wife-taker since he represents a category of
> the wife-taker's ancestors, called "God-the dead," who are greatly feared
> by the wife-taker. He is a kind of intermediary between the wife-taker and
> God, and as such is feared for his ability to inflict death on or give life to
> the wife-taker's house. The origin and creation of each house of the vil-
> lage goes back to the first woman given as spouse to the founder of this
> house, that is, to a pre-existing relationship with the wife-giver's house.
> (1985:119)

Van der Kroef also provides a succinct summary of the fundamental role
of affines (wife-givers, *hula*) as a general source of life in its multiple tangible and intangible manifestations for the house (wife-receivers, *boroe*)
among the Toba-Batak in central Sumatra:

> In the important exchange relationship, the boroe [wife-receiver] is re-
> garded as the "inferior" of its hula [wife-giver] and as dependent on the
> latter for both its spiritual and material well-being. Thus from its hula the
> boroe receives the *sahala,* the life-giving substance which the entire social
> group requires. Not only through marriage is the sahala transferred to the
> boroe, but also through the exchange of food and gifts. Fish has a sym-
> bolic and religious significance in that it is the expression of fertility and
> long life. . . . So whenever members of the boroe visit the hula-hula, the
> latter gives them fish to eat and the fish eaten by the boroe strengthens its
> sahala. The hula-hula also gives the *oelos* to its boroe. The oelos is a "gar-
> ment" or cloth of certain specifications and is believed to be magically

charged with the sahala . . . . Its special religious significance comes to the fore in, for example, the case of a married woman desirous of offspring. Where the marriage remains barren, the husband will visit the hula-hula of his wife and request that the hula give him . . . (the cloth that brings fertility and the life spirit), which is certain to make the wife pregnant. Also, land may be given by the hula to its boroe, and land thus transferred carries with it the same concept of fertility and bountifulness associated with fish and oelos; for the land produces the food from which the community draws its sustenance, and by partaking of this food the boroe shares in the same physical substance of which the members of the hula are "made." (Van der Kroef 1954:848; see also Barnes 1974:247–248)[22]

Van der Kroef's account provides insight into the depth and breadth that affinal relationships may hold for the house and thus paves the way for discussion of further elaborations on the theme of superordinant affinal "caretakers" in following chapters. His observations also concisely illustrate the absolute necessity that the house access sources of original life energies through relationships with potent cosmological outside Others structurally and qualitatively superior to the house. Whether the inherent hierarchical dominance of outside life-givers or life-controllers be constrained or allowed to flourish, it will always exist. In its most extreme expression, recognition of affines as hierarchically superior life-giving or life-controlling Others explicitly underwrites both the structural ranking and the political authority characteristic of centralized polities, where it is particularly heralded in the status and qualities accorded the aristocracy, to which we now turn.

*The real implication of power
is that elites live a life and share
a knowledge system that clearly
separates them from other
people.*

LOWELL BEAN, *"Power and Its
Application in Native California,"*
1977, P. 127

8 |

QUALITIES

AND

ARISTOCRATS

A fundamental anthropological truism stresses the importance of social persona or personhood, the "marked tendency to merge the individual in the group to which he or she belongs" (Radcliffe-Brown 1952:25). More specifically, the concept of social persona speaks to "those attributes, capacities, and signs of 'proper' social persons which mark a moral career (and its jural entitlements) in a particular society" (Poole 1982: 103). Such qualitative characteristics may attach to groups or categories and standardized roles or statuses, each of which is defined by distinctive valorizations that also mark its members or incumbents as more or less interchangeable. Such valuations are universal in social settings (Béteille 1977:11) and may be based on a wide range of specific criteria that can be broadly categorized as either ascribed or achieved in character.

As Goldman has pointed out (1970:xvi), ascribed qualities are more permanent or constant in that they tend to outlast the inherently short-lived (a single life-span or less) nature of most achieved accomplishments. They do so because (or to the extent that) ascribed qualities are defined as reflecting certain valuations, fundamentally ideological and esoteric in nature, that are deemed to be *inherent* in the basic nature of the constituency. "The distinction of blood, of breeding, of genealogy, has been as important as, possibly more important than, any particular behaviour: 'the distinction between gentle and ungentle, [is one] in which there is as much difference, as between virtue and vice'" (Goodrich and Legh, quoted in Goodrich 1990:225 regarding English law; brackets in original). Furthermore, belief in inherent qualitative distinctiveness bespeaks belief in a qualitatively defined universe in which dimensions of space and time encode fundamental existential values. Tangible forms and expressions of the spatial-temporal beyond encapsulate these qualities, too, which is to say that when select individuals or specific groups or categories of people are identified as tangible manifestations of cosmological properties, they are also accorded appropriate qualitative distinctiveness. Consequently, "it is not as individuals that people have legitimate positions in society but because of their positions in the eternal order which they temporarily incarnate" (Bloch 1982:223). "Social polarity is . . . a reflection and a consequence of religious polarity" (Hertz 1960b:96).

In general, the fundamental ordering of a given social "system" reflects the relative valuations accorded the inherent qualities represented by the constituent units (Hatch 1987). These valuations usually compare the "worth" or "honor" of the various houses with each other and with the qualities inherent in outside Others. In previous chapters I have suggested, in general terms, what some of the latter might entail. In summary, groups or categories of Others associated with the spatial dimension of the cosmos, including affines and lateral relatives, are identified with first-principle origins, the primacy of things and beings that are first, the beneficence of communitas, and contractual relationships, while groups or categories of Others associated with the temporal dimension of the cosmos, including emergent house ancestors, are identified with prior house origins, the importance of seniority, jural authority, and processual relationships. In this chapter I wish to review some of the qualities deemed inherent in another distinctive category of spatial-temporal Other: the aristocratic sector of hierarchically ranked societies and centralized polities. We may then correlate the qualities broadly associated with aristocracy with qualities associated with ancestors and with affines.[1]

Actual ethnographic descriptions of aristocracies distinguish groups and individuals with high political-ideological status in a variety of ways, reflecting the fact that the specifics of aristocratic roles vary widely cross-culturally. Nonetheless, on a more fundamental level numerous societies recognize qualities deemed inherent in the members of one or more houses that are thought to set them apart from the rest of the population in certain essentials; in other words, they recognize "the elementary idea of aristocracy . . . : the concept of the inherent superiority of a line of descent" (Goldman 1970:xvi). Goldman notes that "what has given aristocracy its command has not been expediency, but a deep and elementary notion of distinctions of human worth. Specifically, aristocracy is a doctrine of social status. Its right to rule, and to assess standards, is a privilege of worth, one of many. Thus the way to an understanding of aristocracy is not through political theory, but through a theory of social status. When we assess aristocracy as a political system we are drawn to study consequences only and to overlook their sources" (4).[2]

The concept of "aristocracy" appears to be identified with aspects of ideal or superior or powerful humanness in contrast to common, ordinary people, who are deemed to be in some manner flawed, deprived, deficient, or dependent and thus unable adequately to handle important affairs (see note 11; Kan 1989: chap. 4; Nutini 1995:40).[3] As exceptional beings, aristocrats are usually deemed to be "suprahuman" or to possess greater purity, durability, or magnanimity than ordinary persons do. Such attributes essentially recognize closer association of aristocrats with sacrality—that is, with spatial-temporal dimensions that stand beyond the common mundanity of the here-and-now and with related conditions of liminality, communitas, and cosmological origins that also transcend the ordinary (Hertz 1960b:96).[4]

Communitas, including concern with the moral, the sacred or holy, the qualitative and beneficial conditions of existence, aesthetics, and excellence in general, is expressed both within aristocratic groups themselves on occasions when members strive to diminish their own differences by reference to shared aristocratic qualities and in terms of extending prosperity, beneficence, and protection toward commoners (". . . chiefs are expected to use their godly powers for the benefit of people . . ." [Howard 1985:68 regarding Rotuma; Woodward 1989: 133–134]), often as a condition of, or by way of emphasizing, the distance between themselves and commoners.[5] With respect to the latter, Rowlands's comment regarding chiefdoms of the Cameroon grasslands is instructive: "What outsiders erroneously call a chief is indigenously called a *fon*. . . . In European thought 'chiefs' . . . retain attributes of authority and power to command, to punish, to reward and to exploit; all of which are quite foreign to the Mankon notion of *fon* . . . when asked to describe a *fon* . . . informants would never use the language of discipline and punishment but rather the language of generosity, redistribution, and fertility" (1985:53). Emphasizing beneficence and prosperity in this manner does not deny that chiefs may also be quite formidable and that ruling lords may exercise considerable jural authority and may punish and harm as well as help and protect. Rather it recognizes beneficence as the *ideally* more significant, more honorable, higher-ranking, and definitive attribute of cosmologically defined power in general (57). As Hocart put it, there are those who "are still possessed by the idea that the primary function of a king is to govern, to be the head of the administration . . . he is nothing of the kind. He is the repository of the gods, that is of the life of the group," and as such his fundamental purpose is to confer upon the people the blessings of the gods (1970: 98–99).

Communitas is temporarily characteristic of various other categories of liminal persons, such as groups of initiates or mourners during rites of passage.[6] Aristocrats, however, are accorded these qualities permanently as members of a distinctive social sector that, like affines and ancestors, constantly stands outside and thus apart from houses of living common folk. ". . . the system of nobility not only signifies 'generosity', namely nobility, of blood and degree which is known by its insignia . . . but it is also a form of codification, an encoding of knowledge, a hidden language or initiate wisdom . . ." (Goodrich 1990:225–226 regarding English nobility). Consequently, "from a religious standpoint, the separation between commoners and chiefs is close to absolute. They occupy different realms of spiritual existence, and in this limited sense form two classes" (Goldman 1975:48 regarding the Kwakiutl).

This sentiment, and some sense of the specific qualities that differentiate aristocrats and commoners and define aristocrats as Others relative to ordinary people, are widely expressed in ranked societies and centralized polities, and a sampling of some of these terms and metaphors of valuation is informative. For example, according to the Luwu, nobles have "white blood" in varying degrees of purity, while commoners' blood is "red"; "white blood's source is in the Upper World of spirits and ancestors" (Errington 1987:419, 423). Among the Wanano of Brazil, "high-ranked groups are said to be 'succulent' and are expected to manifest this trait through generous display in the sponsorship of large dance ceremonies" (Chernela 1993:6, 129),[7] while persons of

highest rank among the Tsimshian of the Northwest Coast were called
"ripe" or "real" people, being persons with supernatural connections to
give potency to their names (Seguin 1986b:484, 493; Kan 1989:100).
In Yap the comparison differentiates between people (and land) that are
tabugul—sacred, high, pure, clean—and those that are *taay*—profane,
low, impure, dirty (Labby 1976:69, 85). More specifically, to be *tabugul*
was "to control Yap's productive resources in both quantity and quality,
to have shaped the productivity upon which social life was based
through the process of development, to be the source of that productivity and thus to represent, in this sense, the social order. To be *taay* . . .
was to lack that control, to be dependent, to have developed and been
developed by the social order to a comparatively lesser degree (72; see
also note 11 below).

Elaborating on the theme of qualitative contrasts between aristocrats
and commoners in the Tanimbar Islands, McKinnon explains that the
rank difference between nobles and commoners is recognized in differences between "named" and "unnamed" houses, respectively:

> Important, named houses are often referred to as ships, under which
> lesser, unnamed houses "take shelter" or "harbor." Similarly, named
> houses are also known as "buffalo," in contrast to unnamed houses,
> which are referred to as "pigs." More significantly, however, the nobles
> who occupy named houses are thought of as "village people." It is their
> province to know "customary law," to sit in their village, in their houses,
> and negotiate bridewealth and other exchanges . . . according to custom-
> ary law. In so doing, they negotiate the order of human relations and the
> enduring form of culture: they create and recreate them with each negoti-
> ation. The commoners who belong to unnamed houses, on the contrary,
> are "forest people." It is not their province to understand customary law
> in any depth, and they are not allowed to talk it . . . Their special province
> is in relation to the forest—to hunting and agriculture, not to the village
> and customary law. (McKinnon 1991:105)[8]

Ultimately, McKinnon says, nobles "embody the totality of that which
defines humanity," which includes, in this case, opportunity for nobles
(but denied commoners) to establish "ideal" forms of marriage and
modes of exchange that connect nobles "to the past and to ancestral
sources of life" (275, 282). Similarly, according to Rousseau, "almost all
Kayan rituals contain elements which indicate whether the participants
are *kelunan jia* ('refined people') or *kelunan ji'ek* ('inferior people'). . . .

The 'refined people' are deemed to have greater spiritual powers and to have the ability to come into more intimate contact with the supernatural" (1979:218).

Rousseau also notes the close spirit of pragmatic communitas that unites the category of 'refined people' known as the *maren* (the ruling stratum of the Kayan), who maintain close links with each other and "frequently express the view that they must support each other irrespective of kinship relations and that solidarity must be demonstrated even between chiefs who personally dislike each other" (224, 221–222; Richards 1961:137). The nobility of the Jama Mapun of the Philippines expresses a comparable solidarity by maintaining a Hawaiian system of kinship terminology that differentiates the aristocracy as a group and contrasts with the kin term usage followed by the rest of society (Casiño 1976:23–25). Pabir (Nigeria) aristocrats followed a similar practice (Cohen 1976:204).

A closer look at the distinguishing characteristics of aristocrats as Others reveals several additional and ethnographically well-represented criteria. First, as Labby and McKinnon indicate for Yap and Tanimbar, respectively, aristocrats are accorded exceptional access to and identification with contexts of cosmological sources and origins.[9] Contacts with such beginnings, which deepen and extend spatial-temporal cosmological dimensions, can be expressed either in terms of *quantity* (abundance) of links with origins, as in detailed genealogies, or in terms of *immediacy* of contact, as in positional successions, or both, as in primogeniture (an abundance or quantity of first-born or immediate ancestral links).[10] Other mechanisms for expanding spatial-temporal dimensions include detailing and recording the nature of time, including calendrics and the development of writing or other recording systems (Hill 1992:92; Giddens 1984:182); extending cosmographical contacts and acquisitional activities such as long-distance travel and trade (Helms 1993); and encouraging development of the creative arts, especially as they relate to regalia and to ceremonials (Peregrine 1991:8). By elaborating and preferably monopolizing these and other activities (which are preexistent in nonranked societies), aristocrats increase or "unfold" and intricately structure the distance between the here-and-now and the there-and-then of cosmological sources and origins.

Increasing spatial-temporal distanciation, however, increases the necessity of bridging that expanse and making it accessible to society at large. As part of their political-ideological "generosity," aristocrats also provide that service by encouraging their own identification as tangible

representatives of Otherness.[11] But elaborating and heightening the
spatial-temporal dimension and then bridging that distance to bring it
closer to home also separates aristocrats from the common populace
and accords them privileged access to the power believed inherent in origins as well as greater control over the very concept of origins itself, including the diverse ways and means of accessing and expressing it. These
prerogatives constitute a type of resource and "wealth" that aristocrats
value highly and carefully guard. So it is that celebration of a privileged
access to origins is epitomized in the greater sense of "history" that aristocrats openly maintain and exhibit but that is denied to commoners. As
Connerton points out, "What is lacking in the life histories of those who
belong to subordinate groups is precisely those terms of reference that
conduce to and reinforce [the] sense of a linear trajectory, a sequential
narrative shape: above all, in relation to the past, the notion of legitimating origins . . ." (1989:19, 18–20). Numerous ethnographic examples support this statement, emphasizing the distinctive connection
of aristocrats with concepts and "events" of primordial or cultural origins compared with "a certain indifference" to such in "the short and
simple annals of the poor" (Sahlins 1983:523).

For example, Hill notes how the Annals of the Cakchiquel and the
Popol Vuh relate the histories of two noble Mayan houses of Guatemala
to semimythical events linking them to the legendary times of the "fantastic Toltecs" (Hill 1991:286).[12] In Hawaii aristocratic *alii* traced detailed lines of descent back to founding ancestors, while common people
were not allowed to possess genealogies; the latter held identity by virtue
of relationships of subordination to the aristocracy (Bargatsky 1985:
397; Valeri 1990:165, 181 n. 25; see also note 11 below and Friedman
1975:173).[13] Similarly, in the Tanimbar Islands, where, as we have seen,
the distinction between nobles and commoners corresponds to "named"
versus "unnamed" houses, "named houses are marked by their permanent relation . . . to distant ancestral sources of power and established
lines of fertility. Unnamed houses are, by contrast, marked by their im-
permanent and fleeting relation . . . to immediate ancestors and recent
lines of fertility" (McKinnon 1991:104, 97–98). Likewise among the
Tuareg, "it is because of the fact that the dominant group has a genealogy, relating the group to the prophet or to old Arabic tribes, that it ex-
ercises a monopoly of political power" (Bonte 1981:53). For all these
and numerous other ranked societies or centralized polities, as for the
Luapula of west-central Africa, where "the history of the kingship is the
subject of daily discussion at the king's court, where the aristocrats

gather to drink beer," it can be fairly said that "for commoners, precedent is around them in the present; for the kingship, precedent is only in the past of the kingship itself" (Cunnison 1957:27).

Let us turn now to a second distinguishing characteristic of aristocrats as Others. Members of aristocracies, especially politically active persons such as chiefs and kings, are hedged about with an exceptional number of distinctive behaviors—including prohibitions, taboos, or avoidances—that, considered overall, appear designed to deny their "ordinariness" and to identify, exaggerate, or inculcate their qualitative distinctiveness as "suprahuman" beings who are freed from certain of the more "mortal" or "physical" features of human existence (Gluckman 1962:42).[14] Not only are aristocrats often able to avoid the mundane tasks and manual labor that provide subsistence and other basic necessities for commoners (Lloyd 1965:75; Bean 1977:127) but, as Nadel pointed out for the Nuba, "the whole physical life of the chief is dominated by sacred, mystic laws" (1947:345). Kopytoff summarizes some of these conditions, pointing out that a ruler might find his sex life severely restricted and his other elementary physical functions, such as crying, eating, drinking, or defecating, ritually controlled and that he might not be allowed to die a natural death (Kopytoff 1987:66; Fortes 1962b:66; Lambek 1990).[15] Maquet, discussing traditional relations between aristocratic Tutsi and commoner Hutu in Rwanda, explains why this is so. Noting that the Tutsi (who favored pastoralism) not only based their diet heavily on liquid dairy products (milk and also beer) rather than on solid food but also "behaved as if the need for nourishment was, if not shameful, at least beneath their dignity" (1961:19), he continues, "This attitude . . . might be explained . . . on a deeper level as an affirmation of what we might term a fundamental difference between themselves and Hutu. The Tutsi, according to their legends, came from another world. They were human beings like the Hutu, but not in quite the same way and thus were entitled to rule" (19, 147). Tutsi were also taught always to present a demeanor of dignity, amiability, politeness, and self-control since "it was taken for granted that only vulgar persons showed off all their emotions" (118, 117).

In another part of the world, Tlingit aristocrats, as "ideal" persons linked to the center of society and of the universe, avoided consumption of certain foods, especially shellfish (indicative of marginal or peripheral cosmological realms) in order "to maintain their purity and guarantee their material, social, and moral superiority" (Moss 1993:642, 646; Kan 1989:92–93, 98). Persons of high status in Tlingit society, as paragons of perfection, virtue, and morality linked to the sacred, were also expected to be even tempered and mild mannered and to show exceptional control over expressions of emotion. A model person was also expected to be wise, generous, and modest (Kan 1989:96, 101, 319 n. 35). In addition, "because of strong preoccupation with physical perfection, persons with serious bodily defects and handicaps could not aspire to high rank and status in Tlinget society" (60).[16] The bodies of aristocrats were also judged to be purer and heavier (more solid) than the bodies of ordinary people, and these qualities were augmented by a profusion of valuable ornaments, clothing, body paint, and tattoos, which aristocrats, unlike commoners, wore all the time (89–90).

More of the same is found in the various centralized polities of Oceania. To review only a few examples, Maori chiefs ate apart from other people and could not be touched by commoners, while high priests were fed only by their sisters, who put the food directly into their mouths (Goldman 1970:520). On Easter Island "ordinarily, no one dared touch any part of the ariki mau's body. His head was particularly sacred and his hair was never cut . . . No one was allowed to see either the ariki mau or his son as they ate or slept and none but other ariki could enter the royal hut" (112). On Mangareva "royal infants were hidden away as though to emphasize their exclusive cycle of emergence and growth" (158), while in the Society Islands, not only were the clothes, houses, canoes, and litter-bearers of the highest elites deemed sacred but the very sounds in the language that composed their names could not be used for ordinary significations (181). In Samoa, where the glance of the Tui Manu'a withered the fruit on the trees, "his person, his food, and all his intimate belongings . . . were sacred and dangerous" (253).

"Ideal" behavior, perfect physical form, untouchability, freedom from manual labor, and adjurance of "normal" or common physiological needs, including natural death,[17] as well as other attributes not specifically referenced above, such as being ceremonially "fed" by periodic prestations of food and drink by commoners and, in many cases, accorded forms of locomotion, such as being carried on litters (somewhat suggestive of the distinctive modes of transportation necessarily accorded corpses) or on horseback, that contrast with "ordinary" bipedalism, all identify aristocrats as distinctive types of beings that differ from ordinary living humans of the here-and-now.[18] These attributes testify that aristocrats have transcended or controlled the raw, mortal physicality of body and emotion and stand closer to suprahuman (supramortal) states of being; more specifically, they indicate that the inherent quality of aristocracy can be associated with vital attributes of the ancestral dead or even of the gods (Howard 1985:67–73), who are also "ideal" beings freed from manual labor, ritually fed by the sacrifices of ordinary people, released from processes of physicality, and directly conjoined with conditions of origins.[19] In addition, aristocrats, like deceased ancestors, hold permanent liminal status that charges them with the proper nurturing of the polity (Bloch 1992:6).

Indeed, so many of the qualities definitive of aristocracy are ancestor-like in nature that even in unranked and noncentralized polities ancestors may properly be regarded as the original aristocrats. Physically living aristocrats, in turn, with their ancestorlike qualities and their existence in a state of permanent liminality, become for all intents and purposes tangible forms of *living ancestors,* actual embodiments of ancestral natures situated in a condition of high and powerful ambiguity between this world and the other (Leach 1979a:158). This identification (which holds true particularly for the ruling members of aristocracies), is especially telling from the perspective of the ordinary populace who, as aristocrats are "elevated" by association with ancestors and origins, are to equal but opposite effect reduced and "dehumanized" by the judgment that they inherently lack the means for comparable access to broader connections of space and time (see note 11). The ultimate implication of such polarization is that aristocrats essentially come to constitute another category of cosmological Other for the populace at large.

Identification of aristocrats and especially rulers as tangible living ancestors and as inalienably associated with contexts of origins is widespread and well recognized ethnographically.[20] ". . . the chiefs . . . represent the first ancestors and have therefore dual qualities as person and as ancestral spirit" (Goldman 1975:50 regarding the Kwakiutl). "Since each notable person is always in some respect an embodiment of a mythological founder, the entire genealogical network of a community is always a living representation of the beings who existed, or who preexisted in mythological times" (27). "The idea that the reigning king is 'dead', and therefore a spirit or an ancestor, is widespread in southern Nigeria" (Armstrong 1980:403; Fardon 1990:81; Rowlands 1985:54). "The chief becomes an embodiment of his predecessors, a living ancestor himself" (Gudeman 1986:95 regarding the Bemba). "Through the use of the indigenous writing before the conquest, leaders of preeminent chinamitales traced their descent back to the legendary founders of their groups. This was done not only to legitimize their authority but also to establish themselves as possessors of the same supernatural powers those ancestors had" (Hill 1992:92 regarding the Cakchiquel). "[Aren] is derived from the root *ren*, 'to increase'. . . . It is a spiritual substance or quality that is held to be inherent in ancestors, rich men, and other superiors . . ." (Woodward 1989:128 regarding the Ao Naga). In short,

> . . . the king's consumption of food in private, the use of a special vocabulary to describe his actions, and the restrictions on his performance of manual labor all served to constitute the king as someone not living like other human beings, thereby recreating through everyday practices the duality between the king and the kingdom. At the same time the symbolic constitution of the king as someone not living like other humans served to create his ambiguous role as a "living-spirit," a unique symbolic mediator, alive yet somehow not alive, the vital essence of the kingdom yet somehow completely separated from it. (Carlson 1993:321 regarding the Haya of Tanzania)[21]

Recognizing chiefly rulers and aristocracies as living ancestors has much merit in that it entails a cosmological or universal view of the phenomenon of aristocracy in which aristocrats are understood to constitute a qualitatively distinctive category of Others, permanently situated not at the pinnacle of human polities but in an institutionalized liminality. As such, aristocracies are positioned between those who are physically alive but spiritually limited (members of ordinary houses) and those who are spiritually fulfilled but physically dead (true ancestor-beings). Since the pragmatics of aristocratic activities involve the realm of the physically living, however, it is incumbent upon aristocracies, as both physically living and spiritually ancestral, to emphasize their ancestorlike Otherness relative to other living persons rather than to emphasize their physical life or "humanness" relative to spiritualized beings. Hence the emphasis on access to origins. Hence, too, the formal emphasis on the derivative capability either to represent beneficence and provide conditions conducive to prosperity and well-being for those under their charge or to withhold prosperity if recipients are judged unworthy, uncooperative, or unappreciative. "What ultimately distinguishes sub-clans of rank from others is that they are credited with the possession of peculiar powers which make their members, especially their leaders, dangerous men, and therefore entitled to receive the marks of respect and other privileges . . . Thus the Tabalu sub-clan of Omarakana possess the To'urikuna magic of weather and prosperity by which they are believed to be able to bring famine or plenty on the whole Island" (Powell 1960:128 regarding the Trobriand Islands).

In earlier chapters, the capacity and responsibility either for providing prosperity, well-being, and social reproduction or for withholding these benefits were also accorded to another category of physically living Others, one that historically preceded aristocracy. Affinal groups have been qualitatively identified in terms virtually identical to those accorded aristocracies—that is, as a category of sociological-cosmological Other or not-Us (from the perspective of the house) with the power to help or to harm that also provides essential access to contexts of cosmological origins and the life that flows therefrom. In addition, we have seen that hierarchically superior affines become living ancestors for the house by embodying ancestral potencies and legitimacies and tangibly representing the very presence of ancestors themselves on ceremonial and ritual occasions. The significance of all this for aristocracies lies in the fact that aristocrats not only are accorded distinctive qualities as living ancestors relative to the rest of the populace but also very often are structurally (formally) related to that populace as affines (see Chapter 9). Some of the political, economic, and territorial implications of this well-recorded circumstance are appreciated in the anthropological literature, but the fundamental significance of the fact that in ranked societies and centralized polities aristocrat-commoner relationships are cast in the idiom of affinity has not been adequately considered. It is my contention that the qualitative characteristics accorded aristocrats as living ancestors and especially the acceptance of the hierarchical superordinancy of the aristocracy derive in large measure from the qualitative and hierarchical characteristics of affinity and express the formal sociological-cosmological identification of aristocrats by the populace as affinal as well as ancestral Others. The following chapters explore this assertion in greater detail.

9 |

ARISTOCRATS
AND
AFFINES

In *Kings and Councillors* Hocart astutely perceives that the most persistent feature of dual social organizations is mutual ministration, each division doing for the other what is necessary to ensure life and prosperity, generally by referencing dualities inherent in the structure of the cosmos (such as sky and earth), which must be integrated by various rituals, including marriage (1970: chap. 20). Hocart finds considerable evidence of such dualism among both centralized and noncentralized polities. In line with his general thesis that the machinery of centralized government is prefigured in noncentralized forms, particularly in organization for ritual, he also finds that dichotomies established in noncentralized social and ritual settings (as in various expressions of moiety) are equally important to the organization of centralized polities, where the fundamental dualism exists in the division between aristocracy and commoners (290), whose interrelatedness we may then also expect to find expressed in ritual, including marriage.

In *Society against the State* Clastres takes a different approach to the basic dichotomy of the rulers and the ruled by interpreting that fundamental dualism in terms of Us versus Them or the inside versus the outside. He argues that those who would be governed (the Us that is inside society) find it most expedient to interpret power and the political sphere as something best consigned to the outside (nature) and power holders as beings best kept at a social distance and understood as Others (1987:41, 42). In Clastres's study, based on noncentralized South American societies, these procedures explain the apparent lack or rejection of authority such that the erstwhile community leader becomes dependent on the group for his political recognition rather than the reverse (44–47).

The political impotence accorded some South American tribal authorities is far from universal, but a perception by those who are ruled that high authority is properly quartered in the cosmological beyond *is* universal in nonindustrial polities, as is the identification (by those who are governed) of would-be rulers with the cosmological outside. Interactions between the dual organization of rulers and ruled, aristocrats and commoners, thus become interactions between Others and Us and (if Hocart is correct) are informed by the same qualities and valuations that accompany all such interactions of the house and its Others. I have argued in previous chapters that one fundamental way to relate the house to its Others is through the affinal dimension of kinship. This is as true of ranked and centralized polities as it is of noncentralized "egalitarian" ones. Indeed, the remarkable generality, flexibility, and durability of kinship in general as a social and political mechanism (as opposed to its strictly domestic functions; see Sahlins 1976:5, 6, 211; Kopytoff 1987:39; Bloch 1973) seems particularly evidenced in ranked and centralized polities, which are frequently demographically larger and may be ethnically more heterogeneous and where it is particularly true that "people behave among themselves in a certain way and therefore they are related in a certain way: not that people are related in a certain way and therefore they behave in a certain way. This is true of relationships of wider scale, or political kinship" (Cunnison, quoted in Cohen and Comaroff 1976:95).[1]

Affinity is a vitally important component of political kinship in ranked and centralized polities because of the legitimations and the accessibilities it provides. Most significant in this respect are the affinal affiliations of aristocracies, both those that relate aristocratic houses with other aristocratic groups and those that relate aristocratic houses to select commoner houses.[2] The ethnographic literature is replete with evidence of both types of aristocratic marriages, but the typical descrip-

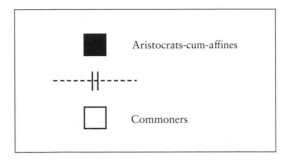

F IGURE 7   Hierarchical superiority of aristocrats relative to commoners as
influenced by affinity.

tive and analytical emphasis focuses on the alliances created and the resulting transfers of valuables or other forms of prestations rather than
on the qualities of affinity that underlie those alliances and prestations
and that are the focus of my concern (Clastres 1987:46). Consequently,
much of my discussion of aristocratic marriages rests on the logic of the
assumption that where alliances are defined in marital terms, affinal
qualities are also involved.[3] If this is accepted, then it follows that aristocratic marriages, like all marriages, are fundamentally cosmological in
qualitative import. This means that they invoke conjunctions between
houses and outside Others and that the relationships established via the
idiom of affinity involve issues of communitas, hierarchy, and legitimacy
based on differential access to contexts of origins. Where aristocratic-
commoner marriages are concerned (and considered from the perspective of commoners), aristocrats as actual, potential, or categorical affines
constitute a category of other people, hierarchically superior and powerful outsiders whose interests and activities are considered morally legitimate when they are directed (communitas-like) toward the better-
ment of spousal houses or of the polity (Fig. 7; cf. Fig. 6).[4]

In aristocratic marriages the political-ideological element inherent in
affinity becomes more explicitly actualized. In more "egalitarian" settings affinal political ideology may remain largely latent or implicit, at
best only periodically expressed, especially in the majority of marital alliances that involve houses that are not engaged in the high stakes of politics and that only have need to activate the ideological (cosmological)
context of affinal/lateral relationships on special occasions, such as mortuary rites or first-fruit celebrations, when legitimizing affinal witnesses-

cum-ancestors are required at house ceremonies or as individuals seek the shelter and support of affinal communitas. In centralized polities, however, the qualitative power of affinity assumes major and persistent political-ideological significance as members of aristocratic houses seek constantly to publicly legitimize both their status as living ancestors and the activities that rely on such identification for political justification.

Affinal relations also provide the aristocratic sector with essential structural ties to the populace at large, particularly as aristocrat-commoner marriages identify select aristocratic houses as actual affines of select commoner houses. These alliances facilitate the broader identification by commoners in general of aristocrats *en masse* as "affines of us all," especially in the communitas sense (often expressed in ritual) of holding responsibility for the general well-being of the polity. Structural ties with the commoner sector by marriage (or some other form of politically instrumental kinship tie) are especially essential for aristocrats in kinship-based centralized polities because their categorical qualitative identification as living ancestors in and of itself does *not* provide structuration between aristocrats and commoners but only between aristocrats and ancestors; even formal genealogies or positional successions per se are important primarily for the links they evidence with ancestral origins. In addition, using the idiom of affinal kinship to effect aristocratic-commoner structuration not only creates essential sociological ties but also does so within a cosmologically informed context that legitimizes (as inherent in affinity) the hierarchical nature of the aristocrat-commoner relationship and places that hierarchy within the broader cosmological context in which aristocrats are identified as living ancestors (Fig. 8). Consequently, the dual roles of aristocrats as living ancestors and as affines are conjoined, as they are in any social setting for any and all affines who ceremonially represent ancestors for a house, and aristocrats as actual or generic affines become identified in general both as guarantors of public well-being and as validators of jural authority within the polity.

The same origins-related affinal legitimation and support also accrue to aristocratic houses, especially by virtue of Outside affinal relations they establish with other aristocratic groupings of their own or other polities. In fact, given that aristocrats are more likely to quantitatively increase their affinal associations, and thus increase their legitimizing witnesses, by contracting multiple marriages and that as formal political agents they have greater need of such legitimation because they operate in a wider public political arena and in more purely or formally

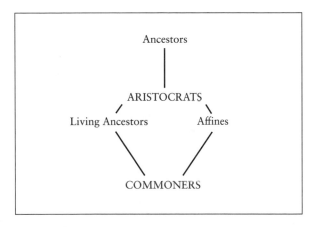

FIGURE 8   Ancestor, aristocrat, and commoner ties
when aristocrats are defined as affines
and as living ancestors.

"political" terms, it may be claimed that in ranked and centralized polities the significance of the political-ideological role of affines and lateral relatives as outside legitimizers becomes increasingly focused upon, or restricted to, higher-status houses. Conversely, the legitimizing element of the ordinary affinal ties of ordinary commoner houses becomes correspondingly less significant in the broader public arena, though still essential for the social reproduction and legitimation of the life of the house itself. In this sense usurpation of the legitimizing power of affinity by aristocrats can be seen to constitute yet another dimension of chiefly or aristocratic monopoly.

In general terms, in ranked and centralized polities, commoner houses encounter affinity through marriages with other ("peer") commoner houses either within or without the polity or by marriages with aristocratic houses while aristocratic houses contract marital alliances with select commoner houses or with other aristocratic houses either of the same polity or of other polities. The political-ideological significance and potential of all these affinal avenues will be further affected by whether the affinal group stands as spouse-giver or spouse-taker relative to the house, given the general precept that to generously give or provide signals a superior or superordinate status while to take or receive signals some manner of inferiority or dependency because it indicates an inability to produce what is needed. To give or to provide also signifies a closer association with ultimate sources and ultimate suppliers (Miller

1988:50). Hence givers and providers either are accorded an inherently closer association with contexts of cosmological origins or are thought to occupy an intermediate or liminal position between such supernatural sources on the one hand and dependent earthly receivers on the other.

The ethnographic literature indicates that in centralized polities both forms of marital alliances may be used to formally relate the aristocratic sector to the commoner sector in affinal terms. That is, aristocratic houses will serve either as spouse-takers relative to select commoner houses or as spouse-givers relative to select commoner houses (usually in addition to marital alliances with other aristocratic houses). Let us consider both affinal settings in somewhat greater detail, bearing in mind that the ultimate political-ideological goal of aristocracies, especially of ruling houses, is to effect a legitimizing connection between prior house origins and first-principle origins as well as to exercise authority as living ancestors and as affines.

In hypothetical terms, when aristocratic houses stand as spouse-givers to select commmoner houses as spouse-receivers, the role of the aristocratic house as affinal Others providing access to first-principle origins through the auspices of the life-giving women they provide as spouses also defines and legitimizes their hierarchical supremacy and qualitative superiority both as affines and as authoritative living ancestors. In this scenario, commoner houses may recognize aristocratic houses as affinal "mother's brothers" or "fathers" and accept the propriety of aristocrats-cum-affines as a legitimate source of social and political well-being (communitas) both for specific spousal houses and for the polity at large. Spouse-giving aristocratic houses, in turn, not only establish affective and structural ties with commoner houses but also acquire wives and legitimating affines of their own by contracting additional marriages with other aristocratic houses that, as first-principle-related affines, are able to witness and legitimate the various ceremonial occasions and other more secular activities of the focal aristocratic house, including events when the house celebrates its own prior origins and relates them to cosmological first principles.

Data to support the hypothetical model outlined here are readily found in ethnographic examples, though specific ethnographic references often differ with respect to which aspects of the overall picture are emphasized. Murphy and Bledsoe, discussing the Kpelle of Liberia (1987), provide an excellent example of how affinity structures the general political hierarchy by defining aristocrats as wife-givers and as affinal/lateral relatives to commoners. The highest offices of Kpelle authority (those at the chiefdom and district levels) are controlled by ruling patrilineal landowning lineages, each claiming to be founder, clearer, "opener," or "namer" of a territory and tracing its ancestral prior house origins to the founding settlers of the land, a type of originating event that presumably also references first-principle origins. Community leaders are formally affiliated with a landowning lineage by receiving a wife from the landowner—usually a landowner's sister or a brother's daughter. This woman becomes not only the mother of the community leader's children but also, by extension, the "mother" of the growing patrilineal descent group as a whole. The landowner's kin group, as affinal/lateral relatives, now stands in the position of "mother's brother" to the community kin group, which in turn is recognized as its "sister's son." More specifically, "everyone in the host lineage is in the category of *MoBro* to everyone in the [community] lineage. The initial marriage is thus considered a pivotal event in determining the (theoretically) perpetual hierarchical relationship between the two groups" (Murphy and Bledsoe 1987:128). The process may be extended even further as the community lineage, in turn, gives wives to still other lineages that then also become "sister's sons" to the chiefdom's landowners.

> The nested structure of hierarchical *MoBro-SiSo* ties ramifies throughout [the] Chiefdom, which is sometimes called by [the] people in English "the land of uncles and nephews." The saliency of these matrilateral ties even misled one of the first ethnographers of the Kpelle, Westermann, to identify them as matrilineal . . . The essential political quality of these matrilateral relations lies in the combination of hierarchy and support, in contrast to the competition and rivalry that often permeate relations within the patrilineages. Ideally, *SiSos* defer completely to their *MoBros*. . . . The *MoBro's* [sic] is his *SiSo's nuu-namu,* 'person owner.' As such, he is the patron who provides political and economic help and can demand labor and support in return. He is the crucial intercessor for his *SiSo* when the latter gets in trouble or is involved in important matters, such as marriage negotiations or disputes. (128)

Indeed, for the Kpelle, "matrilateral kinship provides the unifying metaphor that binds the entire political structure" (ibid.).

Murphy and Bledsoe also relate, however, that hierarchically inferior sister's sons in good standing generally serve as assistants to their superior mothers' brother's lineages in ritual matters, including mortuary duties for mother's brothers, and sister's sons of some importance also hold responsibility as ritual consecrators, ritual guardians, and administrators of portions of territory (128–130, 133–134). This curious service as ritual consecrators, seemingly out of character for subordinate sister's sons, becomes more comprehensible when it is understood that the sister's sons who perform these functions represent lineages that were previous inhabitants of territories that were later taken over (officially "founded") by more powerful though later-arriving mother's brothers' lineages to whom sister's sons' lineages became subordinate by virtue of being given wives. In other words, the ritual potency of such sister's sons lies in their representation of earlier, meaning primary or "first," inhabitants of the land, a status that carries its own independent relationship to a context of first-principle origins. Their services as ritual legitimizers for landowners' lineages, then, constitute a co-opting of this first-principle origins context by the politically superior mother's brothers' lineages for their own benefit (129, 130; see also Part Three below).

Murphy and Bledsoe also draw attention to two other well-known examples, the Nuer of the Sudan and the Kachin of Burma, in which affinal/lateral ties created by aristocratic wife-giving activities structure relationships between aristocratic houses and commoners. Although each situation can become very nuanced and complex, the basic structure is straightforward. Regarding the Nuer (and especially the eastern Nuer, where qualitatively distinctive aristocratic houses are more in evidence), Gough discusses how patrilineages of "nondominant" clans may be structurally associated with "dominant" or aristocratic clans in a kind of "perpetual kinship" in which the aristocratic lineage is regarded as "children of the mother's brother" relative to nonaristocratic "children of the father's sister" or "children of girls," meaning persons or groups of persons attached to aristocratic lineages by maternal or conjugal links, plus descendants of men who married women of the dominant lineage (1971; see also Kelly 1985:182, 206, 221). Such "sister's sons" may have only weak patrilineal ties of their own. "It is because of the incipient social stratification of Nuer society and the prominence of dominant clan groups, that other members of the society stress their cognatic links to the dominant lineage of the community rather than their own agnatic ties; and that the dominant lineages themselves make room in their structure for cognatically attached branches of lower rank . . . the rules bring into each village attached affines of many different clan groups who are not related to, and have no unity with, one another, but who are bound to the village through their individual ties to its 'bulls' [powerful village leaders, usually aristocrats]"(Gough

1971:98, 99). Gough also notes the additional strength in numbers and the loyalty provided for dominant clansmen by groups of sister's sons, tempered by claims that sister's sons may make on the herds and the generosity of their mother's brothers that the latter may feel ambivalent about fulfilling (91, 94, 113). Origins myths mentioned by Evans-Pritchard suggest that the familiar role of affines/laterals as avenues to supernatural powers and contexts of origins, especially first-principle origins, is also a feature of Nuer political ideology, especially in the context of the famous Nuer leopard-skin chiefs or earth-priests.[5] "The leopard skin was given by the ancestors of the dominant lineages to their maternal uncles that they might serve as tribal priests. The structurally opposed lineages of the clan were then in the common relationship of sisters' sons to the line of priests, which thus had a mediatory position between them" (Evans-Pritchard, quoted in Beidelman 1971:389; Kelly 1985:205).[6]

Among the hierarchical *gumsa* Kachin discussed by Leach (1961, 1965) and Friedman (1975), structurally significant political marriages are those in which women of the highest, chiefly descent groups who do not marry into other chiefly houses marry aristocratic men who are village headmen, as other aristocratic women sometimes marry commoner men of their village (Leach 1961:81–86). Consequently, select chiefly houses stand as higher-status wife-giving fathers-in-law (and classificatory or actual mother's brothers) to select aristocratic sons-in-law (actual or classificatory sister's sons), and select aristocratic houses stand as higher-status wife-giving fathers-in-law (classificatory mother's brothers) to select commoner sons-in-law (classificatory sister's sons; 8–9). According to Friedman, the hierarchy of Kachin houses evidenced in the wife-giving/wife-receiving ranking has its roots in the relative success of lineages in demonstrating connections between lineage ancestors (prior house origins) and higher celestial spirits or *nats*, who are the source of all fertility, prosperity, and wealth (first-principle origins) by producing surpluses for community feasts; the greater the surplus, the greater the prestige and the higher the rank of the lineage (1975:170). Ranking is then institutionalized by identifying the ancestors of the lineage producing the best harvests (thereby evidencing the most influential connections with spirits) as the same as the village ancestral spirit (nat) through whom all other village lineages may contact the higher nats. The chiefly lineage, therefore, is the lineage that connects the community not only to its own founding ancestors but also to the higher, first-principle spirits, as evidenced by the placement of altars to both the chiefly lineage's own ancestor (recognized as territorial spirit) and the major celestial spirits in the chief's house and by acknowledgement that only the chief can make offerings to the supreme earth-sky spirit (172–174). According to Leach, the supreme sky spirit is also regarded as an affinal relative of one of the chief's remote ancestors (1965:108). Thus the chiefly lineage is conjoined with first-principle origins by the same (affinal) means by which commoner houses are conjoined with the aristocratic lineage that references first-principle origins for them.

The same themes of aristocratic houses allianced, as wife-givers, to commoner houses, combined with recognition that aristocratic-cum-affinal houses also conjoin hierarchical superiority with privileged access to origins, is exemplified by McKinnon's study (1991) of the ranked (though not politically centralized) society of the Tanimbar Islands of eastern Indonesia. Tanimbar also illustrates that the affinal context for aristocrat-commoner relationships may be referenced in other terms; in Tanimbar they are glossed in sibling- and gender-related terms as well as in lateral kinship expressions.

In Tanimbar, aristocratic houses are known as "named" houses, meaning that "the group has an enduring relation with the founding ancestors, which is a sign of its permanence, its weight, and its value" (McKinnon 1991:98, 104). Named houses establish connections with unnamed houses that lack such attributes by providing them with wives. In the hierarchical relationship between named wife-giving houses and unnamed wife-receiving houses, however, the superordinant, origins-related named houses are also regarded as "male" relative to the unnamed houses, which are "female"; the former also constitute "older brothers" or "uncles" relative to their "younger brothers" or "sisters or aunts" (98). Named houses as "males" maintain the most active or direct access to first-principle origins essential for the reproduction of social and political life. They are charged with, and distinguished by, the responsibility that originally devolved upon their ancestors of moving about in the outside realms of the heavens, the underworld, and the lands beyond the horizon in order to contact distant sources of cosmological power and obtain tangible embodiments of first-principle origins that support the reproduction of their own here-and-now world (56, 62, 79–80; see also Chapter 11). In contrast, members of unnamed houses, as "females," remain at home as fixed and stabilized anchors maintaining more passive, though still essential, supportive ritual relationships with creator-sources (133). Within the ritual order of the named houses themselves, however, it is equally the duty of men to maintain fixed, anchored, stabilizing relationships with founding house ancestors (prior house origins) to enable outmarrying women and other "female-related resources" (land, trees) to extend beyond the house and effect necessary connections with Others (84, 101–103, 107). Unnamed houses, though recognizing immediate house ancestors (father and father's father), acquire access to origins by alliances with superordinate named houses that are identified as "sources" or origin points themselves. Consequently,

> it was only named houses that maintained . . . a center for an enduring ritual relation to the founding ancestors of the house-complex as a whole. The relation of unnamed houses to these ancestors existed only to the extent that they remained attached as younger brothers to named houses. The capacity for named houses to stand for and represent the whole depended upon their position as a ritual center. It was their *tavu* [carved altar panels] and their heirlooms that provided a pathway, both in space and through time to the founding ancestors—to the origins, the base, and the root of all that had issued forth and should continue [to] issue forth from them. (99, 104)[7]

McKinnon emphasizes that "most important, the relation between elder and younger brother houses codes a hierarchical relation between nobles and commoners" (98, 104–105). She further stresses that this relationship between houses is not conceived as an inclusive ideology of descent; rather the relationship between the houses of the elder brother and attached younger brother is viewed as an exclusive hierarchy, a "radical disjunction between elder and younger" based on traditional associations between the respective houses referencing conditions of original migration and settlement and persisting in "a conventional understanding that, being hierarchically related, they are mutually obliged to treat each other well" (100, 101, 99).

The structural ties that relate nobles and commoners, named and unnamed houses (as well as named with other named houses) in Tanimbar society are, however, affinal. The linkages of named houses with other named houses form affinal alliances that endure generation after generation and are considered to have been in existence since time immemorial (104, 123–127, 228). At their highest level of expression, these intermarriages emphasize a communitas-like equality among named houses that references the original transcendental unity of cosmic origins (124–127, 226, 280–281).[8] Yet named houses are also matrilaterally affiliated with unnamed houses as wife-giving sources of life: "One's vital life substance derives from one's ancestors—and in particular one's maternal ancestors" (110, 98, 115). As such, the affinal relationship between named and unnamed houses marks an explicit inequality; those who are sources and givers of life-providing women are clearly qualitatively distinctive and stand hierarchically superior to those who receive women and life. In Tanimbarese idioms, the wife-giving house of the brother (the "male" house) is the "root" of the life that flows to the sister's husband's house (the "female" house) to be actualized in the "sprouts" that are the sister's children (111).[9]

When we turn from aristocratic houses as wife-givers to wife-takers for commoner houses, the basic situation changes and becomes more complicated. One fundamental difference lies in the manner of placing the qualitative emphasis that identifies social standing. When, from the purview of the commoner house, aristocratic affinal Others are wife-givers, the beneficent "gift" of a life-providing woman *elevates* the status of the aristocratic affinal group as qualitatively superordinate to the commoner house. When, however, from the purview of the commoner house, aristocratic affinal Others are wife-takers, the superior status of the affinal Others is initially achieved by *reducing* the status of the commoner house, marking it as subordinate to the affinal group by virtue of its surrender of women (Fig. 9). In addition, given the potential political-ideological import of accessing legitimating first-principle origins that would accrue to the wife-providing house even if common, it is further incumbent upon wife-taking aristocratic affines somehow to actively manifest their own independent and superior access to first-principle origins relative to their wife-providers. This can be accomplished either by redefining "wife-taking" as an alternative expression of first-principle origins in the sense of bringing "order" to otherwise uncontrolled fertility or creativity (see Chapter 7) or by surpassing the inherent worth of the woman received with distributions (e.g., at life-crisis rites or feasts of merit) of items of tangible wealth that also refer to first-principle origins (Ekholm 1978:118–120).

To be appropriate for this purpose, "valuables" either must exceed the woman's "worth" in a quantitative sense or be very durable and long-lasting goods. If durable, they are indicative of the greater permanence of origins-related associations claimed by the wife-taking house, which is meant to contrast with the inherently temporary nature of the affinally contracted link with origins offered by the wife-providing house, which can dissolve upon the death of a spouse (Bloch 1992:81–84). By receiving such goods the wife-providers also must recognize the

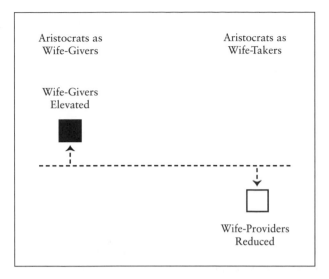

FIGURE 9   Changes in status of aristocrats and com-
           moners related to roles as wife-givers and
           wife-providers.

ultimate superiority of wife-takers as overall provider of first-principle
prosperity, especially if the proffered valuables assist the commoner
house to take wives for itself (Fig. 10).

By relying on means other than the giving of women to maintain their
ultimate hierarchical superiority, wife-taking aristocrats rest their final
political-ideological identification on the ancestral more than on the affinal side of the affine-as-ancestor equation. That is to say, when aristocrats serve as wife-givers for commoners, they are primarily highlighted
as *affines* accessing life-giving first-principle origins for commoner
houses. However, when aristocratic houses are structurally related to
commoner houses as wife-takers and therefore must also serve as generous provisioners of other forms of wealth to preserve their status, they
appear to emphasize primarily their identity as *living ancestors* expressing the quality of well-being for commoners in idioms of abundance or
durability rather than in idioms of life-giving affinity. Consequently,
when aristocrats are wife-takers relative to commoners, the threatening
(to the aristocracy) hierarchical quality inherent in affinal relations may
be greatly reduced and the *affinally* defined "*exclusive*" form of aristocratic-commoner hierarchy (characteristic of aristocrats as wife-givers
for commoners) may be reformulated as an *ancestor*-related "*inclusive*"

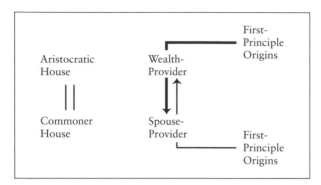

FIGURE 10   Access to origins when commoners are
spouse-providers for aristocrats.

form of hierarchy. This form of hierarchical expression is also readily expressed as political dominance supportive of interests of aristocrats primarily by referring to their inherent superiority not as in-laws but as living ancestors of the polity.

Efforts to reformulate hierarchy as dominance, however, often remain incomplete or become more complicated because attempting to neutralize the political-ideological potential of commoners as wife-providers may reduce but does not totally destroy that potential.[10] Wife-providing commoner houses, like all sources of wives, do in fact offer routes to legitimizing first-principle origins for aristocratic wife-taking houses and, therefore, do have potential to affect the legitimacy supporting the aristocracy. This potential is evidenced in a positive "affinal" fashion when ritual representatives of the common population are required to attend aristocratic burials and royal installations and when commoners are thought to access distinctive supernatural sources, such as earth spirits. Such potential can be evidenced in a negative "affinal" context when wife-takers' failure to honor obligations to wife-providers' houses unleash the evils of sorcery that can challenge the legitimacy of those who rule (Rowlands 1985 : 58–62; cf. note 10).

It is to be expected, however, that aristocratic wife-taking houses would prefer to evidence access to first-principle origins by means other than, or in addition to, recognition of commoners' political-ideological potential. Therefore, although affinal ties with commoner houses remain essential for structural reasons, various structural manipulations (in addition to the wealth-related "adjustment" described above) may also be utilized by aristocrats to reduce the impact of those ties. Thus, for example, commoner houses may be affinally allied only with lower-ranked and politically less significant aristocrats (Rousseau 1979), allowing higher-ranked aristocratic houses to establish more telling origins-related affinal alliances with other highly ranked houses of the same or of another polity. Highly ranked houses may also emphasize outside activities other than marriage, such as long-distance acquisitional trade, in order to evidence their own independent access to first-principle origins (Powell 1960:138–139). Alternatively, the first-principle origins accessed via commoners may be openly recognized by the chiefly ruling house (as, for example, in ritual relations between chiefs and commoner women; see Watson 1958:167), while the rest of the aristocracy focuses (often very competitively) on relations with prior house origins as celebration of their status as living ancestors. Sometimes, too, the potency of commoners as legitimizing affines may be openly recognized only on periodic select occasions, as at mortuary rites and installation ceremonies, while aristocrats emphasize their positions as living ancestors accessing either context of origins on a more constant and permanent basis (Watson 1958).

The ethnographic record illustrates various points asserted above. The Kayan of central Borneo as described by Rousseau (1979) exemplify, in reasonably straightforward terms, affinal structuring between wife-taking aristocratic houses and wife-providing commoners. The Kayan divide the "refined" aristocratic houses of a given village into two categories—the ruling stratum (*maren*) and the lesser aristocrats (*hipuy*), who follow contrasting marital practices. The maren prefer to obtain spouses (either aristocrats or commoners) from villages other than their own, thereby creating an extensive network of intercommunity alliances, although maren men may marry other maren of their own village or even a high-status commoner (1979:219 table 1, 218, 221–222, 226, 230). The hipuy, on the other hand, avoid ties with other villages (as all commoners do) and marry either marens or, more likely, commoners of their own community, preferably of the more socially acceptable *panyin jia*, or "superior" category of commoner (the offspring of hipuy and ordinary panyin), which is distinct from ordinary panyin and from captured non-Kayan slaves, or *dipens* (227, 230–231). Rousseau notes very explicitly that the importance of hipuy as a category of lesser aristocrats is to be found at the structural level, standing as they do between the high aristocracy and the commoner population

(232). Their structural relevance clearly includes their affinal ties with village commoners.[11]

The Trobriand Islands, as is well known, approach the wife-taking privileges accorded leaders of their highest ranked descent groups (*guyau*) in a very different fashion by seeking to increase the number of chiefly alliances with lesser guyau and wife-providing commoners (*tokay*) as much as possible, with the ultimate result that the chief becomes "a glorified brother-in-law of the whole community," as Malinowsky phrased it (1935:192; Powell 1960:124–125; Sider 1967: 99). Indeed, the importance of affinal relations for political structuring between high-rank aristocratic descent groups and commoner houses is such that when no suitable woman is available to establish an affinal alliance, a "male wife" may be substituted (Powell 1960:134–135). Nonetheless, among the highest-ranked leaders most wife-taking extends significantly beyond their own village and village clusters: "Mitakata, the leader of [the] highest ranking sub-clan (the Tabalu of Omarakana village) . . . received gifts in respect of his twelve marriages from seventy-six individual donors, fifty-seven (75 per cent) of whom lived in villages other than those of the Omarakana cluster" (125, 126–129).[12]

In the Trobriands wife-taking of any sort also establishes the superiority of the wife-takers relative to the wife-providers, "plac[ing] the wife-giving group in the position of tributary affines to the individual to whom the wife is given" (135). Yet it is incumbent on highly ranked wife-takers, if they would justify their claims to power and expand their authority, to respond to their wife-providers' tributary contributions of consumable garden products with durable, crafted wealth items that attest to the ability of the high-status wife-takers to effect more lasting, independent access to contexts of origins. "Marriage always entails . . . reciprocal gifts: vegetable food from the wife's kinsmen to her husband; that is, the annual *urigubu,* and in return valuables . . . from the husband's to the wife's kindred. Now people of rank in Kiriwina were able to supply the Sinaketan husbands of their sisters with a large quantity of food. The Sinaketans in return gave to the paramount chief and to other notables *what to these was of greater importance, necklaces and belts of shell discs*" (Malinowsky, quoted in Brunton 1975:547, 553, Brunton's emphasis). Acquisition of such durable valuables, inalienably associated with contexts of cosmological origins (Helms 1988:153–156),[13] in turn provided the Kiriwina leadership with evidence of legitimizing contact with contexts of origins independent of alliances with their own wife-providers (Powell 1960:135, 140–141; Weiner 1976).

Among the Mambwe of northern Rhodesia, where chiefs and chiefs' sons take their wives, including great wives, from among commoners, the inherent qualitative ambiguity between aristocrats as wife-takers and commoners as wife-providers is expressed in the terminology of the relationship in which the chiefly wife-taker is addressed as "son-in-law" by a commoner "father-in-law." (In one version of native myth-history this mode of address is said to recognize the original offer, by a senior commoner, of a daughter in marriage to an impressive newcomer if the latter would agree to become chief [Watson 1958:13, 14]).[14] Commoner affines also play significant roles at mortuary rites, and the chiefly installation ceremony involves an act of ritual intercourse between the successor and the commoner great wife of his predecessor, who appears to formally represent first-principle origins; "the great wife's sexual and procreative powers were (and are) thought to be associated with the well-being of the country. In this sense, therefore, she symbolized the land and the people in their relations to the chief" (167, 138–139, 166). The qualitative identity accorded aristocrats by commoners, however, seems to emphasize the sacred potency not of affinity but of living ancestorness. For example, village headmen, most of whom are of royal lineage, are expected not only to grant usufructory rights to the cultivation of the land but also to perform ancestor-related fertility rituals for both land and people. The power of the royal headmen's supplications derives more specifically from the sacred authority and ritual supremacy of the royal chief, whose sanction, in turn, lies "in his relation to the spirits of his ancestors, who protect the people, guard the land, and control the fertility of both people and soil" (142, 143, 135, 161–163). Royal headmen thus appear to access royal prior house origins (the ancestors of the royal clan); these ancestors, however, also convey first-principle powers (forces of nature, the seasons, fertility, and harvests) that provide the prosperity and well-being attributed to the chief and his ancestral spirits (168).

Another excellent example, also from Africa, is provided by the nominally patrilineal Lovedu, who require the presence of matrilateral relatives at all important house gatherings, including harvest offerings to the patrilineal deities, and who structurally link commoner houses to the royal house by requiring that all district headmen send a daughter or sister to "marry" the royal queen in exchange for the queen's essential rainmaking abilities (Krige and Krige 1943:77, 83, 164–165, 173–174).[15] "Through her wives, the queen becomes 'son-in-law' to all her district heads, and by allocating these wives to other district heads and to noblemen she becomes parent-in-law to them" (175). There are numerous other examples of the structuration created by aristocrats as wife-takers and sisters' sons relative to commoners as wife-providers and mothers' brothers, as well as of the ritual authority held by commoners as first-principle-related providers of women, an authority "at once indispensable and inimical" to those who would rule (Sahlins 1976:28, 26–28, 32 n. 24).[16] The "essential function and position" of the wife-taking ruler as ultimate cosmological affine for people and state was aptly summarized by Josselin de Jong (speaking of the Minangkabau of Indonesia) in gendered and "dualistic" terms: "He was the representative of the patrilineal male principle, which enters into combinations with the matrilineal female principle as expressed by Minangkabau social structure. The different parts of Minangkabau, divided into matrilineal clans and phratries as far as its socio-political organization is concerned are gathered together, find their focus as it were in the Ruler, who acts as a kind of universal husband; the male patrilineal principle (the Minangkabau dynasty) being wedded to the female, matrilineal principle, the Minangkabau territory" (quoted in van der Kroef 1954:857; see also Kemp 1978).

Since aristocratic houses frequently activate affinal ties not only with commoner houses of the polity but also with other aristocratic "peer" houses, either in the same or other polities,[17] it is appropriate to turn from commoner-aristocrat structuration to consider qualitative and structural features of the latter more closely. Aristocratic affinal Others presumably are primarily necessary as legitimating witnesses for rites of social and political reproduction for focal aristocratic houses. Yet the frequent aristocratic preference (especially among highly ranked houses of ruling lines) for rank endogamy might seem to thwart this essential affinal role, given that in sociological terms this very "near" form of affinity would conjoin as affinal Other persons and houses already closely related through consanguineal ties, thereby seeming to confound the two. The Tanimbarese, for example, claim that at the very highest levels of aristocratic relationships differentiations between wife-givers and wife-receivers fold together in recognition that both are referencing a fundamental context of origins that moots the question of their difference (see note 8). In other polities, including the Tshidi of South Africa and Botswana, the content of the relationships may be decided by the more usual tactic of mandating that where consanguine and affinal/lateral ties coincide, as is particularly the case with royal lineage marriages, the qualities of the latter are held to take precedence (Comaroff and

Comaroff 1981:37, 36). The pragmatics of political affairs between wife-giving and wife-taking houses may inform the primary meaning of the relationship, too. Among the patrilineal Tshidi, when politics stipulates political inequality and a hierarchical relationship between wife-giving and wife-receiving houses, the wife-giver will be recognized as mother's brother and the married woman as mother's brother's daughter, but when greater rank equality and agnatic activities are desired, the two parties may choose to emphasize the consanguineal side of the relationship—that is, wife-giver and spouse as father's brother and father's brother's daughter, respectively (36, 37, 41–43; Cohen and Comaroff 1976:97–101).

Royal sibling marriages, the closest possible co-opting of affinity, may resolve the issue by identifying one of the pair with first-principle origins and the other with prior house origins, often glossed on a cosmic scale. Affinal siblingship thereby becomes a living expression of the ultimate conjoining of contexts of origins, and by so doing tangibly evidences for all to see the (hopefully) indisputable accessing of both contexts of origins by the ruling house. By such affinity the cosmologically defined origin of the ruling house itself (represented by one of the sibling-spouses) is constantly legitimated by the perpetual witness of preexisting first-principle origins (represented by the other sibling-spouse). For example, in descriptions of marriage between the Peruvian Inca and his full sister, the Inca is identified as "the son of the sun," an apparent reference to the principle of lineality and thus a statement of prior house origins. His sister-wife, however, is referred to as "the ancestress, Mama Anahuarque . . . , of all pre- and non-Inca people representing the goddess of the earth Pacha Mama" (Zuidema 1989:269). This identification bespeaks a context of preexisting first-principle origins that legitimizes the purported celestial origins of the royal house itself and the linking of the contemporary members of the royal lineage with those origins and then conjoins both contexts of origins through the idiom of a cosmic affinal conjunction.

In addition to seeking legitimizing affinal witness among its own by rank endogamy, an aristocracy may access origins through the kin group of previous rulers, who may ritually legitimize a new ruler by embodying a preexisting context of origins (e.g., Bloch 1989:82–84 regarding the Merina of Madagascar). Consider, too, the frequent preference among rulers for affinal/lateral relatives as councilors and aides (Robinson 1962:123–124). One of the most interesting of this type of affinal/lateral legitimation involves the widespread African institution of the indispensable "queen mother," [18] whose distinctive attributes are readily understandable as an expression of the legitimizing ritual potency held by affinal/laterals as outside Others. Cohen's discussion of the role of this royal relative among the Pabir of Nigeria succinctly describes all these characteristics as well as the solidarity of communitas that the queen mother as affinal Other can provide for the royal house and the polity:

> The queen mother lived in a separate unwalled town a mile or two from the capital. She ran her own administration and visited the king twice a year to discuss affairs of state and to admonish him about good government. She was also the keeper of the sacred royal objects used to enthrone a king. She represents unity and integration. Dissidents may go to her and she will protect them.
>
> More importantly she must never be a real mother to the king. Instead she is a wife to the previous king chosen from a segment of the royal family whose male members are losing their claim to the throne. . . . [This group forms] a separate 'woman's' segment of the centralized society. Thus, the queen concept is used to symbolize wholeness, integration, continuity, and to organize opposition but keep it within the system rather than using it as a reason for cleavage and break-up. (Cohen 1976:207)

In another discussion of the Pabir queen mother, Cohen describes the formal procedures whereby "the *Maigira* ritually creates the new monarch" after the candidate spends a period of time in retreat in her community, making it explicit that "the Queen Mother and her town, Kogu, are thus the sacred givers of royal power" (1977:21, 22). Cohen also notes that the legitimizing objects of royal regalia, of which the queen mother is "official owner," date back to the founder of the dynasty. Summarized within the context of this essay, the queen mother, who connects both contexts of origins as affinal keeper of house regalia, legitimizes the enthronement of a new ruler in her capacity as affinal agent of preexisting first-principle origins, and then confers the regalia that conjoins that new lord with the prior origins of the ruling lineage itself.

Turning from aristocratic endogamy within the polity to marriages with houses of other polities, we find that these ties express in uncomplicated fashion the familiar tenet that entities standing outside the polity encompass power and hold the potential to extend legitimizing blessings and support because they hold a superior position in a cosmologically defined exclusive hierarchy (Valeri 1985:94). Association with and support by this august company may also elevate focal aristocratic houses vis-à-vis other houses of the focal polity. For example, among the

Coast Salish of North America, where "contracting marriage alliances with families in other villages was 'high class'"—meaning that it was the highly ranked or "wealthy" portion of society who did so—there appears to have been a positive correlation between degree of participation in intervillage activities and social repute; "high-class persons" were "those who had formally demonstrated their high status in an intercommunity setting" involving elaborate marriages and potlatches with outside guests, including affines (Elmendorf 1971:361, 363, 368, 370; Kan 1989).[19] The legitimizing power inherent in outside affinal ties was also clearly recognized by the Shilluk of the Sudan, who received certain royal emblems from a Nuban group that was given a Shilluk royal sister in marriage. By virtue of this affinal tie, the Nubans, as "sisters' sons" to the Shilluk royal house (their "mothers' brothers"), were also accorded the right to decide which of several eligible Shilluk princes "was chosen by God to be king of the Shilluk" (Lienhardt 1955:35).

It is noteworthy that the Shilluk aristocracy formally stood as wife-provider to an outside source of legitimating Other in much the same fashion as commoner houses of their own polity stood as wife-providers for Shilluk aristocratic houses. The Shilluk aristocracy, and especially the royal house, thus held an intermediate position, standing on the one hand as a collectivity of royal princes ritually subordinate to an outside affinal/lateral entity (Nubans) and, on the other hand, as an aristocratic sector superordinate to the collectivity of their own affinal commoners. This betwixt-and-between position as wife-provider to one category of outside Other and wife-takers to another explains the several marital prospects faced by Shilluk royal women. On the one hand, royal women could marry Nubans and link the fortunes of the royal house to these outside affinal legitimizers. On the other hand, royal women were defined as nonmarriageable "male" members of the agnatic royal lineage who guarded the distinct identity of that house and its separateness as an entity relative to the commoner populace. Consequently, while men of the Shilluk royal house took commoner wives (although the king himself married a half-sister), it was considered inappropriate for women to marry within the polity.[20] This practice appears to preserve the qualitative unity and superiority of the royal house relative to commoners while still maintaining the necessary structural ties between the two and to emphasize the importance of a complete, unequivocal, and unsullied agnative identity and ancestral lineage for the royal house ("the king at one with his fathers"; Lienhardt 1955:35, 38, 39, 41; Kemp 1978:70–71, 74–75, 79–80; Ekholm 1978:121). The marriage of royal women with an outside Nuban house, on the other hand, effects the even more essential legitimating link with first-principle origins.[21]

The Shilluk example raises another fundamental issue concerning how distinctive identities may define aristocrats and commoners as separate and unique categories of being while the particular idiom of affinity structurally relates this difference through a common dialogue of kinship that is mutually comprehensible. Simply stated, it is essential to realize that aristocrats and commoners may interpret the inclusiveness or the depth of the general affinal relationship that formally conjoins them in different ways. Fortes explicitly describes this situation as it applies to the more tribal Tallensi (1945), but his insight, with additional discussion by Keesing, may be extended to the affinal conditions that relate aristocrats and commoners in ranked and centralized polities.

Among the patrilineal Tallensi, a man not only sacrifices to his own lineage ancestors but also approaches lateral ancestors through the "mothers' brothers" of his lineage, whose defining characteristic as such is that they sacrifice to their ancestors on behalf of their "sisters' sons" (Keesing 1971:156–157). Sisters' sons' interests in the lineages and ancestral cults of their lateral mothers' brothers define these laterals as *groups* of people and as *unified* social entities, *but the reverse is not true.* "A man has no interest in or bonds with any of his sister's children's agnates except her children" (Fortes, quoted in Keesing 1971:164). That is to say, the "[sister's son] is related by descent to [the mother's brother]'s lineage and its ancestors, but [mother's brother] lineage members are related by kinship but not common descent to the [sister's son]" (Keesing 1971:167). I interpret this to mean that the ties of mothers' brothers to sister's sons are perceived by the former as essentially individualistic in nature, at best collective; they are not group oriented nor do they define sisters' sons as a unified group. In contrast, however, the ties of sister's sons to mother's brothers are perceived (by those sister's sons) to be group related and are directed to the mother's brother's lineage as a cohesive entity. Goody describes the same situation, though in a slightly different manner, with reference to the LoDagaba of Ghana: ". . . as far as the system of patrilineal groups is concerned, a man's 'mother's brothers' are located in *one* descent group, his 'sister's sons' in *many*. Moreover, a man's descent group has a classificatory relationship with its 'sister's sons,' which it does not normally have with its 'mother's brothers'" (1959:70, my emphasis).

The general sense of these examples when extrapolated to centralized polities is most important, for it allows the recognition that when aristocrats are perceived by commoners as affinal/lateral relatives, that perception can be extended to define aristocrats in general as a distinct social entity, a *group*. Aristocrats, in contrast, may regard *individual* affinal commoners and their immediate family as kin, but leave open the option of whether or not to extend broader recognition as such to larger collectivities of commoners, depending on what the political theater dictates. Asymmetries such as this help to explain how aristocrats may be regarded by commoners as a qualitatively separate and distinct sociopolitical entity that must be linked to them by some sort of contractual kin relationship, such as affinity, while the aristocracy may perceive commoners more in the aggregate or as collective kin with whom relational ties may be looser and sometimes potentially more processual (Blau 1977:46–47; Goldman 1970:19). In other words, all things considered, commoners may be inclined to view aristocrats in general largely within the context of affinity respectfully expressive of exclusive hierarchy, while aristocrats may be inclined to view commoners in general more from the aristocratic heights of living ancestorness, a perspective that also opens the way for a potentially more dominating sense of inclusive hierarchy.

From the purview of commoners, aristocrats-cum-affines, as a distinctive social entity positioned hierarchically as superordinate cosmological Others, are charged with the political-ideological responsibility of providing access to first-principle origins for the polity as a whole. This obligation may be considered part of the long-term morality inherent in the aristocratic-commoner relationship when it is expressed in kinship idioms, including affinity (Bloch 1973:76–77, 86–87). This identity is also indispensable to aristocrats as a vital means, indeed the most vital and most defensible means, of claiming legitimacy by reference to the will of the gods; anything less exposes their authority to question, and "authority questioned is authority lost" (Pitt-Rivers 1973: 96). Aristocratic claims of legitimizing access to origins are bolstered by the generic ancestor-related identity accorded affines as Others, which admits the feasibility of the role of aristocrats-cum-affines as living ancestors. Status as living ancestors, in turn, can reflect upon and enhance the significance of aristocratic prior house origins, particularly as these are linked to absolute first principles.[22]

Aristocrats are aided and empowered in fulfilling their charge of providing access to origins (that is, to the source of life, fertility, and general well-being) for the polity and, in the process, of enhancing their own legitimacy, by the fact that they also evidence an abundance of affinity, meaning quantitatively more affinal ties relative to commoners: "people who are more real [that is, aristocrats] are 'kswaatk' ['father's side' or lateral relatives] to a wider group of people" (Seguin 1986b:493 regarding the matrilineal Tsimshian).[23] In addition, in keeping with their perennial status as living ancestors, at least some aristocratic affinity is often considered qualitatively to be more permanent than the affinity known to commoners. The general sense of this point is expressed by McKinnon, speaking of the Tanimbarese, who describes how the highest-ranked marriages among select aristocratic houses are seen to constitute an ongoing, permanent cycle of alliances that ultimately references ultimate cosmological origins and sources of life (1991:127–133). All other affinal connections "implicate only the bloodlines of particular people and the more ephemeral affinal relations of recent marriages. The latter are given a subordinate value and . . . are not thought to involve the fixed order of relations between houses" (223, 225).

Considered overall, affinity and the qualities that accompany it not only structure aristocratic-commoner relationships but also define the qualitative characteristics of aristocrats in kin-based societies to such a substantial degree that they can be said to be both directly and indirectly (through the definition of living ancestors) definitive of much of that which qualitatively marks and defines aristocrats as aristocratic in these polities.

PART THREE

*. . . the trick of history is to
maintain both the invariance of
structure . . . and the value of
temporal precedence . . . .*

RICHARD PARMENTIER,
The Sacred Remains, 1987, P. 15

10

STRUCTURE

AND

COMMUNITAS

In politically centralized polities, the fundamental question and perception of who or what chiefs and aristocrats "are" legitimizes high political-
ideological rank and office, defines to a great extent the specific tasks associated with these positions, and may help to determine how these
tasks are carried out (Feinman and Neitzel 1984). More specifically, the
aristocratic sector of a ranked society or centralized polity, if it is to successfully claim its authority and protect its legitimacy, must create and
reserve for its members, not just as individuals but as a *group,* a unique
existential identification as Other relative to the population at large.
Identification as Other, in turn, by definition assigns to the aristocracy
the qualitative attributes of communitas by virtue of which aristocratic
rulership identifies a spirit of unification among its own members and
holds responsibility for procuring, protecting, and enhancing the well-
being of the general populace. As outside Other, the aristocracy, as a distinctive category of beings, must also effect structural ties with the wider
populace. This is typically (though not necessarily exclusively) achieved

by arranging marital alliances with some element of the commoner population as well as with aristocrats in other polities.

Aristocrat-commoner marriages further identify the Otherness of the aristocracy relative to the rest of the polity as affinal in character. Aristocratic affinity, which largely informs aristocratic communitas, assists in the additional identification of aristocrats as living ancestors, an exalted status that is given tangible expression by (among other things) distinctive sumptuary laws that also stress the Otherness of the aristocracy. Identification as the polity's affines and as its living ancestors provides essential associations with various contexts of cosmological origins, and it is by virtue of its privileged access to origins that the aristocracy and its activities are most fundamentally defined and legitimized. Successful maintenance of this privileged access over several generations institutionalizes aristocracy and chiefships ("complexity is a consequence of the sustained concentration of control over critical resources"; Peoples 1993:9; cf. Harrison 1990:139; Allen 1984:35–36).

In previous chapters these definitive qualitative and structural aspects of aristocracy and chiefship were separately examined. In historical reality, of course, they should be more or less expressed in tandem. In this chapter, therefore, I focus specifically upon some of the ways in which this can be accomplished. Examining the conjunction of structure and quality also permits general consideration of developmental patterns and processes, for in actual historical circumstances the attribution of distinctive origins-related qualities to would-be aristocrats and the development of distinctive structural ties between aristocratic and commoner sectors often proceeds at different rates or as separate processual "events." This differentiation occurs primarily because aristocratic Otherness and aristocratic communitas are not created solely by affinity and thus do not emanate entirely from the structural creation of aristocratic-commoner affinity; they can also be defined, at least in part, by additional mechanisms or circumstances that may identify a group as effecting closer, even monopolistic access to legitimating cosmological origins. These means can include claiming to be the original or at least the prior inhabitants of a region relative to newcomers or, alternatively, arrival in a given region as powerful newcomers from a geographically distant (outside) place claiming attributes that, in the eyes of the autochthonies, attest to unusual and superior ideological/cosmological associations. For a group already in situ, it can also involve reaching outward to establish contacts via diplomacy, pilgrimage, or long-distance trade with geographically distant peoples and places that are situated in supernaturally defined cosmographical realms and are identified with concepts and conditions of origins.[1]

Aristocratic-commoner structuration and qualitatively characteristic aristocratic communitas emerge historically in distinctive developmental formats. Very frequently (probably always) one or the other of these two aristocratic requirements is already presaged or actually evidenced in precentralized political-ideological conditions (Spencer 1994:35); successful political hierarchy and centralization lies in adding the other element to complete the creation of aristocracy and chiefship. In other words, if, in a noncentralized setting, marriage ties already structure relationships between a distinguished house and a number of other houses, then the challenge for political centralization lies in identifying and elaborating additional circumstances that can attest to a privileged access to cosmological origins for that house and that will further qualitatively define the collectivity of its membership as living ancestors. Alternatively, again in a noncentralized setting, qualities and abilities attesting to exceptional associations with the supernatural outside (i.e., evidence of access to origins and a concomitant communitas) may already be accorded members of a particularly prominent house, and the challenge for achieving political centralization will lie not only in extending those associations but also in developing structural mechanisms, including multiple affinal ties, that can relate this house to the wider polity on a broad front.

This developmental contrast can also be stated in terms of differential orientations to spatial-temporal cosmological axes. That is to say, when structural affinal ties already exist between a potential aristocratic house and other houses, qualities associated with the "spatial" cosmological axis (i.e., contractual associations referring to first-principle origins, primacy, and other things that are first and communitas in the sense of affinal benevolence) are in place to inform the developing aristocratic role. The further enhancement of aristocratic political ideology then requires the addition and elaboration of qualities associated with the "temporal" cosmological axis (i.e., institutionalizing a further identity as living ancestors processually associated with prior house origins, seniority, and the exercise of jural authority). Alternatively, when "temporally" defined cosmological identifications are associated with a senior, jurally authoritative house, then fuller elaboration of an aristocratic identity requires the addition of qualities associated with the "spatial" cosmological axis (i.e., contractually accessed first-principle origins, primacy, and other things that are first and the communitas of affinal benevolence).

These several hypothetical patterns refer to "internal" or "emergent" political conditions where aristocratic elaborations of structure or communitas, space or time, develop locally and essentially reflect the inability or unwillingness, for any number of reasons, to adequately restrain aspects of house or group ranking or hierarchy already inherent in the precentralized political environment (Rousseau 1985; Béteille 1977; Tonkinson 1988; Collier 1988; Horton 1972:112, 116). But they are equally relevant when political centralization results from "external" or "impositional" factors involving the addition of a group or category of outsiders to an already inhabited region, either by peaceful migration or by conquest. Sometimes this condition is only alleged and may not express actual historical realities, for a claim of foreign origins may simply be a metaphorical signifier allowing a potential aristocratic group to claim unique origins or qualitative distinctiveness relative to the rest of the polity.[2] ("Creation, migration, and parturition are so many versions of the same story"; Sahlins 1983:529 regarding Maori origins tales.)[3] Whether myth or actual history, however, when foreign (outside) origins are claimed, both structure and communitas and spatial and temporal qualities must again be factored into the centralization process.

For example, when an indigenous population recognizes an actual or potential aristocratic sector as "newcomers," that recognition essentially identifies the aristocracy as an inherently distinctive category of beings deriving from a spatially distant, cosmologically charged outside realm qualitatively associated with conditions of first-principle origins, primacy, and things that are first. Marital alliances contracted between these newcomers and the indigenous population provide the necessary structural connection between aristocrats and commoners and further enhance the Otherness of the newcomers with the communitas and hierarchical supremacy of affinity.[4] Once identified in such "spatial" terms, it remains for the aristocratic sector to develop its "temporal" identification by defining or elaborating connections with home or polity ancestors that will grant them seniority in addition to primacy and thus legitimate their jural authority. Circumstances will be somewhat different, however, if the newcomers are incorporated into the polity in a subordinate status relative to indigenous or "original" houses. The latter, who now have the potential to constitute the aristocratic sector, can initially define and legitimize their political-ideological superiority by reference to the temporal cosmological axis—that is, to already established relationships to the polity's prior origins and thus to seniority and rightful jural authority, and also to the first-principle origins that accrue to those who are "first." Marital alliances with subordinate newcomers will not only create necessary structural ties but also further assert the hierarchical superiority and Otherness of the aristocratic sector in "spatial" affinal terms that further associate the aristocracy with first-principle origins, primacy, and the communitas of affinity.

These several hypothetical developmental patterns can be illustrated in part or in whole by ethnographic and ethnohistoric particulars that augment previous examples and highlight some of the mechanisms by which aristocratic-commoner structuration and qualitative distinctiveness are given tangible expression in various historical settings. We can begin with consideration of the spatial/temporal, structural/qualitative patternings that can occur "in situ" when the process of community fissioning common to noncentralized settings is impeded.[5] Reduced fissioning automatically encourages the "emergence" of an incipient hierarchy and a potential for political centralization based on the higher status and ritual authority already accorded (as it often is in noncentralized societies) to community founders or "owners of the land" or their descendants who, by virtue of the privileged access to origins accruing to "first" or "prior" settlers, are already qualified to act in ritual and sometimes in jural capacities for the entire community (Horton 1972:94–96, 112). In fact, the primacy or seniority inherent in being "first" or "prior" can be evidenced, or at least implied, even when fissioning occurs.[6] Rosenberg has argued cogently that when fissioning takes place among hunters and gatherers, especially as a result of population pressure, "the departure of less-well-integrated visitors is a more likely outcome than the departure of long-time band members" (1990: 408–409; see also Levy 1992:22–24).

In more settled noncentralized settings it is also common to encounter "offspring" or "satellite" houses or communities that still recognize ties with "parent" houses or communities on the basis of the latter's closer identification with ancestral origins. Although such offspring communities or houses are often economically independent and to varying degrees politically autonomous, they are likely nonetheless to be regarded as ritually "incomplete," meaning that they cannot approach the ancestors directly but must recognize the greater religious and social authority of the parent house or community that can access origins and approach the ancestors: "Satellite villages may be autonomous with regard to social, agricultural, and ritual life on virtually all occasions, but in the final instance they are not. Mother villages have ultimate ritual jurisdiction, having the authority to pronounce upon questions of existential concerns and are the arbitrators of life giving knowledge. This fact . . . makes the mother villages adamant in their exclusive right to the execution of their authority" (Howell 1991:227, 228, 231, regarding the Lio of eastern Indonesia).[7]

Townsend, speaking of the Fox Islanders of the eastern Aleutians, has emphasized the importance of kin-group ranking based on priority of settlement within autonomous communities as more sedentary conditions develop. Townsend explains how, by virtue of direct descent from a founding ancestor, a headman and his family may form an elite unit within a larger kin group, a process that can become a key factor (Giddens's "key institutional transformations"; 1984:246) in the eventual emergence of dominant aristocratic lineages if and when, for any reason, resource competition tightens (Townsend 1985:144–146, 150–155; Netting 1990:58; Levy 1992:22, 24–25). Building on this point, as it were, Cohen provides an excellent analysis of political centralization processes among the Pabir variant of the Bura-speaking people of northern Nigeria (1976; 1981:97–101). The initial step was taken when, in response to pressures emanating from the state of Borno (Bornu), Bura villagers began to reduce and reverse their usual fissioning pattern, moving from more scattered locations to more densely populated walled communities that offered greater safety from Borno raids (Netting 1990:57–58). This process led, in turn, to increased and expanded jural authority for the traditional village leaders who, as "shadows" or "souls" of their villages, were already recognized as chosen heirs of their respective founding lineages and had already been granted senior authority by other lineage elders that allowed them to sacrifice to and consult with supernatural powers regarding dates for first plantings (Cohen 1981:98–99; 1976:203).

The next step toward political centralization saw further elaboration of some of these jural and priestly roles in order to identify a founding lineage not only with prior village origins but also with more elevating or distancing absolute, first-principle origins. This was accomplished by associating a potential aristocratic house with the powerful state of Borno, a cosmographically "distant" or outside locale that the Pabir now identified with "origins." Consequently, the emerging Pabir aristocracy copied titles, court procedures, and pre-Islamic religious ideas as well as distinctive dress and house styles and other sumptuary distinctions from Borno (Cohen 1976:200, 201).[8] Some aristocratic Pabir rulers were even accorded a legendary heroic forebear said to have originally come from Borno, thereby directly relating their own prior house origins to the context of first-principle origins associated with Borno. Pabir rulers developed further tangible evidence of their cosmographical outside associations by developing an important trade in salt and establishing ties with chiefs of surrounding peoples (Cohen 1981:99–100). They also enhanced their identification as "living ancestors" by emphasizing temporal associations with the dead, conducting sacrifices at royal tombs for the welfare of the people and performing other rituals to assure rain and good crops (Cohen 1976:203–204). The growing body of aristocrats, composed of the leading village lineages, further accentuated their social, political, and ideological "distance" from the common population by exchanging daughters in marriage among themselves, although they often continued to find spouses among the ordinary populace in the traditional exogamous fashion (204–205), thereby maintaining necessary structural ties with the wider populace while presumably further enhancing, by the qualities of affinity, their increasing access to cosmological origins.

The qualitative distinctiveness associated with "founder" houses can also underwrite the emergence of such groups to aristocratic status when, instead of "rising above" other houses (Kopytoff describes this process as "mobility by levitation"; 1987:51), aggregates of other people are incorporated "beneath" their authority. Here again aristocratic qualitativeness initially rests on cosmologically defined primacy or seniority as being first or prior inhabitants in the area or as having the closest genealogical connections to a putative founding ancestor. ". . . the fact that the first occupants of the defined tract of land have a relation to it which differs from and is more intimate than that of later comers provides the germ of a potential differentiation between royal and non-royal lineages" (Horton 1972:112, 100). The Gola of Liberia are a case in point. Typically each of the small Gola chiefdoms

> involved a central village surrounded by satellite hamlets in which the dominant class of the population was a land-owning patrilineage made up of the descendants of the founder. The related sub-lineages were ranked according to distance from this founding ancestor. A large proportion of the population of these minute societies, however, was contained in numerous attached lineages of non-related immigrants—whether Gola or non-Gola—who had been incorporated by patronage or intermarriage, and whose members were granted theoretically tentative rights to the use

of lands. In addition to these, the small households of the various clients, slaves and other dependents of the wealthier families contributed still further to the social heterogeneity of the chiefdoms. (d'Azevedo 1962:12)

Miller also describes this very common phenomenon with reference to peoples of west-central Africa, especially Angola (1976; 1988; see also 1981), noting that, in societies (such as that of the Mbundu) where technologies were limited and reliably productive land was often scarce, acquisition of people—affines, wives and children, even strangers represented idiomatically as dependent kinsmen—provided political superiority for those who would be lords, patrons, or masters (Miller 1981). In such a setting descendants of the first settlers on the land "justified their primacy over a majority of more recent arrivals, whom they accepted only on condition of subordination to the heirs of the original occupants" (Miller 1988:44–45; 1981:50). More specifically, "masters had to preserve the ideology of the lineage and its proclamations of legitimacy deriving from local birth in order to create the difference that justified their superiority over aliens" (Miller 1981:51).[9] Miller goes on to note that chiefs of landowning lineages, who were also responsible for producing vitally important rain, further integrated their positions and presumably enhanced their qualitative distinctiveness as Other as guardians of spiritually charged relics that were associated with traditions of origins.[10] It should be noted, however, that "origins" in this context refers not to the origins of the populace or the chiefly house per se but to the appearance of the particular mode of political organization that surmounted traditional lineage fissioning to create more centralized polities. The legitimizing political-ideological imagery, however, is presented in familiar cosmological terms of first-principle origins: "the mythical and heroic ages of the past usually purport to describe the formation of present social structures through presenting a contrast between a former period of chaos and the emergence of orderly modern social arrangements" (Miller 1976:56, 59–74).

Mbundu rulers strengthened structural relations with the wider populace by accepting the daughters and nieces sent to their courts as wives (as well as the sons and nephews loaned as pages) (Miller 1988:61). In addition, rulers whose legitimating titles identified their status as "sons" of the original title-holding lineage "extended their influence into the lineages living further away through the distribution of subordinate noble titles derived from their *ngola* [the power of the iron relics]" (Miller 1976:77; see also note 10). Such titles were preferably distributed to the sons of rulers' wives and their successors.[11] They directly identified these new subgroup lords with cosmological origins by referencing the name of symbolic ancestresses, just as the chief was referred to by the name of the legendary "founder" of the polity.[12] Mbundu chiefs also distributed such largesse as could be accumulated through trade and continued the long-standing practice of granting access to land and to rainmaking rituals to lineages of newcomers seeking a place to settle (62, 70, 87).

Parmentier, discussing Belau (Caroline Islands, Micronesia), provides another excellent example of the emergence of "founder" houses to aristocratic status. He describes how the contrast between politically influential chiefly titleholders and their families on the one hand and politically dependent families on the other is expressed in village complexes in which a dominant "capital" village, populated by highly ranked descendants of earlier ancestors, is surrounded by satellite hamlets populated by more recently arrived immigrant groups and families who formerly lived in the capital village but broke away (1987:60, 64). Some of the most important chiefly titleholders further legitimize their links to prior house origins by retracing ancestral migration routes and holding regalia symbolic of the sea journey by which the first ancestors arrived at the islands (70). The most highly ranked village, however, emphasizes the autochthonous (first settlers and first principle) quality of its origins in order to anchor its claim as the sacred center of all Belau (241, 244).[13] It is also the prerogative of highly ranked persons to create various spatial/temporal social relationships or "paths" in exchange, cooperation, or warfare. The right and the capacity to create such relationships, normally regarded as the privilege of gods or of heroic ancestors (114, 134), clearly seems intended to qualitatively relate high-ranking persons to ancestral precedent, for expert knowledge of ancient, ancestral "paths" (which continue to guide contemporary affiliations) is an essential part of chiefly responsibility (115). Satellite houses, however, can participate in such external relationships only by following the paths established by chiefly houses. Chiefs, chiefly houses, and capital villages also construct Belauan history since only aristocrats' activities are regarded as significant historical processes, and only they have the power to construct the "official" record of the past (123, 237, 241); this procedure, we may add, also maintains politically legitimizing connections with ancestral origins.

In the previous examples, where aristocratic houses either emerged in situ from a broader population, "submerged" less fortunate houses beneath them, or structurally incorporated newcomers as subordinate commoners, chiefs and aristocrats seem to have worked primarily to establish and maintain "distance" from commoners and to develop the qualitative character of their aristocratic statuses. In other settings the range or political effectiveness of structural ties linking aristocrats to other houses of the polity may be the more problematical issue. In some ethnographic accounts this situation may reflect the organizational weakening of formerly more centralized polities as allies defect or kinsmen betray (Sahlins 1962:380–381) or when (perhaps as a result of Western colonialism) formerly high chiefs and aristocrats have been demoted to community elders, though they continue to exhibit the "poses and paraphernalia" of ritual associated with greater days (Kopytoff 1987:52; Gluckman 1965:175; Sahlins 1962:316–319). In other cases aristocratic qualitative distinctiveness may simply have preceded structural alliances in a developmental process that is (or has the potential to be) moving toward increasing political centralization.

A good example is provided by the Yao of east-central Africa, where qualitatively distinctive chiefs enjoyed superior privileged access to ancestral prior house origins. (The powerful nineteenth-century Yao chief Mtalika "dared to take the offerings of flour from the graves of his ancestors, as a sign that his power derived from their strength as well as his own"; Alpers 1969:414). The high rank and legitimacy of such chiefs was also based on primacy of occupation of the land, on being "first" to establish settlements even though historically the Yao had arrived as migrants and invaders from the east and claimed "primacy" of settlement only after subjugation of the indigenous population (Mitchell 1956: 62).[14] In spite of aristocratic Yao claims to both contexts of origins, structural ties that would bespeak the effective subordination of villagers to this higher political-ideological authority appear to have been somewhat problematical given the "almost autonomous" nature of the villages that composed a Yao chiefdom (31; Alpers 1969:408, 414).

Yao chiefs, in fact, often appear to have been regarded more as headmen writ large, for although all of a chief's territory was officially under his authority, no formal administrative machinery was ever established. Powerful headmen, who also competed with chiefs for followers, at times acted contrary to chiefly wishes, especially in more distant portions of the domain where the chief might be known in name only (Mitchell 1956:36; Alpers 1969:415). All this suggests that the further development of institutionalized political centralization, if such were to be, would lie largely in the strengthening of politically effective structural ties between aristocracy and ordinary villagers. Even so, formal structural ties were not entirely lacking. Yao chiefs were related to some village headmen by consanguineal kinship and to others by affinal links established through marriage with headmen's sisters and daughters; recognition of common clan names provided connections with still others (Mitchell 1956:70–71; Alpers 1969:416). Such relationships also became fixed and highly formalized over the generations through principles of perpetual relationship and positional succession (Mitchell 1956:121–122), although they still allowed considerable de facto autonomy for village leaders and effectively relegated a Yao chief's major responsibilities to the conduct of his qualitative capabilities.[15] These included "a certain amount of ritual in terms of ancestor worship," especially prayers for rain, which only the chief could offer since no one else could approach the chiefly ancestors, and monopoly over long-distance trade, which also involved chiefly access to origins since caravans could not set out unless they had the blessing of the chief's ancestors and were also ritually guarded en route (34, 37, 52–53, 76–77; Alpers 1969:410, 416–417). ("Mkumba held rights to the ivory in his area and made sacrifices for rain—the main attributes of chiefship"; Mitchell 1956: 48). Mitchell summarizes and underlines the qualitative, essentially communitas, nature of Yao chiefship by noting that "the chief is a representative of his people and it is his particular duty to ensure their welfare and that of the chiefdom as a whole" (54).

Much of the legitimacy and qualitative distinctiveness accorded to Yao chiefship rested on the fact that the Yao originally arrived in "their" territory as outsiders. In such situations, which are very common in chiefdoms, the original homeland becomes a place of cosmological beginnings and the arrival at the current locale is defined as a pivotal cosmological "event," whether effected by peaceful migration or by militant means. When the purported original migration lies in the distant past (and regardless of whether it is historically accurate), remembrance of this ancient context of origins and privileged identification with it can define degrees of political and ideological distance and order and a distinctive qualitative character for those currently in authority. For example, Rowlands describes how, among most chiefdoms of the Cameroon grassfields, chiefly heads (*fons*) of royal clans claimed a common origin from a prestigious center in the Tikar region of the Upper Mbam Valley:

> The founding ancestors of these polities are said to have migrated together in a mythical past and after various travails come to settle in their present

locations. Each living *fon* recognized (and still does) common descent and relative rank with his 'brothers' expressed in terms of genealogical distance and the details of the migration myth. A regional hierarchy of polities of different size and status was seen as the product of a shared common ancestral substance, embodied in the acquisition by *fons* of common elements of regalia, masquerades, music and dance as well as rituals for pollution removal and the paraphanalia of a distinctive form of regulatory association. It was access to the legitimacy of origin which defined a *fon* from an ordinary clan or lineage head in his chiefdom and set him apart in terms of access to superior ancestral blessing. (Rowlands 1985:62–63)

When the original migration is "historically" more immediate and the political charter relatively new, the legitimation and qualitative distinctiveness that would-be aristocrats seek via access to such origins make emphasis on places and contexts of origins even more compelling, as Kopytoff has discussed at length with reference to traditional African polities (1987; Beck 1990). In these cases, when, for any of a number of reasons (Kopytoff 1987:5–6), groups of houses leave an established polity and move to a new locale, they may claim legitimate authority both by virtue of holding primacy as new settlers ("founders") and by reference to the "parent" polity from which they came. The latter now becomes a place of origins, both in the sense of defining the proper (i.e., moral) first-principle charter of political order that is to be implemented anew in the new settlement and in the sense of identifying the prior origins of the now independent, new founding houses: ". . . we find a constant reiteration of outside origins in African oral traditions; one never allowed oneself and others to forget that 'we are from . . .' elsewhere. At the same time, however, these claims of alien origin had to be reconciled with the equally important but contradictory contention: that of 'being first' in the area . . ." (24–25, 26, 71–75).

Should the site of the new polity already be inhabited by an autochthonous (or at least prior) population, as was the case with the Yao and many other groups, the legitimacy of being "first" requires finer definition for the corporate body of immigrating outsiders. Sometimes the previous inhabitants were simply chased away ("We came and we found the such-and-such, and they fled"; 54). Sometimes, in recognition of their absolute primacy of settlement, the autochthonous population, as original first-principle "owners" of the land, were granted select ritual or administrative responsibilities in the new order, a process of accessing preceding first-principle powers and people that has direct parallels and precedents in the general co-opting of affines' legitimating first-principle powers. In either case, whether dealing with affines or autochthonies, the dominant houses, "even while insisting on their role of founders, were co-opting their predecessors into the political rituals precisely because they were predecessors" (57, 55–56).

However, given that things and beings associated with cosmological conditions can be defined in very negative as well as very positive terms, it is also understandable that the cosmological identification accorded the autochthonous era and the autochthonous population by dominant newcomers has often associated the former with conditions of precivilized primordial chaos that existed before truly creative, positive first principle origins (represented by the immigrant newcomers) brought moral order to the universe (27, 56–57; Eliade 1959a:10, 11).[16] In this interpretation the particular social and political arrangements introduced by newcomers as Others are identified with the "true" context or "pivotal event" of proper first-principle origins, and the legitimacy of the authority of the dominant arrivals is based on the new cosmologically defined political-ideological era that they introduce and establish (Kopytoff 1987:57, 63) and into which they incorporate the original inhabitants as "latecomers."[17] Should later migrating populations eventually supersede the first group of newcomers, the process may simply be repeated, each group defining its own arrival as a pivotal first-principle creational event marking the passage from disorder to order (58), the cosmologically defined wholeness and propriety of social and political life overall being interpreted as the sum of the contributions of each (Sahlins 1983:527–528; McKinnon 1991:65, 67, 74).

There are many situations in which prior inhabitants accord qualitative distinctiveness to aristocratic newcomers on the basis (whether mythical or historical) not of relatively peaceful migration but of conquest. This attribution reflects both successful force of arms and what that success implies about the dominant newcomers' association with superior supernatural powers and access to origins; "the Sufi *babas* who led Turkish warrior bands in the conquest of Asia Minor and the Balkans represented a variant type of warrior chieftaincy combined with religious appeal. Success showed the hand of God" (Lapidus 1990:33). In addition, as with more peaceful migrations, qualitative distinctiveness in conquest situations also rests on conquerors' associations with spatially "distant" outside realms or places of origins from which they have come as outside Others and with which they are inalienably associated. "The myth of sovereignty based on the invasion of foreign, youthful chiefs from overseas or from a distant land . . . found in Western Polynesia, Fiji, Indonesia, and Central Africa, to name a few examples, contrasts an indigenous people ruled by generous ritual chiefs to conquering political chiefs who represent political-magical power and military violence and who are associated with external relations" (Friedman 1992:844).

In fact, because it supports a crucial identification of qualitative distinctiveness based on differential access to contexts of origins, an identification as outsiders, be it by migration or conquest, historically real or only imputed, is often crucial for aristocratic sectors and chiefly rulers and may be emphasized for just that reason:

> High-level leaders of the larger tribal polities in Iran were almost always somewhat distinct socially and symbolically (as well as economically) from the people they led. They were often said to originate from groups with whom the affiliated people traced no actual or fictive kinship ties. In fact, their status as leaders often derived in part from their distinctive, exclusive identity. Many leaders descended from people who were originally said to be outsiders or strangers, and they preserved the separation such an identity implied in order to exercise power and authority more effectively. They set themselves apart ideologically to legitimize their distinctive social position, material privilege, and political authority. They invoked genealogies to define and maintain their exclusivity, and their lineages were often highly endogamous. (Beck 1990:195)

Since aristocratic houses cannot be Other without reference to a focal Us, however, aristocratic exclusivity cannot be total, as Beck goes on to note: "Occasional marriage outside the lineage was also important for it served to expand political contacts and create intratribal (between the ruling lineage and others in the tribe) and especially extratribal alliances. A tribal elite claiming Kurdish origin and ruling over Baluch in Baluchistan demonstrates these processes, and one finds similar histories and legends of origins for other high-level tribal leaders in Iran" (ibid.).[18]

Much of the fascination in investigating access to origins lies in seeing the multitude of approaches to contexts of origins and the flexibility with which these diverse references can be adapted to fit changing political circumstances or manipulated to facilitate political adjustments, not only in a comparative cross-cultural sense but also in the changing political parameters of a given polity. In recognition of this point and to conclude this discussion, it seems appropriate to augment the abbreviated examples previously cited with a fuller, more detailed synopsis, which I have reworded and reconceptualized to some extent in terms relevant to this essay, of some of the major processes involved in the formation of political centralization among the Ekie of Zaire as discussed by Fairley (1989).

Prior to political centralization, the Ekie were organized into politically autonomous village groups that were ritually ranked, apparently on the basis of differential access to prior house origins. In each village group one village was recognized as the parent community holding ritual precedence over its fellow villages while significant ritual precedence was accorded the oldest village group; the village group that traced its history to the original "founding father" of all held ultimate ritual authority. Lineage elders, who seem to have dealt with jural matters, enjoyed the legitimacy deriving from their closer association with their respective prior house origins, while connections with first-principle origins essential for general fertility and the collective prosperity of the Ekie as a whole was mediated by the *tshite*, a position vested in one particular house and the highest Ekie ritual status, who linked the Ekie with their common collective ancestors (Fairley 1989:292–293).

It then so happened that the Ekie faced encroachment by the expanding Luba state. Allied with a neighboring people, the Ekie were able initially to ward off the Luba, but in the process they granted sanctuary to a group of injured Luba warriors (known henceforth as the Bena Totue), possibly with intent to ease relationships with the Luba, with whom the Ekie began a period of peaceful coexistence. (It is important to note that the Bena Totue were never integrated into Ekie society and to this day constitute a distinctive "Luba" sector of the population that retains its own corporate cultural identity; 295). Another party of Luba then arrived and, like the earlier contingent, were encouraged to settle and were offered Ekie wives. The leader of the new Luba, described metaphorically as a skilled hunter who was wise, just, and generous, became involved in Ekie politics as a mediator of disputes and attracted a following of Ekie who relocated to his village, where the Luba leader held independent authority as "chief of the children" (ibid.). This newcomer, however, was also identified as a royal member of the powerful Luba court (he and his followers may have originally moved to the Ekie as a result of Luba succession problems), and he presumably employed this spatially situated outside association with a high-status Luba house to enhance political-ideological separateness for himself and his following from the general Ekie populace.

The successor to this first Luba-related political leader established additional "temporal" contexts for legitimacy and authority based on inheritance of his office and an associated relationship with prior house origins (296). This successor, Nkole, also began an expansionist program against neighboring groups (the only legitimate use of force in the Ekie chiefship), and his success attracted numerous Ekie interested in participating in the campaigns. These Ekie warriors were then encouraged to establish new villages in the expanded territory, villages whose leadership was appointed directly by Nkole and was loyal to him (ibid.). Ekie warriors, some of whom became village chiefs, now formed a new, presumably somewhat aristocratic sector in the conquered territories with wealth and position derived from services rendered the Luba leader (296–297, 302).

At this point Nkole co-opted the legitimating first-principle authority of the *tshite,* the traditional Ekie ancestor-priest, by incorporating this high ritual office into his growing bureaucracy in the role of adviser and confidante. The first-principle legitimacy affirmed by Ekie collective ancestors and manifested by the *tshite* was also used to ritually confirm kingly investiture, kingly ritual purity, and kingly burial. In effect, it identified and legitimized the king as the living ancestor of the developing polity, the role the *tshite* formerly had played: "once the *tshite* was integrated into the small bureaucracy, Nkole became the chief intermediary between the [Ekie] and their ancestors" (297, 298). The kingly "living ancestorship" acquired and legitimated by the ritual relationship with the co-opted *tshite* was expressed idiomatically in affinal terms; "an indigenous description of the *tshite*'s new role often employs conjugal terms: . . . Tshite is the wife of Nkole" (297).[19] Use of the idiom of affinity, which seems to symbolically parallel the initial Ekie offer of wives to the original Luba migrants, presumably further identified the qualitative distinctiveness of the kingship by redefining its political-cosmological Otherness as that of wife-taker relative to the commoner population.

Nkole further defined and legitimated the political-ideological distance and qualitative distinctiveness of the king (and protected his position from other Luba contenders) by establishing "prior house" associations with the original Bena Totue. This he achieved by instituting a series of sacrificial offerings at the burial site of the leader of the original Bena Totue (the first Luba to appear among the Ekie), who was now also recognized as the Luba ancestor of the current chief and whose acceptance of the sacrifices was interpreted by the Bena Totue community as approval of Nkole's leadership. The sacrifices also extended the ruler's new temporal connection with the original Luba founder to include a spatial cosmographical link to the authority of the outside Luba empire, the original source of the first Luba migrants. As part of this process the Bena Totue were assigned a key ritual role in rulers' confirmation proceedings, presumably as "outside" witnesses referencing both the Luba empire as original point of origin and the approval of their own founding ancestral leader, whose sacred burial site (actually a lake), now reconstructed as a place of origins and of kingly sacrifice, was situated within their territorial domain (297–298).

Ultimately, as a result of all these origins-related temporal-spatial extensions and co-optations, the political-ideological authority of the Luba-related Ekie king as royal living ancestor replaced the political-ideological authority accruing from the original collectivity of Ekie ancestors as Ekie elders accepted the king, rather than the *tshite,* as the highest-ranking ancestor-related intermediary with ultimate contexts of origin (298). Yet the rulership in general, though greatly elaborated with respect to its cosmological connections, remained relatively uninvolved in daily village affairs (the royal court was supported economically by revenues from conquered enemies rather than by Ekie commoners), where traditional elders, as living representatives of their own immediate houses and village ancestral orders, continued to wield significant jural authority and to offer moral guidance to families regarding behaviors that would guarantee the life-enriching blessings and benevolence of house ancestors. Through the activities of these village elders, principles of authority and moral rectitude, legitimated by allegiance to house and village contexts of origins that predated the cosmological embellishments necessary for political centralization, continued to flourish (299–302, 309), a reminder of the constancy and power of things and relations that are first.

11

> *The hierophany of a stone is*
> *pre-eminently an ontophany;*
> *above all, the stone* is, *it always*
> *remains itself, it does not*
> *change — and it* strikes *man by*
> *what it possesses of*
> *irreducibility and absoluteness*
> *and, in so doing, reveals to him*
> *by analogy the irreducibility*
> *and absoluteness of being.*
>
> MIRCEA ELIADE, *The Sacred and the*
> *Profane*, 1959, P. 155

TANGIBLE

DURABILITY

Cosmologies based on the consubstantiality of life (Goldman 1975:22) recognize a dynamic universe defined and characterized by impermanence of form, transitoriness of being, and transformations from one form or state of being to another. Aware of such shifting and elusive cosmological qualities, human beings, blessed or cursed with the consciousness that defines cosmologies in such fluid terms, expend considerable time and energy attempting not only to explore but also to stabilize and harness the energetic forces attributed to the universe and to tangibly shape and concretize these dynamics in order to create at least the illusion of a certain amount of stability, order, and durability in the worlds and affairs of spirits, gods, and people.

From the human perspective, stabilization of an inherently dynamic world can be best effected or is most crucially recognized at the temporal/spatial "extremes" of cosmological existence by classifying things and beings according to the places and conditions of their original cosmological beginnings and by defining moral proprieties and social order within the currently existing house. Cosmological stabilization and order can also be recognized in the seeming permanence and "longevity" of certain tangible things found in the world, including rocks, minerals, shells, trees, and mountains, in the dependability of animal behaviors, and in the amazing cyclicality and predictability of celestial and astronomical movements and "events." It is also found in the lasting durability of the bones, teeth, claws, and (to a lesser degree) pelts, skins, and feathers of animal forms of Others inhabiting the cosmological outside. In the world of the human house, stabilization and a certain sense of durability are expressed by careful ritual regulation of crucial transformative events, such as births, initiations, marriages, and especially deaths, and of encounters with other cosmologically significant life-forms, especially other people, ancestors, and animals.

The ritualistic particulars that effect stabilization at these times include both highly formalized behavioral regularities (Bloch 1974) and the manipulation of durable tangible objects ("regalia") that embody various mystical powers and, by their durability, keep these powers available, controlled, and harnessed for considerable periods of time.[1] Such objects also bridge the boundaries separating the house from Others and assist the necessary passages and transformations that take place between these two worlds. So it is that the skeletal remains, especially the long bones and skulls, of the dead (or of the conquered enemy), durable crafted heirlooms associated with ancestors, and the bones, teeth, claws, pelts, skins, and feathers of animals (or crafted representations thereof) are essential elements of many house rituals. In addition, cosmological stabilization and order can be expressed by the presence of affines and laterals at house ceremonies and by the constant attainment of spouses from affinal Others (guaranteed sometimes by the levirate or sororate so as to obviate short-term individual dissolutions) so that the social reproduction that gives "durability" to the existence of the house generation after generation will be assured.

In previous chapters considerable attention has been accorded to affines and laterals as tangible and, in a sense, durable (that is, of necessity the role will always be there) expressions of cosmological powers, specifically as tangible living representations of ancestors. Indeed, it is this very tangibility, this sensorily manifested expression of the existence of ancestorness, that makes the presence of affines and laterals so essential at house rituals and their conveyance of the legitimizing power of ancestors so potent. In directly comparable fashion, chiefs and aristocracies must express the same qualities of tangibility and durability if they, too, are to become effective living ancestors. Unlike affines, however, whose public roles as tangible living ancestors are largely limited to periodic ceremonial events of the house, chiefs and aristocrats must express living ancestorness on a constant, full-time basis. Consequently, they must be much more concerned with consistent manifestation of their tangibility. To this end chiefs and aristocrats strive not just to access contexts of origins but also to take unto themselves durable regalia associated with forms of Other (including animals, ancestors, and other people) that expresses not just the potency but also the stability and order of the universe at large. Thus chiefs and aristocrats value ancestral bones or symbolically equivalent forms of crafted heirlooms, pelts, feathers, bones, and teeth (or crafted representations thereof) of select animals or potent gems and stones, shells, and metals in addition to the "regalia" composed of retinues of numerous spouses and other court favorites.[2] These include "foreigners" in various capacities, who signify not only politically significant outside (including affinal) ties but also "tangible" aspects of the potency of other people.

All these types of tangible and durable "things" are also considered as forms of chiefly "wealth"; wealth in this sense is a collective "substance" that not only tangibly evidences access to origins but also permits the enhancement and elaboration of the qualitative aspect of chiefly living ancestorness with a quantitative factor expressed by accumulation of goods and beings that come from outside realms (Fig. 11).[3] Variation in the type and quantities of accumulated wealth items can also reflect the types of outside Others contacted or changes in those contacts. For example, a great deal of ethnographic evidence indicates that acquisition of wealth items may rapidly escalate as contact with other people increases, and it seems likely that, in general, increases in this type of (potentially) wealth-producing outside contact may occur at a faster rate (especially following European contact) than do increases in wealth-producing activities involving ancestral dead per se or animals (although contact with other people may also increase wealth-producing appropriation of select animals for trade purposes).[4]

Peaceful wealth-producing contacts with other people are usually subsumed within the general rubric of trade, and ethnographic analyses of various forms of trade conducted by members of centralized polities (including diplomatic gift exchange and long-distance acquisition) and of the goods acquired thereby have provided many insights elucidating the role of wealth in enhancing and evidencing aristocratic qualities and identity. But trade obviously abounds in noncentralized settings, too, and examination of methods and circumstances of acquisition and ex-

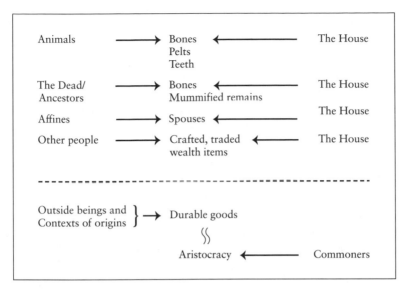

FIGURE 11   Wealth items expressive of contexts of Others and origins.

change in these polities can cast light upon some of the conditions that also hold potential for eventual aristocratic or chiefly trade. These are particularly interesting when they relate trade with other people to activities or contexts associated with animals and ancestors, as, for example, in northern North America where the ceremonial etiquette and alliances accompanying the fur trade with Europeans, which provided considerable wealth for many influential native leaders, were directly modeled on indigenous ceremonies (the Feast of the Dead) associated with secondary burial rites originally developed by the Huron and then widely disseminated to assist the fur trade (Hickerson 1960; Nekich 1974).[5] Among the Yao of East Africa, in comparable fashion, community ritual that safeguarded the chief's trade caravans, as they moved back and forth between Yao territory and coastal trading towns, was directly adapted from the ritual that, in pre-caravan days, had protected elephant hunters confronting the dangers of the outside world (Alpers 1975:19; Helms 1993:156).[6]

In noncentralized polities acquisition of wealth can also enhance vital origins-related qualities such as seniority: "Since in the native view the older a person is, the more material possessions he has, the conceptualisation of the highest ranked lineage as owning more than any other lineage in the clan is congruent with interpreting it as the 'oldest.' Again, the Bororo consider a man who owns a large amount of traditional property as possessing implicitly the esteemed moral qualities of sobriety, knowledge and self-discipline. All of this legitimates the higher ranking lineages' claims to moral authority and responsibility for the clan" (Crocker 1969:48; cf. Levy 1992:32).

It is also significant that the ultimate source of wealth is often thought to be the ancestors, leading to the conclusion that quantity or "surplus" of wealth must represent the "work of the gods" and that persons or houses with wealth, by definition, must stand closer to ancestral origins. "The capacity to produce a large surplus demonstrates the importance and influence of lineage ancestors with the higher spirits who appear as the source of all prosperity and wealth" (Friedman 1975:170, 172, 173, regarding the Kachin). By the same token, variations in fortune can either enhance or reduce qualities of origins-related honor that, in turn, may enhance seniorities or primacies of being first for some houses while demoting the statures and increasing the dependency of other houses.

> . . . the sheer circulation of imports of any sort nurtured social and political stratification in Africa. Goods from the Atlantic accelerated the rates at which the powerful dislocated the weak and at which people of all sorts were uprooted from their home communities and moved to those of new lords or masters, from villages to kings' courts, from old patrons to new patrons, or from lineage leaders to merchants. In the time-conscious societies of western central Africa, where antiquity meant prestige and power brought seniority, these displacements and reintegrations weakened the growing majority of the newcomers and consolidated the dominance of the few earlier arrivals at the tops of the hierarchies. (Miller 1988:94)

Expressed in somewhat different terms and circumstances, just as successful hunts have potential for fostering expressions of individual inequality among hunters and gatherers (Woodburn 1982a:440; see also Godelier 1982:32), so acquisition of other forms of wealth, equally representative of appropriations from the outside world (Ingold 1982:532), help to define the origins-related qualities of aristocracies relative to commoners. This is especially so since, in centralized polities, the latter, lacking renowned ancestors and privileged access to origins, also lack, or should lack, heirlooms and other forms of wealth; "one way titleholders as a class maintain their social position is by making sure that nontitled persons (*remeau,* "naked") do not acquire valuables, or if they do acquire valuables, to scheme to relieve them of their wealth" (Parmentier 1987:78, 39, 69, regarding Belau; Townsend 1985:150).

> Named houses, moreover, maintain an enduring ritual relation to the founding ancestors through which the potential for life may be realized . . . The relation of unnamed houses to these ancestors exists only to the extent that they remain attached to named houses as younger brothers. Younger brother unnamed houses remain on the periphery, while at the center, and at the origin, remain the elder brother named houses— their permanence and weight embodied in the hard bones of their ancestors, in the enduring metals of their heirloom valuables, and in their continued connection to their ancestors, once evident in the exquisite altar panels that formed the pathways of their descent. (McKinnon 1991:106 regarding Tanimbar)

Even when aristocrats cannot entirely monopolize the acquisition of wealth, the aristocratic right to appropriate and control the treasures of the outside world may still be celebrated by acquisition of greater quantity or variety of goods as signifiers of origins-related abundance (Miller 1988: chap. 3; MacGaffey 1986:29; Chernela 1993:150).[7] Quantity, and thus abundance, can be expressed by size, too: "Can't you see he is a chief? See how big he is" (Gifford, quoted in Sahlins 1990:53 regarding Tonga; Sider 1967:90). In the *Traiphum,* a traditional Buddhist cosmography, "the more merit a person had, the better looking, stronger, and richer he was . . . Often the idiom was size. Rulers had bigger houses and held bigger ceremonies than the ruled. Indeed, one word for 'big' (*yai*) meant 'to rule' (*pen yai*) and another (*luang*) came to mean 'royal'" (O'Connor 1989:32).

All of this reiterates Turner's insight (1969:95) that liminal or anomalous political-ideological entities (such as living ancestors) require a rich variety of symbols to delineate and enhance statuses that, being by definition betwixt and between, have no direct foundation, and thus no inherent attributes of tangibility, in the basic social and cosmological realms and categories that organize the universe for a given people. Yet these liminal or anomalous positions represent the seats of some of the most focused intellectualizing about inside-outside relationships and demand definition and identity in cosmological terms. Hence the emphasis upon, elaborations of, and attempted monopolies over tangible expressions of durability and tangibility by those most "professionally" dependent on liminality, including aristocratic "living ancestors," who often seem relentless in their pursuit of numerous wives, the construction of monumental mounds, tombs, and palaces, the acquisition and accumulation of exotic goods from distant locales or of highly aesthetic goods crafted by their finest artisans, and the production of "surplus" at home and who glory in elaborate displays and distributions of such wealth.

Given not only the high visibility and great elaborations of aristocratic wealth detailed in the ethnographic literature but also the highly "processed" nature of many of the goods involved, resulting either from artisanal crafting or from Western manufacturing techniques, it should be reiterated that, in nonindustrial settings, wealth items and concepts of wealth are, at heart, closely related to the most basic and most ancient categories of outside beings the house and the polity have known.[8] In other words, "wealth" is simply a more sophisticated rendering of concepts about animals and animal products,[9] ancestors or the dead and the bones of the human dead, or other people, especially spouses and affines. It is axiomatic, therefore, that wealth should also be widely used in ceremonies that interrelate the outside realms of animals, affines and other people, and ancestors with the house (aristocratic or otherwise) or the polity.

With reference to ancestors and the dead, it is not simply that a certain accumulation of goods may be necessary in a functional or implementive sense before commemorative mortuary rites can be held (Bean 1972:135–136; Trigger 1990:129), or that the role of the dead and the scale and centrality of mortuary rites may increase significantly as goods become more readily available (Kan 1989:271), or that the availability of new types of goods (for example, European brandies and rums) may enhance the ability of chiefs, aristocrats, and elders to contact ancestral spirits (Miller 1988:84; Harrison 1987; MacGaffey 1986:17). All of these are "subsidiary" uses for goods that essentially derive from ancient and fundamental beliefs that human bones themselves (or comparable mummified remains) constitute a potent form of tangible wealth that enhances accessibility either to ancestral dead (Weiner 1992:57) or to comparable outside, origins-related locales whence good things derive (Sahlins 1990:29–30)—bones that can be replicated by or associated with other types of goods, especially goods from distant places.[10]

Given this parallel, it is not surprising to find that providers of valued goods, including traders, may be among those prominent persons apotheosized as ancestors (Parkin 1991:206–209) or that the bones of long-dead heroes, including successful warriors, lovers, and traders (all of whom must interact with other people), may become valued relics, as on Sudest Island where success in trade is enhanced by use of bespelled coconut oil that has been boiled with a human relic (Lepowsky 1989: 204–205, 219–220). In some societies the deceased, faced with travel to a distant land of the dead, may be depicted as a trader in full regalia (Chowning 1989:104–105 regarding the Molima of Melanesia) or at least is thought to do a little shopping along the way (Metcalf 1982:227 regarding the Berawan of Borneo). Finally, considered in broad cosmological perspective, wealth contextualized as ancestral bones may be seen as representative of the "processual" context of origins representing the temporal and relational nature of prior house origins that associates the current house membership with its founding ancestors. This interpretation may help explain why principal ancestor shrines also served as charnel houses and storehouses for wealth objects and weaponry among chiefdoms of the North American Southeast (Brown 1985:97).

The ethnographic literature also attests widely to the valuable role played by affines in effecting the acquisition of wealth, and affinally associated wealth, like ancestor-related wealth, may have its own unique qualities. With respect to the latter point, in contrast to "processual" wealth associated with house ancestors and house origins per se, affinal wealth in and of itself may be understood to represent the "contractual" context of absolute origins. As such, it refers to potent treasures that (like potential affines) exist independently of the house in the cosmological beyond, things whose acquisition heralds the association of the house with first-principle origins. With respect to the former point, affines often encourage acquisitional encounters with other people by creating both the necessary contacts and the essential peace of the trade for members of the house. The literature often speaks, too, of the wealth that may be acquired from potential affines through brideprice and of how access to wealth by other means may enhance the affinal prospects of house members by increasing their ability to pay bridewealth (Vansina 1990:104, 152, 237).[11]

It is noteworthy, too, that affines may be called upon to create, by skilled crafting and artistry, various forms of wealth, including ritual and ceremonial items, required by the house for political-ideological purposes. For example, speaking of the role of affinal/lateral kin (who also represent the opposite moiety) among the Tlingit, Kan says that "the ego's ceremonial regalia were made by his or her opposites, with men carving staves, helmets, house posts, and other wooden objects and women making ceremonial garments. If the person were a high-ranking aristocrat and had to build a new house, his brothers-in-law performed the work. Throughout his or her life, the person wore a series of garments . . . made by his or her opposites. Even the funeral pyre and the box for the cremated remains were . . . constructed by members of the opposite moiety" (1989:152; Seguin 1986b:488; Sider 1967:101; Crocker 1979:284–285; Morphy 1991:135–136). This role suggests that affinal qualities may be comparable in some respects to qualities generally associated with skilled artisans in nonindustrial settings. This is not surprising given that both are outside-affiliated roles that relate the house (or the aristocracy) to outside contexts of origins by creative acts of artistry or of human reproduction that replicate the original creative acts of first-principle deities, ancestors, or culture heroes.[12]

Items of tangible wealth not only associate their acquirers with categories of Others and contexts of origins but also connect and interrelate the several origins and outside Others to each other and to the membership of the house or polity, particularly during important political-ideological ceremonies such as mortuary rites, initiations, and political successions. Underlying these interrelations, making them "work," is the sense that fundamental qualitative comparabilities are involved when the house deals with animals, the ancestral dead, other people as trade partners or artisans, and affines. "The language of mortuary exchange is the same as that of *kune* (*kula*) and marriage. The metaphors are spatial, of places linked by . . . (roads)" (Macintyre 1989:145, 146–147, regarding Tubetube). These comparabilities, in turn, express the interrelatedness of a cosmological whole encompassing the house or the aristocracy, categories of Others, and contexts of origins, all of which can be very effectively and succinctly expressed by the various tangible items employed by the participants, both visible and invisible, of house or polity ceremonial events. A very good example is found in Hugh-Jones's discussion of the significance, for the Barasana of Colombia, of the ceremonial *He* (meaning "sacred" or "otherworldly") instruments (flutes and trumpets) that are associated with the long bones of the ancestral anaconda, the roar of shamanic jaguars, and the *He* people, humanity's first ancestors. The term *He* also refers to guests, including affines, who, like the ancestral *He* people, take part in the relevant ceremonies by bringing food and playing *He* instruments that they have brought (Hugh-Jones 1979:133, 138–140, 148–151, 153–155; see also Kan 1989; Weiner 1992; Damon and Wagner 1989).

In spite of qualitative ideological comparabilities, however, tangible "outside" goods may be accorded different political value or legitimizing "weight." It may be expected that goods obtained from nonaffinal trading contacts, for example, may be deemed relatively less durable or less temporally significant than goods that attest to the potency of affines or aristocrats as living ancestors or that express the suprahuman reality of prior house or founding polity ancestors. By the same token, goods indicative of first-principle origins may carry even greater lasting value and legitimizing force by virtue of their association with absolute cosmological beginnings. That is to say, tangible items relating to animals or affines or other people as origins-related outside beings that pre-exist the house or the polity may hold more fundamental "worth" than ancestral heirlooms per se, so that high lords and rulers with long and honorable family ancestry, bedecked with the most skillfully crafted and politically redolent inherited ancestral regalia and privy to a wealth of traded valuables, must be enthroned on seats draped with simple jaguar skins or carved with the likenesses of similar beasts of the wild in order to express their full and true legitimacy.[13]

Regardless of relative "worth," however, valuables that are inalienably connected to the diverse contexts and signifiers of origins connect the immediacy and ephemeralness of the here-and-now with the "lasting" realities and enduring legitimacies of the spatial/temporal there-and-then, and it is ultimately for that reason that they are sought by house and aristocracy. Human life and the life of the house or the polity are inherently fragile, especially in low-technology societies, but durable goods and, by extension, the values and qualities they embody are more lasting. And as long as wealth and the values of wealth endure, so do the qualities of ancestors, affines, and animals referencing prior origins or absolute first-principle forms of being (Eliade 1959a:155). By co-opting these personages, their qualities, and their durable, tangible manifestations or "regalia" for their own ends, houses and aristocracies, too, strive perhaps futilely but always hopefully to endure.

We should take seriously each culture's conception of its universe, because it probably tells us more about the generative rules for behaving than any other aspect of a cultural system . . .

LOWELL BEAN, *"Power and Its Application in Native California,"* 1977, P. 128

12

CONCLUDING

REMARKS

Geertz has stated that "religion is sociologically interesting not because . . . it describes the social order (which, in so far as it does, it does not only very obliquely but very incompletely), but because, like environment, political power, wealth, jural obligation, personal affection, and a sense of beauty, it shapes it" (1966:35–36). It has been the intent of this study to elucidate some of the ways in which certain cosmological aspects shape and inform low-technology societies, particularly the politically and ideologically charged "exclusive" hierarchies that define and regulate relationships between Us and categories of outside Others whose identifying qualitative characteristics as affines or as aristocracies are also, at heart, cosmologically derived.

As numerous ethnographic studies have documented and numerous scholars have appreciated, the particulars of cosmologies have provided essential and unexcelled models of and for human living. These formats not only enhance a reassuring sense of regularity and encourage order in human affairs but also provide avenues toward the legitimate expression of virtually all the diverse activities that sustain human life. In addition, they express psychologically necessary personal aspirations, provide growth points for cultural change, and activate the conditions with potentiality to produce such change. " . . . each culture's conception of its universe . . . probably tells us more about the generative rules for behaving than any other aspect of a cultural system—it explains from the 'top' and provides the baseline for all action in culture" (Bean 1977: 128). Cosmological formats do this by identifying the proprieties, the archetypical standards, that "economic," "social," and "political" affairs must try to evidence if they are to be socially acceptable. Foremost among these is recognition of the legitimizing primacy of cosmological origins and the strongly positive social valuation and validation accorded the actors and the activities that seek to access them.[1]

The flexibility, adaptability, and changeability of human affairs rest on the fact that the limited number of contexts of cosmological origins can be accessed by many different means, all of which are more or less interchangeable in terms of this fundamental value. This point is most significant for the world of politics, for it underlies, generates, and explains the dynamics of political ideology and political economy. Stated in the simplest terms, most, perhaps all, of the resource-enhancing competitions; the social alliances, factionings, regroupings, and consolidations; and the craftings and acquisitionings of bodies of esoteric knowledge and of valued tangible goods either at home or from abroad that constitute the heart of active political life constitute different ways of accessing origins, and from the perspective of political practitioners, if the means to do so is blocked in one direction, it may be approached by another. Recognition of this point opens the way for a greater appreciation of how polities can adapt and change, for understanding the necessity of evidencing access to legitimizing and empowering origins, one way or another, can explain why politically influential groups and individuals do what they do; their activities serve either to express individual abilities to tap into origins-related contexts (as tribal leaders do in noncentralized polities) or to evidence relative closeness to places or conditions of origins (as chiefs and aristocratic groups do in centralized polities).

I have also argued in this essay that cosmological qualities referring to origins are essential to the qualitative definitions accorded important segments of the "social order," most notably affines, one of the most fundamental conveyors of origins-related legitimacy, and aristocrats, political agents who express most completely and most consistently the importance, the means, and the consequences of sustained access to origins. I have further argued that, from the point of view of "ordinary" persons, the origins-related qualities and activities associated with affines and aristocracies identify members of both categories as tangible forms of cosmological Others, specifically as living ancestors. Identification of cosmological Others in terms of ancestry and of affinity relative to a focal house also clearly extends the use of the kinship idiom into the wider cosmos, with the result that the sociological-ideological "distance" inherent in relationships between those of Us in the here-and-now and Others in the there-and-then can be bridged and mediated by long-term ties.

The idioms of affinity and ancestry also identify essentially two general political-ideological orientations (cf. Leach 1961:104) by which the house may effect connections with Others and with origins. In the "contractual" approach the house views the outside, its Others, and its contexts of origins as separate, independent, and generally preexistent of itself. In the "processual" approach the house views the outside, its Others, and its contexts of origins largely as extensions of its own corporateness. Common to both contractual or processual perspectives, however, is the universal assertion that whatever is situated in the outside realms of spatial/temporal distance qualitatively transcends, for better or for worse, that which is purely local and purely immediate. Qualitative distinctiveness, in turn, translates into hierarchical structuring, which thereby stands identified as a universal feature of cosmological patterns. All these factors are tangibly or literally expressed in the political structures and processes that associate legitimizing affines and origins-seeking authority figures with the house and in the general developmental options open to ranked and centralized polities. Figure 12 summarizes these points, which have been examined at some length in previous chapters.

In some polities the full implications and political-ideological impact of the qualitative and hierarchical distinctiveness of outside Others can be controlled (generally by being limited to special ritual events), though perhaps never totally denied if it is true that "order is seen to consist mainly in inequality (or difference . . .)" (Aquinas, quoted in Dumont 1982:238). In others, however, most notably chiefdoms, these implications and imports not only are explicitly expressed but are even encouraged to flourish. Several important points can be derived from this fact. First, by explicitly recognizing the qualitative distinctiveness and hierarchical superiority of living forms of cosmological Others who are directly connected to the house or the polity, such as affines and aristo-

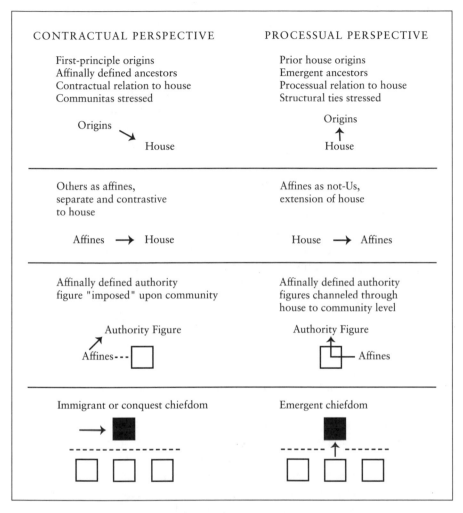

FIGURE 12 Contractual and processual perspectives of Others and origins.

crats, the interface between the house or the polity and the more distant reaches of the greater outside is also highlighted and elaborated by the liminal or ambiguous status of those same affinal and aristocratic groups that "relative to their subordinates in the hierarchy, function as self contained wholes; relative to their superordinates as dependent parts" (Dumont 1982:222 n. 1). It would seem to follow, then, that scholarly investigation into the development of centralized polities should focus on this cosmological interface linking the Us and the Other as much as it has on the material interface linking the cultural and the natural (cf. Dove 1992:247).

The second point suggested by the open recognition of the qualitative distinctiveness and hierarchical superiority of Others in centralized polities is a reiteration that cultural developments, including increased organizational complexity, rest on undeveloped potential already present in preceding less complex settings. That is to say, explanations for the hierarchical structuring and qualitative inequality characteristic of chiefdoms should not assume that such features are new cultural creations whose origins must lie in unique activities peculiar to would-be chiefs or in exceptional possibilities inherent in the ecological environment, though these clearly are not irrelevant to the total process (see Earle 1991, 1987). Rather it should be understood that principles of inequality and hierarchy are already present in the conceptual "environment" in noncentralized settings and that their formal or public expression in chiefdoms reflects the successful overriding of previous efforts to keep them at bay or under wraps, a far easier analytical task than trying to explain the appearance of inequality and hierarchy in chiefdoms as a new and unique phenomenon.

The third point to be drawn from the argument that inequality and hierarchy are inherent and universal aspects of cosmological structurings and of concepts of Otherness that emerge to full tangible recognition and expression in chiefdoms is that the concept and the reality of aristocracy is made possible by, or is a function of, developing complexities in cosmologies as much as by changes in social demographies or supportive ecologies and economies. More specifically, the emergence of aristocracies and chiefships reflects elaborations in concepts about cosmological Otherness and the nature of the relationships between categories of Others and the houses of the polity. This is why I have focused on the concept of aristocracy as a group rather than individual identification and have interpreted chiefs and other aristocrats as a category of Others (affines-cum-living-ancestors) writ large rather than as ambitious individual heads of houses writ large. Similarly, if I were to further pursue the qualitative antecedents of aristocratic attributes, I would inquire more deeply into the nature of cosmological Otherness, including Masters of Animals, totemic landscapes, and the human dead, rather than into the attributes of house elders or big men per se, for I am persuaded that the concept of aristocracy is rooted in the personification and literalization of concepts about the nature of the universe rather than in differences in the individual skills or attributes of persons of the house or polity per se. Concomitantly, I argue that, at heart, the hierarchical ethic informing relationships between aristocrats and commoners is more accurately understood as based on differences in kind indicative of "exclusive" forms of hierarchy rooted in the structure of the cosmos rather than on differences in degree indicative of "inclusive" forms of hierarchy rooted in the consanguineal corporate kin group (see Carlson 1993:315, 324, 327)—that is, in the qualities originally accorded firstborns rather than in those of seniority.

It is no coincidence that both heaven and the emperor are high and far away, for at its heart the legitimacy and the activation of political authority rest on the manipulation of an awareness of Other worlds and of Other beings. Such Others are effective and essential, because they alone have direct access to origins, to that which is truly authentic, to that which sets the standard, to that which is, by definition, superior to anything that follows, since that which follows, including the life of the house or of the polity in the here-and-now, can be at best only an imperfect copy of the archetypical original.

APPENDIX

Geographical Distribution of Select Ethnographic Sources

The following ethnographic sources were especially useful with respect to some aspect of the study and were quoted most extensively in the text. It should not be assumed, however, that they present complete examples of any of the models proposed. The sources are listed here alphabetically by author under major geographical headings.

NORTH AMERICA

Bean 1972; Cahuilla, southern California
Goldman 1975; Kwakiutl, Northwest Coast
Ingold 1987; Circumboreal peoples
Jonaitis 1991; Kwakiutl, Northwest Coast
Kan 1986, 1989; Tlingit, Northwest Coast
Levy 1992; Hopi, American Southwest
Schlegel 1992; Hopi, American Southwest

Seguin 1986a, 1986b; Tsimshian, Northwest Coast
Townsend 1985; Fox Islanders, Aleutians

MIDDLE AND SOUTH AMERICA

Chernela 1993; Wanano, Brazilian Amazon
Crocker 1969, 1979; Bororo, central Brazil
Goldman 1963; Cubeo, Northwest Amazon
Hill 1984; Wakuénai, Venezuela
Howard 1991; Waiwai, northern Brazil–Guyana
Huxley 1995; Urubu, northeastern Brazil
McAnany 1995; lowland Maya, Mesoamerica
Reichel-Dolmatoff 1985, 1986; Tukanoan Desana, Colombia
Stone 1989; lowland Classic Maya
T. Turner 1984; Kayapo, central Brazil
T. Turner 1979; Gê and Bororo, central Brazil
Viveiros de Castro 1986; Araweté, Brazilian Amazon
Zarur 1991; Bororo, central Brazil

MIDDLE EAST AND AFRICA

Alpers 1969; Yao, Malawi
Beck 1990; Iran
Burton 1983; Nuer and Nilotic peoples, southern Sudan
Carlson 1993; Haya, Tanzania
Cohen 1976, 1977; Pabir, Nigeria
Comaroff and Comaroff 1981; Tshidi, South Africa and Botswana
d'Azevedo 1962; Gola, Liberia
Dieterlen 1973; Mande, Upper Volta, West Africa
Ekholm 1978; west-central Africa
Evens 1984; Nuer, southern Sudan
Fairley 1989; Ekie, Zaire
Fardon 1988, 1990; Chamba, Nigeria and Cameroon
Fortes 1945; Tallensi, West African Sudan
Goody 1962; LoWiili, West Africa
Gough 1971; Nuer and Nilotic peoples, southern Sudan
Gudeman 1986; Bemba, Zambia
Harris 1962; Taita, Kenya
Kelly 1985; Nuer and Nilotic peoples, southern Sudan
Kopytoff 1987; African frontiers
Krige and Krige 1943; Lovedu, Transvaal
La Fontaine 1962, 1975; Gisu, Uganda
Lienhardt 1955; Shilluk, southern Sudan
MacGaffey 1986; BaKongo, Zaire
Middleton 1977; Lugbara, Uganda
Miller 1976, 1988; Mbundu, Angola

Mitchell 1956; Yao, Malawi
Murphy and Bledsoe 1987; Kpelle, Liberia
Parkin 1991; Giriamba, Kenya
Richards 1961; Swazi, southeastern Africa
Rowlands 1985; Cameroon grasslands chiefdoms
Uchendu 1976; Igbo, Nigeria
Watson 1958; Mambwe, northern Rhodesia

SOUTH AND SOUTHEAST ASIA

Barnes 1974; Toba-Batak and Kédang, Indonesia
Barraud 1985; Tanebar-Evav, Moluccas, Indonesia
Bloch 1992; Ladakh, northern India
Endicott 1979; Batak, Malaysia
Friedman 1975: Kachin, Burma
Fürer-Haimendorf 1969; Konyak Naga, Assam-Burma
Howell 1991; Lio, Flores Island, Indonesia
Leach 1961, 1965; Kachin, Burma
McKinley 1976; Iban, Borneo
McKinnon 1991; Tanimbar, Moluccas, Indonesia
Metcalf 1982; Berawan, Borneo
Pauwels 1985; Tanimbar, Moluccas, Indonesia
Rousseau 1979; Kayan, Borneo
Traube 1989; Mambai, Indonesia
Valeri 1994; Huaulu, Indonesia
Van der Kroef 1954; Toba-Batak, Sumatra
Vitebsky 1993; Sora, eastern India
Woodward 1989; Ao Naga, Assam

OCEANIA

Battaglia 1990; Sabarl, Louisiades
Bloch 1992; Orokaiva, Papua New Guinea
Brunton 1975; Trobriands, Melanesia
Campbell 1989; Vakuta, Papua New Guinea
Dalton, 1996; Rawa, Papua New Guinea
Errington 1974; Karavar, Melanesia
Errington and Gewertz 1986; Chambri, New Guinea
Foster 1990; Tauga, Papua New Guinea
Harrison 1990; Manambu, Papua New Guinea
Keesing 1982; Kwaio, Solomon Islands, Melanesia
Kelly 1993; Etoro, New Guinea
Macintyre 1989; Tubetube, Papua New Guinea
Maddock 1989; Australia
Mead 1938, 1940; Arapesh, New Guinea
Myers 1986; Pintupi, Australia

Parmentier 1987; Belau, Micronesia
Petersen 1993; Awok, Micronesia
Pomponio 1992; Mandok, Melanesia
Powell 1960; Trobriands, Melanesia
Sanday 1986; Hua, New Guinea
Scheffler 1965; Choiseul, Solomon Islands, Melanesia
Sider 1967; Trobriands, Melanesia
Thune 1989; Normanby Island, Papua New Guinea
Turner 1988; Fiji

NOTES

1. THE SETTING

1. Definitions and descriptions of the concept of chiefdom abound. Useful overviews may be found in Anderson (1994b: chaps. 1 and 2), Spencer (1987), and Earle (1987), among others.

2. The terms "elite" and "aristocracy," though closely related, are not synonymous. In addition, I find the term "aristocracy" to be more appropriate for my analysis and use it in preference to the more commonly encountered "elite" throughout the study. In the sense that both terms identify a "superior" social sector that stands apart from the rest of the population, the terms are basically interchangeable and use becomes a matter of personal preference. However, "aristocracy," unlike "elite," explicitly includes the context of political authority and government in its basic dictionary definition. Since the importance of the aristocracy/elite in this study lies in the nature of their political legitimacy, I will generally use the term "aristocracy" rather than "elite" in my discussions.

3. By "consubstantiality of life" I refer to beliefs that the definitive nature of the cosmos and of all things and beings that it contains lies in a shared dynamic of life forces; that the essence of something or somebody lies in fundamental energetics rather than in physical or material characteristics per se.

4. "We should then say, speaking roughly, that there are two ways of somehow recognizing *alter:* hierarchy and conflict" (Dumont 1982:239).

5. In relating processes of political authority to cosmological conditions of origins, ancestors, and the encapsulation of cosmological energies and powers, I am deviating from the frequent practice of associating political ideology with powers of "nature" (e.g., Bloch 1989:77, 80). The two are, of course, intimately related in traditional thought. Though not totally interchangeable, they reference much the same thing.

6. As MacGaffey (1986:42) has succinctly noted, distinguishing between the mystical and the empirical by way of reducing one to the other or of discarding one or the other as less relevant is a characteristic of our Western epistomology. It is "only the nonbeliever who believes that the believer believes in God; to the believer his belief is knowledge, that is, perceived and experienced fact" (1986:1).

7. On these points I am in full agreement with Giddens: "I do not at all want to deny the influence of the surrounding natural habitat upon patterns of social life, the impact that major sorts of technological invention may have or the relevance of the material power resources that may be available and harnessed to human use. But it has long been conventional to emphasize these, and I think it very important to demonstrate the parallel significance of authoritative resources [including the organization of social time-space]. For . . . we are still prisoners of the Victorian era in so far as we look first of all to the transformation of the material world as the generic motive force of human history" (1984:258–259).

2. THE HOUSE

1. Typically, in its physical form, when the house is identified as a microcosm of the universe, the roof is the sky, the house posts are sky-supports, such as mountains, the floor is the earth, and the center of the house is the center of the world (e.g., Hugh-Jones 1979:151; González and González 1989).

2. Hodder emphasizes that "the domus is not equivalent to 'the private.' I do not wish to assume that the house is a private domain in opposition to an outside public world" (Hodder 1990:68–69).

3. See also papers in Carsten and Hugh-Jones (1995) and work by Parmentier (1984:657–658); Errington (1987:405); Vansina (1990:73, 75); Bloch (1992: 70, 74–75); Kan (1989:24); Appell (1976b:70); McKinnon (1991:33). References cited are chosen as representative examples of the approach indicated.

4. Drummond has succinctly stated the matter a little differently, arguing that, since the shifting bands of nonhuman primates seldom constitute fixed groups, the concept of group is a complex conceptualization unique (presumably) to humans. "The idea of group, of a cultural We, is not somehow given, not provided by our heritage as social animals, not, as Derrida . . . would say, *present,* but is constructed through a tremendous effort of will from the puzzling and conflicting facts of human sexuality, reproduction, and social relations" (1981:639).

5. "Here-and-now" refers to settings and interactions that, as Giddens has described it, are characterized by only short distances in time-space separations: ". . . the setting is such that all interaction has only a small 'gap' to carry over in crossing time and space. It is not just physical presence in immediate interaction which matters . . . it is the temporal and spatial *availability* of others in a locale" (Giddens 1979:207).

6. See also Lévi-Strauss (1987:180); Bloch and Parry (1982:33); McKinnon (1991:97–98); Errington (1987:406); Howell (1991:230); Fox (1987:177); Goldman (1975:64); Taylor and Aragon (1991:44).

7. My methodological use of the concept of the house as the inside group or Us contrasting with affinal groups as outsiders or Others deviates from the inclusion of affines within the concept of the house in certain ethnographic contexts (e.g., Pauwels 1985:132 regarding Tanimbar in the southeast Moluccas). Lévi-Strauss also includes affinal features in his general discussion of the house (1987:12), and in some cultures the house may show a tendency toward endogamy (Bloch 1971:61–62). In comparable fashion I also seek to situate the dead and ancestors outside the house per se, though crucially linked to it, rather than to view these beings as constituting part of the house in the strict sense of its situation in the here-and-now. The expression of this aspect of the interpretive model will also vary in specific ethnographic situations, as is always the case when applying models. My reasons for structuring the presentation in such fashion will become clearer in later chapters.

3. THE DEAD

1. There is, of course, a tremendous range of attitudes and responses toward death and the dead in non-Western, nonindustrial societies. Some are rather perfunctory, such as those held by hunters and gatherers constituting what have been termed "immediate-return societies," where, as the Baka put it, "when you're dead, you're dead, and that's the end of it" (Woodburn 1982:195). Similarly, the Krikatí of Brazil try to forget the dead as soon as possible to prevent them from continuing relationships with the living (Lave 1979:30). Nonetheless, belief in spirits, ghosts, or other intangible manifestations of the dead or even of the living is extremely common cross-culturally (Rosenblatt, Walsh, and Jackson 1976:51–52). The reality of such concepts for those who believe them is very graphically conveyed by Seeger, who points out that the reality of the spirit realm is as real to the Suyá of Brazil as Europe or China is to Americans. "Those places become part of our lives and experience even though we may never have been there. The same thing was true of Suyá experiences with spirits" (1987:57).

2. Lévi-Strauss sees this role performed by children at Halloween and Christmas in Western culture and suggests a similar role for Southwest Pueblo children when katchina figures (costumed and masked beings who are the incarnated dead and deities) return annually to the communities (1993:44–45). A comparable identification may be attributed to the very young, only recently arrived

from the other world and all too frequently, in nonindustrial societies, too soon returned (Fardon 1990:35–36).

3. The alleged burial, among the Dinka, of the Master of the Fishing Spear while he is still living is a most dramatic example of this condition (Lienhardt 1961: chap. 8; Deng in Huntington and Metcalf 1979:175–176; Counts and Counts 1985:17–18).

4. Persons suffering from certain extremely serious illnesses, such as brain death, are also classified with the dead in Western society (Counts and Counts 1985:22).

5. The approach of death, of course, is one of the qualitative factors defining "old age."

6. In Irish farmhouses, typically built in rectangular form on an east-west axis, the largest room was in the middle and contained the hearth and fireplace at the west end. A door beside the hearth led behind it to the west room, a place with "a sacred and special quality" associated with the dead. In comparable fashion, "the Batammabe [Dahomey, West Africa] believe that the ancestors, the source of their lives, continue to dwell among them. They leave them the ground floor of their houses, and there they erect their altars. Animals stabled there are only eaten at sacrificial feasts and are considered food of the dead. Old people, too weak to climb the stairs every night, sleep downstairs, too, and so come closer to the ancestors whom they will soon join" (Englebert 1973:117).

7. In Karavar (Territory of Papua and New Guinea), where a successful man accumulates quantities of cowrie-shell "money" (*divara*) for distribution at social events, the death of an unambitious "rubbish man" who did not accumulate *divara* led to the comment that "today Taki died. But in truth he has been dead for several years, for he has not had any *divara*" (Errington 1977:30).

8. In many "tribal" societies, especially the so-called "equal bridewealth societies" (Collier 1988), bones often are also believed to represent the part of a person produced by, or containing particular properties associated with, kin or house membership as opposed to other associations. For example, in the procreative process the flesh and blood portions of the body, which eventually decompose, may be thought to be produced by one parent and the durable bones by the other. From the point of view of wider group associations, bones may be associated with ego's house and constitute a shared identity with its membership, past, present, and future, while the temporary, perishable portion of the body will be attributed to the affinal side of the parental relation. Bones thus create a sense of perpetuity by connecting the house with its dead over the generations (cf. Weiner 1982:57–58, 62, 1992:57; Traube 1980:98; Collier 1988: 133; Macintyre 1989:138; Bloch and Parry 1982:22–27).

9. Francis Huxley, discussing the Urubu of Brazil, recounts how the Indians suspected that he might be immortal because he was tall—that is, he had "lengthened" long bones. Many asked him to pull at their arms and legs to make them taller and so, presumably, give them long life (1995:201).

10. Among many native populations of Mesoamerica, Central America, and South America, hard seeds may be called "bone." Conversely, bones are regarded as a form of seed because of their regenerative power (Labbé 1986:116; Furst 1978:23). The Mambai of East Timor cherish various types of metal ob-

jects—swords, spears, breast disks—"which mythological traditions trace back to the bones of Father Heaven" (Traube 1980:99). On Vanatinai "success in obtaining valuables is attributed to the power of one's exchange magic, such as bespelled scented coconut oil, which has been boiled with a human relic, sometimes that of the deceased for whom the feast will be held" (Lepowsky 1989: 219–220).

11. Such bones are decorated and ornamented with leaves, feathers, or woven bands; that is, they are crafted into aesthetic objects probably to enhance their potency or to define the category of that potency (see Helms 1993: chaps. 4 and 9).

12. For example, a child or youth may have died too young to have accomplished anything significant, a man's life may not be considered notable in achievements, or a woman's role may be regarded as less significant in the public forum.

13. Basically the same treatment for the same reason may be accorded enemies from the outside who are captured alive, brought to the village, fed and feted, and then executed. See, for example, Huxley (1995: chap. 19).

14. In Ingold's view, with respect to circumpolar hunter-gatherers, personhood is held to transcend the human/nonhuman dichotomy, and humanity is simply "an aspect of incidental form rather than essential content" (1987:248). So it is, too, that the Uduk of Sudan "see themselves as members of the great family of hoofed animals, and kin to the wild antelopes" (James 1990:198) and that the Ma'Betisék (Malay Peninsula) believe that animals and also plants possess human characteristics (Karim 1981:45). See also the discussion about the lives of yams in New Guinea by Tuzin (1972) and papers in Ingold (1988).

15. Concerning animal lifestyles, the Makuna, also of Colombia, "believe that in another dimension of reality, all animals are people; they have houses and gardens, musical instruments and ritual ornaments, chants and dances, as people do. They are grouped into communities inhabiting particular territories and also have their headmen, or 'masters of the animals'" (Århem 1992:51).

16. "Dead Soras become part of the soul of their living descendants' crops" (Vitebsky 1993:31).

17. The term "enate" denotes relatives and relationships traced through females.

18. In an interesting variation on this theme, the Sumbanese say that "dead souls are like brides," meaning that "they must be carefully ushered out of the ancestral house and (despite a certain emotional wrench) prepared for a journey to another home. The ritual incorporation of the dead into the village of the ancestors provides an exact parallel to that of the bride" (Hoskins 1987:177). More specifically, "both assume the same position, sitting motionless in the right front corner of the house; the heads of both are veiled in red cloth; both are attended by women who weep and perform exhortatory chants in anticipation of the addressee's departure; and both are carried from the house by men while the women attempt to hinder their passage" (Forth, quoted in ibid.). This imagery applies to the dead regardless of gender; all dead are "feminised" (Hoskins 1987:177; see also Weiner 1987:265 regarding the Foi of New Guinea).

19. The *susu* is matrilineal; fathers constitute affinal "outsiders."

20. The Maï are described as "our tall fathers-in-law" or "our gigantic potential affines," indicating the superiority and the dangerous character of the Maï and the obligation people have to feed them (Viveiros de Castro 1986:217).

4. ANCESTORS

1. "To be seen is the ambition of ghosts; to be remembered is the ambition of the dead" (Goodrich 1990:292). Understandably so, considering the possible fate of those who are forgotten: "As long as the dead were remembered by their living matrikin and could participate in their potlatches, they remained immortal and sat close to the fire in their noncorporeal houses . . . The forgotten ancestors, on the other hand, moved further and further away from the fire, suffered from hunger and cold, while their 'houses' in the cemetery crumbled" (Kan 1986:200 regarding the Tlingit). In comparable fashion, disowned ancestors and forgotten dead among the Manus suffered the ignominious fate of being turned into sea slugs (Fortune 1935:6). Elsewhere, among the BaKongo of Zaire, the dead fell into oblivion by becoming termite hills (MacGaffey 1986:74) while Ob Ugrians believe that a man's soul shrinks after death, as his life is played in reverse, until he becomes a small black beetle (Ingold 1987:246).

2. Speaking of the stylization accorded ancient Egyptian tomb paintings, Kent Weeks gives a vivid example of the transformation from individual to social personage: "An artist may have been commissioned . . . to carve representations of nobleman N in N's mastaba. For all we know, N may have been an aged, bald, short, hunchbacked albino; but we may be certain that such features would not have appeared in his representation unless, like the dwarf Seneb, those attributes were in some way necessary for the role he was assigned to play in the Afterlife or . . . were significant attributes of that role. As holder of certain titles, our nobleman would have been shown to be Egyptian, male, well dressed in a specified costume, middle-aged, and in good health (albeit with the slight degree of corpulence appropriate to his well-fed and sedentary existence). In short, he would have been shown as a successful gentleman" (1979:71).

3. Compare the model of the "superordinate society" developed in Helms (1993: chap. 11).

4. Recognizing that "there is no invariable one-to-one correspondence between social structure and patterns of ancestor worship throughout the world" (Kerner 1976:206), I have hesitated to associate ancestral contexts with particular types of social organization. Nonetheless, broad correspondances seem to exist. For example, strongly temporal contexts of ancestral identification appear in strongly lineal societies such as those found in Africa, while strongly spatial ancestral concepts appear in some hunting and gathering and simple horticultural societies, including "tribes" in tropical America. Cognatic and bilateral societies, not surprisingly, are among the many groups that incorporate both spatial and temporal ancestral contexts.

5. Compare the model of the "acquisitional society" discussed in Helms (1993: chap. 12). A type of processual imagery can be found, however, in some myths recounting the creation of life-forms. The emergence of the first people

from the body of the primordial ancestral anaconda of the South American trop-
ics is a well-known example (Chernela 1988:36–37; Hugh-Jones 1977:192–
193), although in other versions of this scenario the first people are the offspring of marriage between a culture hero and an anaconda woman (Howard
1991:64).

6. Chernela (1988:35); Reichel-Dolmatoff (1985:113–115); Ingold (1987:
251); Kent (1989:12, 13); Lévi-Strauss (1969a:67, 123–124, 82–83); Karsten
(1968:426).

7. An interesting parallel is suggested by the Herrero of South Africa, among
whom an individual recognizes the emergent ancestral spirits of a "patrilineal"
association while inheriting cattle "matrilineally" from a mother's brother, provided cattle are construed as constituting links with a type of ancestral first-
principle origins, as is often the case among African pastoralists (Radcliffe-
Brown 1965:23; see also note 22).

8. The societies in question would have been organizationally relatively
simple, very mobile and flexible social groups with considerable choice of personal residence and interpersonal ties (see Woodburn 1982; Kelly 1992:43–48).
The possible historical origins of ethnographically known immediate-return societies are somewhat controversial. It has been suggested that their egalitarian
organization may be the result of relatively recent encapsulation by politically
dominant neighboring societies. The alternative view posits that immediate-
return societies could have existed in the past as well as in the present. See discussion by Barnard and Woodburn (1988:27–28) and Woodburn (1988).

9. Some historically known nonsedentary hunting and gathering societies
and small hunter-gatherer-horticultural groups believe that human deaths have
some limited effect on hunting success or that human souls or the human dead
metamorphose into animals. In other cases human shades may be associated
with the "wilds" in general or simply disappear as "finished" (Woodburn
1982:190, 193, 196, 204; Melatti 1979:61; Zarur 1991:37; Pearce 1987:309;
Glazier 1984:138).

10. Consider also Collier (1988:24, 27, 36–37) regarding the nature of
hunting, courtship, and in-law relations among "bride service" societies.

11. More complexly organized hunter-gatherers, those with "delayed-
return" systems (such as Australian aborigines), do place considerable emphasis on burial location both as a means of referencing the dead and, more important, of creating an emotional identification between an individual and a place
(Myers 1986:132, 135, 152). See Chapter 6.

12. By the same token, the presence of agriculture does not automatically signify economic dependence on cultivated foods. The Shavante of Brazil, for example, are energetic hunters and gatherers but unenthusiastic gardeners who
find the drudgery of horticultural work boring. Aboriginally they planted low-
maintenance crops (maize, beans, pumpkins) for harvests that "were thought of
less as providing the essentials for the life of the community than as bonuses to
be used for celebrations," particularly initiation ceremonies (Maybury-Lewis
1974:48).

13. Logistic mobility refers to movement of individuals on periodic forays
away from a more fixed place of residence. It may be contrasted with residential

mobility, the movement of entire communities from place to place. See Kelly (1992:44).

14. Hodder's discussion (1990:138, 130) of increasing emphasis on "boundaries" and "entrances" as evidence of the creation of links between the house and other "foreign" houses in early neolithic Central Europe is also appropriate here. Hodder suggests, among other things, social gatherings where "foreigners" are involved in feasting and food exchanges (138).

15. Goldman has suggested that "men could not have advanced politically until they had emancipated themselves from religious identification with the animal world, and with its shamanic accessories" (1975:4). See also discussion by Tapper (1988:54–57).

16. Consider, too, the decrease in wall depictions of wild animals as well as fewer wild animal bones in Near East neolithic settlements (Hodder 1990:294).

17. Use of ethnographic analogies, though valuable, is admittedly problematical in a discussion of this sort since it is unlikely that ethnographically known societies will exactly fit the economic and societal particulars used to define the proposed historical settings. For example, most delayed-return societies, including the Manambu, in which the house has developed as a corporate entity will probably evidence cosmological and sociological adaptations in which the temporal ancestral cosmological axis is at least somewhat developed although spatial imagery may still predominate. Manambu cosmology is considered here partly because the Manambu, though sedentary, are economically still largely nonagricultural and because Harrison's analysis so clearly states cosmological features that are postulated to have predominated during the earlier era of pre-agricultural sedentism under discussion.

18. The Makuna of Colombia, somewhat settled hunters and fishers who do some farming and who believe that "in another dimension of reality, all animals are people" and live in communities as people do, also claim that "the relationship between the human and the animal world is comparable to the relationship of reciprocity between different groups of people, particularly groups that intermarry." Such "affinal" relationships assure the fecundity of both people and nature (Århem 1992:51).

19. Among the Manambu the dead join the totemic ancestors in mythical origin-villages (Harrison 1990:46).

20. Consider the practice followed by the LoDagaa of West Africa whereby grandparents are buried inside the courtyard of their house while other people are carried into the bush for inhumation (Goody 1962:147).

21. Myerhoff, speaking of the Huichol, characterizes the bond between hunter and game as more of a partnership while the agriculturalist serves as caretaker or servant of his crops (1979:108). Major responsibility for processes of growth and development of wild resources, especially fish and game, may be attributed instead to supernatural guardians, such as Masters of Animals, as "form-givers" (Ingold 1987:247–248). At the same time, resource management among prehistoric hunter-gatherers may well have included the tending of plants for several millennia prior to subsistence dependence on domesticated plants (Schoenwetter 1991).

22. The products of domestication, particularly domestic animals, presum-

ably would have provided another realm of "beings" available for cosmological conceptualization. Among some pastoralists and cattle-herders, certain domesticated animals are clearly associated with the temporal cosmological axis of the house; consider, for example, the significance of sheep bones among Mongol pastoralists (Szynkiewicz 1990), the famous Nuer cattle as discussed by Evans-Prichard (1940:209, 222, 36), and the "cow of divine origin" of the Shilluk (Lienhardt 1955:32). Among other pastoralists domesticated animals can relate to the Otherness of the spatial, affinal axis, as seen in the symbolism of cattle sacrifice and cattle as bridewealth among the Dinka as discussed by Bloch (1992:66–69). In still other instances or in other interpretations, however, domesticated animals, such as cattle or pigs, seem to represent subhuman alterity—that is, what humans would be like if they lost touch with their ancestral natures or their human intellect (Bloch 1992:32–40, 65; Kent 1989:15–16; see also Tapper 1988).

The passivity of domesticated plants as life-forms probably precluded their receiving much attention as a cosmologically significant category of being. Nonetheless, cultivated plants may be accorded life-force derived from the human dead, as among the Iban of Sarawak, where human souls are ultimately transformed into dew that nourishes the rice, thereby ensuring the presence of ancestral "soul" in the grain (Sutlive 1978:63–64). See also Erikson (1990) regarding maize harvest likened to hunted game and related to visits of ancestral spirits, as well as Kent (1989:17 n. 6) and Bloch and Parry (1982:28) regarding the intellect and emotional life of Melanesian yams and taro that are also metamorphosed house ancestors. Maize as the original embodiment of life is also a common theme in Mesoamerica and Central America. The Bribri of Costa Rica (to cite one example) assert that all native peoples known to them as well as they themselves originated from corn seed brought by the creator deity, Sibu, to a hill in the headwaters of a river. Some seeds turned into animals that migrated away and became the different tribes that are neighbors to the Bribri (Bozzoli de Wille 1975:30).

23. See, for example, Hodder (1990:40, 79, 94, 172, 246); Harkin (1992); Mbiti (1969:25–26); Metcalf (1982:243); Middleton (1982:151–152); Goody (1962:84); Price (1995:142).

24. See discussion of "naturally endowed" powers in Helms (1993); also Hocart, *Social Origins,* p. 35 (quoted in Becker 1975:24).

25. Associating "contractual" or "managerial" relationships with the spatial cosmological axis and "processual" relationships with the temporal axis directly suggests Sahlins's recognition of a "double axis" in which distinction is made between relationships of authority linking members of the lineal line of the house and constituting the "armature for the formation of social groups" and "an axis of complementarity" involving brother-sister ties and the mediation of the house with an affinal group via marriage (1976:28, with reference to Polynesia). Consider, too, Bloch's delineation, expressed in terms of time scales, of short-term and long-term relationships as they relate to "of the present" ties of the house with neighbors-cum-affines and "of the ancestors" relations of the house with its dead, respectively (Bloch 1971:219–220, with reference to the Merina of Madagascar). Bloch also notes that this contrast is "really what

underlies the contrast many anthropologists make between descent ideology and social action" (220).

26. The precedence of the spatial axis over the temporal axis suggested here as a general principle is nicely expressed in a somewhat different form in the ethnographic particulars of Araweté cosmology. Noting that the vertical opposition of earth and sky can be transformed into or articulated with a horizontal axis, Viveiros de Castro says that "when a horizontal transfer of the sky/earth axis occurs, it corresponds to the opposition east/west. In such cases, the relationship between the human world and the animal world (represented by the Masters of Animals) prevails over the relationship between humanity and the 'vertical,' humanlike gods . . ." (1986:86).

27. Temporal and spatial sources of political-ideological legitimation not only can be, and have been, mutually valued and conjoined to varying degrees but also consciously *dis*connected. For example, Peter Brown describes (1981: 124–125) the rise of the Christian church in western Europe as involving the devaluing of the traditional (pagan) spatial aspect of the cosmos, such as sacred trees and water sources, in favor of recognition of the worthy Christian dead (and their shrines) and their living representatives (e.g., bishops) as the proper cosmological touchpoints.

5. AFFINES

1. The identification of a closer form of affinity, of affines as "not-Us," may be seen as an expression of the "naturalization of society" while the identification of more distant Others as affines may be seen as an expression of the "socialization of nature."

2. The associations of these persons with ego, like those characteristic of ego's own affinal relatives, frequently express qualities strongly contrasting with qualities operative among the members of ego's house per se.

3. Dumont further explains that "there is likely to be an affinal content in terms which are generally considered to connote consanguinity or "genealogical" relationships (such as "mother's brother"). This is obviously so when there are no special terms for affines, for otherwise we should have to admit that in such cases affinity is not expressed at all" (1983:73, 75–76).

4. See, for example, Grinker (1990); Watson (1982:173); Radcliffe-Brown (1952:91–92); Seeger (1981:121–123); Maybury-Lewis (1979a:230); Lévi-Strauss (1969a:116, 118, 261); Macintyre (1989:134–135, 146); Josephides (1985:65); Seguin (1986:488); Suttles (1991:92); Bloch (1992:70).

5. This same ambiguous cosmological/sociological status also makes in-laws, affinal groups, and affinal relationships particularly significant subjects for study since such contexts often provide growth points for cultural development (Dove 1992:247).

6. Affines can also be considerably discomforted by such roles, for should misfortune befall a member of the house, it is among affines that the cause may be sought and toward affines that retribution may be directed: "Associated with . . . feelings of shame [because of the death of a child or spouse, assumed

to be under the care and responsibility of the affines] is a more basic fear that they, as affines to the deceased, may become prime targets for sorcery accusations" (Campbell 1989:54 regarding Vakuta, Melanesia).

7. Success for men formerly meant hunting luck, nowadays good jobs or scholarly prowess. For women success refers to childbearing (MacGaffey 1986:83).

8. In a somewhat different perspective, Horton, discussing the Ashanti, contrasts the spiritual power that supports a person's life of social conformity within the house (matrilineage) with that which supports his relationship with his father and which is seen to underlie an individual's personal idiosyncrasies, including "his deviations from the social norm, whether these be creative inventions or destructive aberrations such as witchcraft attacks on rivals" (1983:69). This latter power, associated with lateral and affinal relations, is accorded an external source, coming under the aegis of "forces of nature" as opposed to the "forces of society" that direct life within the house (ibid.; see also Sharp 1988:36). The Chamba relate comparable affinities or associations of patrikin with socially correct living and with human ancestors and associate matrikin with "the wild," animality, and the aberrations that can derive therefrom (breech birth; anomalous dentition when upper teeth are cut before lower, a condition related to animality; and witchcraft; Fardon 1990:31–32, 39–40).

9. Weiner recounts an interesting variation or limitation on this general practice of seeking ritual knowledge and assistance through affinal relationships among the Bimin-Kuskusmin who, loath to reach outward beyond the limits of the house (patrilineage) to affines for ritual needs, instead tap into the ritual power recognized in lineage women and specify sisters as ritual leaders and sources of spiritual powers. The sister in such a role is "perceived to embody androgynous elements that contain both male and female reproductive qualities" (Weiner 1982:63). See also Howell regarding the ritual powers of wives who are also regarded as metaphorical sisters among the Lio (1992:131).

10. Also noteworthy in this context is Sahlins's comment regarding western Polynesian societies in which primary economic and political control is reserved for the paternal line while " 'descendants of the woman,' although excluded from succession, retain a ritual authority at once indispensable and inimical to those who would rule" (1976:28, 32 n. 24). Likewise among the Kédang (eastern Indonesia), spiritual authority is held by wife-givers while elders of the house exercise temporal authority (Barnes 1974:275–276, 251–252). Half a world away "it was from his wife that the Kwakiutl male acquired ceremonial privileges so central to his social standing" (Jonaitis 1991:12).

11. This interpretation constitutes a variation on the "center" versus "periphery" perspective of some "dual organizations." See Maybury-Lewis (1979:234–235); Seeger (1981:66–67); Drummond (1981:639–640).

12. "The distinction between us (*kwoiyi*) and others (*kukidi*) runs through the Suyá social universe. The contrast between them has a variety of referents which depend on context. It can be used to indicate Suyá as opposed to non-Suyá, consanguines as opposed to affines, and close consanguines as opposed to more distant ones" (Seeger 1981:122; see also 31–35 for a summary of Suyá dual organization).

13. Hocart further stressed that "the most persistent feature of the dual organization is not intermarriage, but mutual ministration" (1970:284).

14. Such ritual roles also can be exceedingly important as a means to identify and define the corporateness of affines relative to the corporateness of the house. It is sometimes the case that "affinal relations, once the immediate dues of marriage are discharged, are most specifically defined by potential funeral obligations" (Fardon 1990:108 regarding the Chamba).

15. See ethnographic details in Macintyre (1989:139); Chowning (1989: 100–106, 120–122); Pauwels (1985:135–136); Watson (1958:138); Murdock (1934:313); Hoskins (1987:186–189); Maybury-Lewis (1974:281); Kan (1986:195, 196, 1989:24, 151–155, 242); Weiner (1976:62–64); Barnes (1974:176, 179–180).

16. This interpretation, in which the categories of house and cosmological Outside, of living and dead, are bridged by affines, is influenced by Terence Turner's structural interpretation of *rites de passage* in which "the elementary structure of *rites de passage* identified by Van Gennep is really composed of a pair of cross-cutting binary contrasts. These can be conceived as intersecting vertical and horizontal axes. The horizontal axis consists of the contrast between the two categories (e.g., 'boy' and 'man') between which the passage takes place. The vertical axis comprises the relationship between this pair of categories and the higher-level transformational principles that regulate the passage between them. The point is that the structure of *rites de passage* models both of these axes simultaneously, in a way that defines each as a function of the other. The rites of separation and aggregation, in other words, mark the vertical (interlevel) separation between the level at which the initial and final social states or status-identities of the transition are defined and the higher level comprised by the principle of transformation between them, as well as the horizontal (intralevel) separation from the first of the two statuses and aggregation with the second. The liminal base of the ritual, as this implies, is the direct expression of the higher level of transcendent, transformational principles which form the ground and mechanism of the social transition in question. . . . the basic interpretation of liminal rites . . . is that they are an integral part of *processes of structuring . . .*" (1977:68, 70). The structural implications of higher-level affinal liminality, which relates affines to cosmological beings, particularly the ancestral dead, and to conditions of origins, will be addressed in Chapter 6 and in Part Two, where the transformational qualities and status of the category of affines will inform the structural position and qualities of political elites. The qualitative characteristics of affinal liminality are pursued here.

17. See also Fardon (1988:155–156) regarding consociation versus adsociation.

18. Myers provides an excellent discussion of the role of outside persons, including persons from geographically distant locales and affines, in initiation rites of the Pintupi of the Western Desert of Australia. With behaviors closely paralleling mortuary experiences, Pintupi parents mourn the impending ritual "deaths" of their sons and separate themselves from them as the boys enter the liminality of initiation. During this experience parents' places are taken by

"brothers-in-law" who protectively and benevolently guide and assist the boys in the ritual passage from boyhood to marriageable adult (1986:228–236).

19. In the same sense, noninitiation constitutes a state of deprivation or subordination relative to jural positions of the house or polity (Lévi-Strauss 1993:45).

20. In directly parallel fashion, the more fleeting conditions of communitas-imbued liminality experienced by initiates prior to their return to society may also be associated with conditions of death (V. Turner 1979:236; Eliade 1959a: 188–190; van Gennep 1960:75, 81, 114), or the role of initiators may be associated with the dead (Lévi-Strauss 1993:45).

21. It is also tempting to speculate whether, in the historical development of cultural institutions, conditions of group communitas may have preceded development of the house as the focal corporate social entity. If so, the assignment of communitas to settings or groups jurally, temporally, or cosmographically "beyond" the house (such as initiation rites, affines, the dead), can be interpreted as the historical result of the development and emergence of the house as a social entity with its own distinctive internal structures that has pushed conditions of communitas aside or confined them to settings, circumstances, and relationships outside itself. This speculation is fueled by Ingold's argument that hunting and gathering societies are *not* significantly structured by the obligations of kinship relations but by collective conditions of companionship, sharing, and "face-to-face" relationships (1987:116–117). It is encouraged, too, by Myers's discussion of the character of the local camp or "mob" in Australia, in which corporate identity is contingent (rather than enduring) and people form recognized social groups essentially through the sharing of activities. (Local leaders gain prestige by successfully sustaining a "mob" at their location.) These local camps can be socially fragile and easily dispersed, but while they last, they are sustained primarily by "positive feelings" embodied in exchange (1986:164–166).

22. "... in some myths of the Jikany tribes [of the Nuer] the leopard-skin [insignium of priestly office] was given by the ancestors of the [territorially] dominant [agnatic] lineages to their *maternal uncles* that they might serve as tribal priests" (Evans-Pritchard, quoted in Turner 1969:119).

23. In this respect, beauty contrasts with dominance, "a dynamic process *internal* to the whole" (Turner 1984:359).

6. ORIGINS

1. "A *place* is a social construct; a location only becomes a place when significance is conferred on it" (Turner 1988:421). As Myers notes, with reference to the Pintupi, "It is activity that creates places, giving significance to impervious matter" (1986:54). More specifically, as Vansina indicates, "The most important spaces were linked to the spot of creation, having temporal as well as spatial value" (1985:125; see also Rodman 1992).

2. For ethnographic examples see Kelly (1985:171); Evens (1984:327); Burton (1983:110–113); Pomponio (1992:96, 97); Parkin (1991:37, 227–228);

Metcalf (1982:216–218); Fortes (1945:219, 208); Dieterlen (1973:634–637); Turner (1988:429).

3. The people of Tanimbar include stands of long-lived trees in the "estates" that define their houses and their histories. Many other cultures do the same, and references to sacred groves as ritual centers that are associated with house ancestors, and especially house founders, are numerous in the literature (e.g., Brain 1979:397; Winter 1956:123; Fortes 1945:79, 219; McAnany 1995:75–77). It has been suggested by Rosenberg (1990:410–412) that identification of stands of trees with particular kin or local groups may have been instrumental in the processes of sedentism, which historically led to the original development of houses as corporate groups.

4. The comparison between prior house origins and first-principle origins that I suggest here has been stated before in slightly different terms by other researchers. Goldman, for example, notes that Cubeo phratries (clusters of descent groups) are sanctioned "not from descent from a common ancestor but emergence from a common place" (1963:96); and Myers, discussing the cultural creation of the landscape in Pintupi country, distinguishes between "historical" actions of humans and "transhistorical" actions by mythological personages of the Dreaming (1986:55). Barnes sees the contrast in terms of two aspects of government, temporal (concerned with corporate responsibility) and spiritual (concerned with life-forces and well-being) (1974:251–253). See also Evens's (1984:324) distinction between "first in time" and "first in importance" (note 11 below).

5. See also Dieterlen (1973:643–644) regarding the river Niger and its sacred sites as related to the body of an original creator being.

6. A comparable sense of timelessness underlies the significance of Mecca as a dreamed-of (though rarely actualized) pilgrimage site for West African Muslims living in the Sudan (Yamba 1992:110, 115, 116, 118). For these pilgrims, first-principle origins are associated with future time as well as with past time, for "the past and the future have the same ontological status, both being conceived as absolute and unchanging in accordance with the will of God" (116).

7. "Furthermore, psychologically, the second act no longer presents anything new; it marks the beginning of habituation" (van Gennep 1960:178).

8. "All that openeth the womb is mine," says the Book of Exodus (13:12).

9. Conditions associated with primacy could include celestial phenomena, particular cardinal directions and related movements (clockwise or counterclockwise), concepts of heat or light or of things that are elevated. See, for example, Gossen's (1979) description of the Chamula of highland Chiapas, Mexico.

10. Chernela goes on to note that the geographical locus of the births along the river also relates higher-ranked groups with the most abundant sources of fish (1993:93).

11. Evens discusses the subtleties conjoining concepts of seniority and the firstborn among the Nuer. "*Buth* . . . denotes 'first' as in 'first-born' and 'leader' or 'guide' . . . . But of course the idea of first directly entails that of second, third, and so on . . . . [*Buth*] confounds two logically distinct senses of 'first': 'first born' expresses the sense of 'first in time', whereas 'leader' or 'guide' expresses

the sense of 'first in importance'" (1984:324). Evens goes on to discuss the meaning implicit in the Western term "leader," typically construed as "authority," but which can also mean "moral supremacy" or guide and thereby conveys the idea of "author" in the sense of creator or original source, pointing to the context of "first in time" (ibid.).

12. Male captives were returned, allegedly reluctantly, to their own tribe.

13. This circumstance may also identify Europeans as Others related to the dead when they appear among a native population sans children and other kin and evidencing a certain discomforture or uneasiness about the strange world they are visiting. "Perhaps this is why both Mead and Fortune were asked on several occasions to transmit messages to the dead kin of Chambri" (Errington and Gewertz 1985:448).

14. McKinley's excellent essay should also be consulted for discussion of headhunting as an activity conducted in cosmological outside realms with intent to acquire essential fertility and other spiritual benefits necessary for social reproduction. Parallels with affines as outside strangers, sometimes enemies, who also are essential for social and ideological reproduction are obvious.

15. Positional succession means that when a person dies, a member of the same kin group (lineage, house) is designated to take his place in the kinship structure and to assume most of his kinship and (if the deceased has been married) affinal relations. See, for example, Gray (1953).

16. Raven once invited the dead to a feast but found they could not consume corporeal food, only food placed in the fire. This is why today ancestors are fed through the fire and living guests eat the rest of the food (Kan 1986:199, 1989:185–186).

17. Speaking of practices among Koyukon Athabascans (distant relatives of the Tlingit), Kan notes that when gifts of furs and blankets are given to guests, they are actually placed on the guests, and "their departure is described as the dead leaving their relatives forever" (1986:206, 1989:189; see also 257–285).

18. Kan further notes, with respect to the general role of affines and guests at times of death, that "the guests were also described as having given the mourners 'good fortune' or 'blessing' . . . , an act usually associated with benevolent superhuman creatures" (1989:155).

19. The ceremonial ministrations of affines are even more impressive when additional symbolic and cosmological aspects of the potlatch are considered. "Through transformation the participants in the Northwest Coast ritual became more than just individuals, and the dimensions of their actions transcended the limitations of everyday space and time. Each chief became the representative of his house and his house's spiritual authority, linked to the ancestral past by costume and to cosmic forces by paraphernalia such as Raven rattles and speaker's staffs. The careful placement of hosts and guests on mats around the room reproduced the geographical distribution of the world's villages—the social map recapitulating the cosmic map. The ceremonial house itself stood for the universe as a whole, its various rooms differentiating the various parts of the world, its vertical beams representing the axis mundi which links the human realm to the spirit realm, its great horizontal beam standing for the vault of the sky and the Milky Way. Thus, once the universe was contracted to the size of the cere-

monial house whose boundaries had been expanded until they were coterminous with the entire universe, the actions of distribution that occurred at feasts recapitulated the process of distribution at a cosmic level" (Walens 1982:188).

7. HIERARCHY

1. Hatch (1987) emphasizes the valuing of prestige or social honor and distinction as a fundamental source of hierarchy in all societies.

2. But see Woodburn (1982a) regarding the "assertive egalitarianism" of immediate-return hunting and gathering societies.

3. Harrison (1985a, 1990); Hill (1984); Kopytoff (1987:18, 35–36); Rousseau (1985); Claessen and van de Velde (1985:248–249); Johnson (1982); Brown (1991:402–403); Bloch (1989:137–151); Kelly (1993: chap. 7).

4. See, for example, Levy (1992) regarding the Hopi; Chernela (1993) regarding the Wanano; Collier (1988: chap. 3) regarding "ranked acephalous" societies; Woodward (1989) regarding the Ao Naga.

5. The Orayvi clan ranking also conforms with unequal economic prospects related to ecological stress.

6. A comparable distinction has been suggested by Kelly, who identifies a "moral hierarchy" in which "moral worthiness is ascribed to age and gender categories" and a "prestige hierarchy" that encompasses "achieved statuses that differentiate among members of certain age/gender categories" (1993:473). These distinctions appear to be similar to "exclusive" or qualitative hierarchies and "inclusive" or quantitative hierarchies, respectively.

7. This concept is by no means foreign to Western philosophy (Dumont 1982:221–222; Aristotle 1995: chap. 5). Indeed, the first meaning of "hierarchy" in *Webster's New International Dictionary* refers to "divine order," specifically, "a rank or order of holy beings, especially of angels"; also "dominion or authority in sacred things." A cosmic hierarchy also informed the structure and valuations accorded the medieval Great Chain of Being (Lovejoy 1942). In Renaissance thought such cosmic order was regarded as the basis of well-being and cosmic disorder as the cause of evils and commotions; "take but degree away, untune that string, and, hark, what discord follows!" (Shakespeare, *Troilus and Cressida*, 1:3, ll. 108–110). In Dante's terms, "all things whatsoever observe a mutual order; and this is the form that maketh the universe like unto God" (Paradiso, 1:103, quoted in Burckhardt 1987:86). The sentiment may be implied, too, in the well-known hymn "All Things Bright and Beautiful," which proclaims that "the rich man in his castle / the poor man at his gate / God made them high and lowly / and ordered their estate."

8. Myers is speaking specifically of the hierarchy of human ritual generations that transmits knowledge of the Dreaming among the Pintupi.

9. If they were qualitatively identical to the house, they could not be in another cosmological realm.

10. Howard provides a comparable interpretation with respect to some aspects of gender relations among the Waiwai of Brazil. She notes that, since men

pursue hunting and women agriculture, men are linked to more spatially distant forests and women to nearby gardens. As a result, men in general traverse greater distances than women, "both outward and upward, signalling the mastery of powers that are more difficult to control, more dangerous, and more potent because more foreign (logically and spatially) than humankind." Consequently, men have greater power over people and resources, exercising control in public politics, while women deal with domestic household affairs. "This aspect of male/female relations is conceptualized socially and spatially as a hierarchical differentiation" (1991:61). See also Myers (1986), regarding the hierarchy of initiated and uninitiated persons among the Pintupi, and Godelier (1986:136–137) with respect to the related social hierarchies of men/women: initiated men/uninitiated men: dead (ancestors)/living: sun-moon/humans, recognized by the Baruya of New Guinea.

11. Exclusive hierarchies referencing distinctive contexts of origins can be found in dual-organization societies, too. The relationship between the moieties described by Crocker (1969) for the Bororo seems to express an "exclusive" form of hierarchy in that the two moieties, as ranked halves, differ qualitatively with respect to the natures of their respective ancestors. The founding culture heroes of Bororo society were members of only one moiety, and only that moiety originally possessed the most prestigious ritual "rights," though they gave them later to the second moiety. However, the "original" moiety still "owns" important spirits, which they allow the "second" moiety to represent. The original moiety thus seems to be associated with ultimate origins while the second looks to the first as source of important prior origin attributes.

12. There seems to be at least one other way in which contexts of origins may inform ranking. Some noncentralized societies recognize multiple sources of prior house origins and rank house units according to their respective origin points. The Manambu, for example, ceremonially rank descent groups with respect to the relative prestige accorded the different sources (other neighboring Sepik River societies) from whom the descent groups received their rituals and ceremonial appurtenances (Harrison 1987:498, 502–505). This condition may apply within a single house, too, as on Choiseul Island, where a core group of virilocal men who trace descent from the ancestral founder of the descent group solely through men, and thus are said to be "born of men," hold primacy over persons "born of women," meaning offspring of house women for whom no bride price was paid and whose husbands reside uxorilocally. These "secondary" members hold only limited rights in the property and affairs of the house and "live under" the authority of those "born of men" (Scheffler 1965: 46–47, 100–101).

13. A parallel in the animal realm may be seen in Ingold's recognition that when humans encounter animal beings in myth, or when the living hunter encounters his prey, the animal being is regarded not as a particular beast but as an archetypal representative of the animal "master" or "guardian" who holds a higher outside order or rank relative to the hunter. The imagery of the animal master as the affinal "father-in-law" of the hunter affirms the parallel (Ingold 1987:247, 251).

14. I prefer the phrase "wife-receivers" to the more commonly used "wife-takers" in this context since, as the discussion will indicate, the latter phrase may also be used in a separate setting of affinal superiority.

15. See also Turner (1979:160); Harris (1962:70); Myers (1986:174); Valeri (1994:15–16); Errington and Gewertz (1986:102); and also Collier (1988) regarding "unequal bridewealth" societies.

16. Woodward also makes clear the cosmological structuring that parallels the affinal hierarchy in this ethnographic case. "The ancestors of the sky-world occupy a position structurally analogous to that of wife-givers, while those of the underworld are analogous to wife-takers. There must be two lands of the dead because the living must have both superior and inferior extrahuman relationships" (1989:127).

17. In this context bridewealth frequently stands as a replacement for the first-principle mechanism (wife) to assure that the wife-givers will be able to obtain wives for themselves or serves as compensation for a related sense of loss (Lévi-Strauss 1969a:466–471; Vansina 1990:107–109; Collier 1988:146; Kelly 1993:449–450).

18. Turner (1984); Crocker (1969, 1979:299–300); Traube (1989:323); Hinnant (1989:69, 71); Errington (1987:432–433); Maybury-Lewis (1989b:112). See also note 11 above.

19. It seems reasonable to assume, too, that the explicitly cosmological structurings that are offered in native systems of thought as explanations for the existence of hierarchical dualisms (e.g., between "upper" and "lower" moieties; Dillon and Abercrombie 1988:66–67) are also expected to encompass asymmetries in affinal relations.

20. Kelly also offers an excellent explanation of how the beneficent communitas quality of affinal/lateral relations can be squared with the demands of the superordinate position also held by affinal relatives (1985:220–221).

21. Included here are the conditions that "the upper levels of the system . . . comprise the generative principles and . . . the 'common ground' of the discrete categories and relations comprising the lower levels"; that the "upper levels will, in general terms, be seen from the standpoint of the lower levels as standing to them in a relation of becoming to being, generalized potential to specific realization, dynamic to static, and transcendent to immanent. The upper level will also tend to be seen, from the standpoint of the lower level, as both the indispensable, generative ground of the system, a source of powers of a higher order, and at the same time as a domain of relatively uncontrollable and therefore dangerous powers" (T. Turner 1977:57–58). In more specific terms, Judkins, discussing mortuary rites, notes the hierarchical nature of the relationship of general mourners to close relatives as mourners and sees a structural analogy with the "dominant-submissive classes" characteristic of other life-crisis rituals, such as initiation (1973:90). The hierarchical nature of affinal-house relations most likely underlies and conditions the particular roles often accorded affines relative to the house at such times.

22. "The hula-hula can also bestow cattle and livestock on its boroe, in hopes that the cattle will increase in fertility along with the recipient boroe" (Van der

Kroef 1954:848). To reverse the relationship between wife-receivers and wife-givers is unthinkable; "it is sacrilegious for the boroe to give land to its hula-hula." As the Batak put it, "Water cannot return to its source" (850).

8. QUALITIES AND ARISTOCRATS

1. Regarding "aristocracies" or "elites" as a concept for investigation in general, see Marcus (1983, 1992); Goodrich (1990:225–226); Nutini (1995:1–43). See also note 2 in Chapter 1 regarding my preference for the term "aristocracy" rather than "elite."

2. Compare Campbell (1989:110, 113) on thinking about shamans and shamanism in terms of role, quality, attribute, and act.

3. Aristocrats need not be demographically in the minority, though they often are. It must also be recognized and appreciated that the "superior" status of aristocracies could not be recognized as such without the contrastive polarity of the "commonness" of the general populace.

4. Victor Turner once asked, "Whatever happened to liminality in *post*tribal societies?" (1977:39). One answer is that liminality became part of the qualitative distinctiveness of aristocrats, as Turner himself recognized to some extent. See also comments by Terence Turner on liminality and processes of structuring (1977:70 n. 6).

5. Describing the communitas of shared aristocratic qualities, Sahlins says, "Alike in their ancestral claims to sacred life-giving powers, the sources of reproduction in every form, the several great chiefs too had their similar tabus, signs of their own consecrated status. Ultimately the sacred ancestral sources were one, converging on the same original. The sacred ali'i were thus united in a universal genealogy" (1990:42 regarding Hawaiian chiefs).

6. See Turner (1969:107) regarding the institutionalization of liminality and communitas in monastic and mendicant orders. Also van Gennep (1960:11, 191–192) regarding prolonged, autonomous, or "independent" states of temporary liminal identity, such as novitiates or betrothal.

7. Compare the identification of classic Maya nobility as "waterlily people," indicative of purity and productivity (Schele and Freidel 1990:94).

8. Compare the Tlingit word for aristocrat, "person of the village," and that for a person of low status, "person of the beach" or "person of the rocks" (Kan 1989:92–93; Moss 1993:641).

9. "The kingship is held by the royal lineage—a group which in many kingdoms traces its descent from the supposed founder of the town" (Lloyd 1965:100 regarding Nigerian kingdoms; Friedman 1975:173; Nutini 1995:62, 75, 86–87).

10. Positional succession refers to the practice in which the successor to a deceased individual assumes the name, social position, and social responsibilities of the deceased and is even addressed by kin terms appropriate to the deceased. When applied to the leadership of social or political entities, such as a lineage, positional succession means that however long the group has existed, the

founder is always present in the living incumbent who holds his name and that incumbent is always, by definition, sociologically senior among the living. See, for example, Cunnison (1957), Mitchell (1956:121–122); Watson (1958:145–159).

11. Only those who are "independent" or "complete" social persons can legitimately effect broader connections in space and time (Maquet 1961:162–163; Handler 1985:693–696; Errington 1987:423; Turner 1984:341, 358). As Parmentier points out with respect to Belau (Caroline Islands, Western Micronesia), "Only a high-ranking or wealthy person is daring enough to 'invent a path' or 'plant a relationship' not followed before—in fact, rank can be seen as the culturally constituted capacity to create 'types' of relations. Such action is normally thought to be more the domain of gods or heroic ancestors" (1987:114). In contrast, one common way of expressing commoners' subordinate status and "disconnection" from aristocrats identifies their inability to make such connections and, therefore, their perpetual dependency, including lack of privacy, comparable to that of children relative to parents, juniors relative to elders, or, for that matter, the living relative to house ancestors. Differential access to supernatural realms is, of course, found to greater or lessser degree in all societies (see Brown 1981:124 for one example).

12. The two noble houses are the Xahil family of the Cakchiquel Maya and the Canek family of the Quiché Maya.

13. Similarly, among the Tlingit, "aristocratic youngsters received special training in the sacred oral traditions of their lineage and clan. Only they were expected to know the complete (i.e., correct) versions of the origin myths of their matrilineal groups . . . " (Kan 1989:94).

14. "One is born a Brahman, but one must learn to act like a Brahman" (Van Gennep 1960:105); see also Valeri (1990:179, 181) regarding genealogical birth chants as a way of "consecrating" a newborn noble in Hawaii.

15. In addition to such strictures in everyday life, other exceptional behaviors sometimes expected of chiefs and kings at installation ceremonies also dramatically separate the ruler from ordinary society. These actions could involve committing incest with mother or sister, engaging in ritual cannibalism, or killing a kinsperson (Muller 1981:241–242; MacGaffey 1986:176).

16. In reality, "aristocratic families could 'wash away' their children's blemishes by giving away property" (Kan 1989:311 n. 26).

17. Aristocratic approaches to death seem either to deny that death can affect high nobility (as when chiefly deaths are hidden from the populace or only announced euphemistically or when rulers are killed before death can occur naturally) or to associate nobility with the process of death as a transitional or liminal state of being to an exceptional degree, as when aristocrats, as war captives, are subjected to prolonged death experiences that they are expected to face (transcend?) with suprahuman dignity. In either case, aristocratic deaths are expected to differ qualitatively from the normal expirations of ordinary people (or to ennoble ordinary people who are faced with comparable situations—e.g., war captives or women who die in childbirth). The common practice of interring aristocratic remains with sacrificed retainers or spouses is also interesting in light of the common practice whereby living Others, such as affines, ritually

prepare and escort the corpse from the house to whatever fate awaits in the beyond. For elites of centralized societies the escorts seem to be expected to accompany the deceased into the other realm more literally or more completely.

18. In considering the qualities that differentiate aristocracies from commoners, I consider these types of behaviors more informative than the higher material standard of living—better diet, larger houses, etc.—also evidenced by aristocrats and frequently noted ethnographically. These I view in general more as derivative, rather than definitive, of aristocratic qualities per se.

19. "[Religious man] does not consider himself to be *truly man* except in so far as he imitates the gods, the culture heroes, or the mythical ancestors" (Eliade 1959b:99–100).

20. The close identification of persons of political-ideological authority with deceased ancestors and with associated qualities of liminality and beneficence is also commonplace in noncentralized societies, where house elders or senior ceremonial leaders are usually accorded such identification. Rowlands (1985: 51–52) provides an excellent description of such from equatorial Africa, and Rubinstein describes how senior ritualists among the Malo (Melanesia) could approach "the status of a living ancestor, a man so imbued with power through his connection with the supernatural that he had begun to slough off his earthly nature" (1981:139). I do not consider this material in this study since I am interested in the identification not of individuals per se but of entire groups of persons or of individuals chosen from select high-status houses, as living ancestors. In so doing I also downplay the fact that in a given polity aristocratic descent lines and houses often vary in the extent to which they are expected or allowed to express various distinguishing sumptuary laws and thus vary in the extent to which they are "ancestral." This is an important point but not immediately relevant to my argument.

21. Regarding the king's consumption of food in private, and in light of later discussion, Carlson's further explanation is very interesting: "At the level of the secular order, human beings ate in the presence of others; the *omukama* ate in private, *secluded as women were just after marriage*, to foster the idea that he was not in need of normal sustenance" (Carlson 1993:328, my emphasis).

9. ARISTOCRATS AND AFFINES

1. The same condition may hold in noncentralized polities, too, especially if membership in kin groups is rather flexible. On Karavar Island (Melanesia), for example, "a big man is defined by his ability to draw followers to him. He is regarded by his followers as their matrilineal senior—usually their mother's brother. . . . Because they are his followers, they are his kinsmen; they are not his followers because they are his kinsmen" (Errington 1974:35, 42).

2. The affinal relationships established by commoner houses with other common groups in centralized polities, which are important for the houses involved in ways discussed in previous chapters and which prefigure the significance of aristocratic alliances, are often less important in broader political terms and will not be considered further here.

3. ". . . values must be looked at as strategic components of attempts to contrive an image of the interaction. Values . . . may . . . be an expression of the terms within which one party wishes the interaction to be viewed" (Cohen and Comaroff 1976:102).

4. It can be further postulated that, in the view of commoners of centralized polities, the categories of Others inhabiting the cosmological environment include aristocrats, ancestors, and affines. This in turn suggests comparison with the categories of cosmological Others posited for noncentralized societies as animals, the dead, and other people. Comparing the two lists suggests that the major contrast is found in animals versus aristocrats as expressions of Others, a parallel perhaps more appropriately glossed as Masters of Animals versus Aristocrats (Ingold 1987:247). This comparison opens possibilities that go beyond this work.

5. Prior house origins for Nuer lineages were accessed by certain cattle (those whose milk production supported the household) owned by the men of the lineage. "A man establishes contact with the ghosts and spirits through his cattle. If one is able to obtain a history of each cow in a kraal, one obtains at the same time not only an account of all the kinship links and affinities of the owners but also of all their mystical connexions. Cows are dedicated to the spirits of the lineage of the owner and of his wife and to any personal spirit that has at some time possessed either of them. Other beasts are dedicated to ghosts of the dead. By rubbing ashes along the back of a cow or ox one may get in touch with the spirit or ghost associated with it and ask it for assistance" (Evans-Pritchard, quoted in Kelly 1985:232).

6. Complete discussion of the Nuer also involves the Dinka, many of whom are Nuer sister's sons. Kelly discusses Dinka "mother's brother"/"sister's son" alliances, both in general and as they pertain politically to the two basic types of Dinka clans, "priestly or spear-master clans" and "commoner or warrior clans," whose relationship should also be "one of matrilateral kinship" (1985:172–181, 184, 219).

7. For example, named houses assemble their "younger brother" unnamed houses to participate in first-fruit observances that honor ancestors ("feed the dead") whose productive powers provide the crops for everyone (McKinnon 1991:102).

8. At the top of the affinal ordering among named houses, "the differentiation between male and female, wife-giver and wife-taker, superior and inferior, source and issue are recomposed into a transcendent image of unity" and of origin (McKinnon 1991:127, 133, 226, 280–281; see also Davenport 1994).

9. Unnamed houses also are linked as wife-givers to other unnamed houses, but these alliances are deemed to be more particularistic and more ephemeral in nature. Having no inherent permanence, they also have little hierarchical relevance and "bear no relation to the founding of the fixed order of the world" (McKinnon 1991:106, 104, 223, 225, 226).

10. The same result—hierarchy reformulated as dominance—can also come about not only when affinity is neutralized and superceded but also when the negative side of aristocratic affinal supremacy is actively stressed, as among the Bamileke of Cameroon, when chiefs gave women in marriage to sons, servants,

and impoverished subjects without requiring a return of bridewealth so that the husbands would perpetually be in their debt in what amounted to "a vast pawnship system" linked to the slave trade. "When the obligations of affines were not honoured, marriage alliance degenerated into a kind of transaction without social responsibility akin to trading for profit where individual self-gain takes precedence over the morality of social relations." Such moral bankruptcy on the part of powerful "marriage lords" was further backed up by threats of sorcery directed toward husbands' families (Rowlands 1985:58–62).

11. In light of the ambiguity inherently surrounding the ideological (especially first-principle) basis for wife-taking aristocratic superiority, it is noteworthy that in Kayan mythology the ruling stratum (maren) is portrayed as originally the youngest and the weakest of four mythical sons (representing the four social categories), who was a loser in the original cosmological competition for authority. Though loser, however, the first maren was elevated to power by the primordial father to punish the arrogance of the original winner, the eldest son, or dipen, who henceforth would be reduced to dependent slavery and serve his youngest brother (maren) who, in his demonstrated weakness, clearly needed someone to look after him (Rousseau 1979:219). The myth thus ascribes legitimate authority to the maren but only by default, not as inherently deserved, and denies legitimate authority to dipens (the lowest or most extreme form of commoner) also by default (poor behavior), though admitting that it is inherently deserved.

12. The annual harvest gift presented to a woman's husband is known as *urigubu*. Powell notes that twelve marriages was noteworthy (especially given fifty years of missionary teaching) but not an exceptional achievement. In former times "the Tabalu *guyau* of Omarakana cluster could have acquired forty or more wives during a successful political career" (1960:136).

13. Origins-related *kula* valuables may also be displayed or distributed at mortuary feasts. In the Trobriands the body of the deceased is covered with *kula* valuables for a few hours (Brunton 1975:549, 550, 557 n. 7). See also Dalton (1996:399–400) regarding the identical nature of bridewealth and death payments among the Rawa.

14. Mambwe aristocratic-commoner marriages overall also include opportunities for commoner men to establish alliances with chiefly daughters and sisters. The Mambwe, in fact, seem primarily intent on attaching commoners to royal authority by whatever kin tie is convenient (Watson 1958:18, 71–77, 82, 83, 136, 137, 143).

15. Foreign chiefs requesting rain—or peace—will also send "wives" to the Lovedu queen. The rainmaking powers accorded the queen seem to identify her with first-principle origins: "During life, she is not merely the Transformer of the Clouds, but she is regarded as the changer of the seasons and guarantor of their cyclic regularity; when she dies, the seasons are out of joint and drought is inevitable. Her very emotions affect the rain: if she is dissatisfied, angry, or sad, she cannot work well, and in 1935, when the first rains did not come till December, the drought was attributed to her being upset at her daughter's liaison with a commoner" (Krige and Krige 1943:271).

16. Not to be overlooked are ranked societies in the Americas, such as the

Hopi community of Orayvi, where "marriage alliances tend to integrate the body politic by uniting households of different rank" (Levy 1992:68), or the chiefdoms of the Southeast, where members of aristocratic houses married commoners and where it is likely that noblemen served as resident administrators in the commoner communities where they had married commoner women (Anderson 1994b:89).

17. Polygyny frequently allows chiefs to select great wives from appropriate aristocratic houses and secondary wives from commoners (Fürer-Haimendorf 1969:57–58; Cohen 1976:204–205).

18. "The ruler cannot rule without a mother" (Claessen 1981:78).

19. Poor people had to marry within their own village (Elmendorf 1971: 361). Well-born individuals were, ideally, those whose parents came from different villages.

20. Lienhardt explains further that "it would be unfitting for the king, who greatly transcends commoners, to appear as wife's father [i.e., as wife-provider] in relation to a commoner [as wife-taker]" (1955:35). According to Lienhardt, the rank exogamy of royal men and the single status of "male" royal women, when considered together, express a triumph over matrilateral kin and the importance of the principle of the agnatic integrity of the royal house.

21. The Shilluk approach to the "problem" of the connubial status of royal women is not uncommon, but there are others. In Tonga a particularly interesting solution has been found by maintaining immigrant lineages as "foreigners" with whom royal daughters may marry. This approach removes daughters' affinal houses from active political contention (as "foreigners" they are considered ineligible) but recognizes and appropriates the cosmological value of these outside affinals by identifying them as ritual attendants (Sahlins 1976:43, 44–45). See also Parmentier (1987:244–245) regarding Belau (Caroline Islands) for a variation in which the highest-ranked village exchanges women exogamously but is able to deny the alliances that might be expected to follow, thus maintaining a fiction of consanguineal isolation that protects its rank. Other examples of how ranked polities approach the common problem of handling several affinal patterns at once may be found in Kemp (1978); Errington (1987); McKinnon (1991:26–28); Goldman (1970:52–53).

22. These associations with origins are in addition to whatever first-principle origins may be ritually accessed by commoners, perhaps as preexisting autochthonous inhabitants of a region. Commoners' own more limited prior house origins remain of interest only to them.

23. The same can also be said for tribal Big Men (Brown 1970:102).

10. STRUCTURE AND COMMUNITAS

1. For particulars and further discussion of these types of contact, see Helms (1993, 1988).

2. "A particular lineage is recognized as having the right to provide the ruler, and this claim is supported by a legend . . . associating them with the origins of

the nation; their founding ancestor is believed to have first entered the country over which they rule, emerging from the earth or from a river, or descending from the sky, or to have led the people there from some other place, miraculously overcoming difficulties on the way" (Mair 1965:113 regarding polities of east and south Africa).

3. Regarding claims to alien origins for rulers, Horton also opines that "one suspects that they are as mythical as the claims to a divine aura often made by the same rulers" and that they are made for the same reasons (1972:116)—that is, to establish distinctive qualitative value. Some migration and conquest scenarios, however, may be based on actual historical events.

4. These conditions are often described in origins myths and tales in personalized, archetypical metaphors concerning the arrival of an *individual* founder. These stories frequently constitute stylistic reference to the actual arrival of a kin *group* (Kopytoff 1987:23). For example, among the Mambwe of Rhodesia, the founder of the royal clan was said to be a stranger from the west who arrived among settled cultivators as a hunter and married the daughters of local houses. Present chiefs are descendants of those unions (Watson 1958:13–15).

5. Regarding fissioning in noncentralized societies, see Cohen (1981) and Carneiro (1967:239–240, 1987). Nzimiro (1965:122–123) and Trouwborst 1965:170–171) discuss various factors that encourage mobility and migration in centralized and noncentralized societies.

6. Harrison decribes how "the fission of a descent group [among the Manambu of New Guinea] is an asymmetrical process in which an expanding junior branch secedes, taking important entitlements with it. It is the principle of seniority that creates the asymmetry. As long as the group's seniors are in control of the group's secret lore and ritual entitlements, the group is likely to remain intact. But if these entitlements escheat to a junior branch, the scene is set for fission, because it is only by fission that the juniors can legitimise their new status" (1990:126–127).

7. Other representative examples may be found in Goldman (1963:27–28, 34–37, 40–41), regarding satellite communities and sib centers among the Cubeo, and in Bean (1972:87–88), who discusses the Cahuilla of southern California.

8. Stone (1989) provides a thoughtful example of this type of political-ideological elaboration from the Classic Maya as it is evidenced on stelae relating lowland Maya (especially Piedras Negras) lords to Teotihuacan. Stone argues cogently that this connection with a powerful Mexican highlands polity served to "disconnect" or distance Maya lords from their subjects, thereby justifying "the implementation of an exclusive dynastic line which defines itself in terms of palpably different qualities not seen in the general population. These exotic qualities may include a prestigious nonlocal origin or affiliation" (153). Elite claims of foreign affiliation and identification continued to be used in the Post-Classic and Colonial eras as a means of political-ideological manipulation (167–169).

9. Miller emphasizes that the rich and powerful valued the loyalty of their dependents more than their labor, and therefore required periodic signs of respect

that promised prospective support more than immediate labor that would fill storehouses with surplus foods that would soon decompose (1988:47, 53).

10. The sacred relics of Mbundu chiefs included carved wooden figures linked with agricultural success and associated with rain and bodies of water (rivers, lakes) and small pieces of supernaturally charged iron.

11. "If possible, they took a wife from the lineage and awarded the original title to a biological son born of this marriage; they trusted him, and later his successors, to represent royal interests to their kinsmen and related lineages" (Miller 1976:77, 78).

12. This was not the name of an actual person but of the body of concepts that underlay the organization of the polity (Miller 1976:79).

13. ". . . the trick of history is to maintain both the invariance of structure (for example, that the position of the capital village in a district is a matter of timeless, cosmologically grounded legitimacy), and the value of temporal precedence (for example, that the chiefly line traces its migration back to a point prior to that of other, lower-ranking lines)" (Parmentier 1987:15).

14. In recognition of the potency of their autochthonous status, however, indigenous leaders were accorded high rank in Yao society because they represented the original expression of first-principle origins. Newcomers who arrived after the Yao invasion recognized the primacy of the Yao chiefs.

15. Among the Yao, as among numerous other nineteenth-century African polities, the rise of influential families also involved the acquisition of non-Yao women by raiding or by the slave trade. These women became junior wives to politically ambitious leaders and, in addition to providing labor, bore children to increase the size of their captors' houses. Since Yao society was traditionally matrilineal, a man's children by slave women belonged to his house (where they were referred to as "grandchildren") rather than his wife's and obeyed his authority rather than that of his wife's brothers (Alpers 1969:411–413).

16. Those who are ruled may view the dominant aristocracy in comparable terms, as do the Goba of Zambezi, who see their rulers as quintessential aliens and therefore in the same class of beings as slaves and wandering homeless ghosts (Kopytoff 1987:62).

17. It is tempting to see a parallel here, in general terms, between the manner in which the "chaos" of autochthonous existence is transformed into a "morally ordered" existence by the arrival of outside Others and the potentially "unlawful" (meaning immoral or "chaotic") conditions threatening any given house anywhere before it is affiliated with affinal Others who, by providing for proper (meaning moral) means for social reproduction, bring moral order into the life of the house. To the extent that migrants intermarry with autochthonous populations, the parallels are merged.

18. The consequences of failure to effect such structuration can be readily discerned in the unstable nature of the Turkish chieftaincies discussed by Lapidus (1990:33).

19. In Fairley's interpretation, which is complementary to mine, this description indicates both the subordinate status now accorded the *tshite* and the interdependence established between the *tshite* and the king, who become the cooperative parents of Ekie society (1989:297).

11. TANGIBLE DURABILITY

1. Exactly what constitutes "durability" or even "tangibility" is, at heart, defined by every society and may or may not fit Western ideas about these qualities.

2. Durable items like shells and metals may also be symbolic of bones. See, for example, Weiner (1992:60).

3. Alternatively, of course, while success in the acquisition of aristocratic wealth can signify enhanced connections with categories of cosmological Others, diminution of wealth can signify reduced connections and, correspondingly, reduced aristocratic potency.

4. Western contact may, however, bring changes and dislocations that increase the more malevolent side of contact with the supernatural. See, for example, Harms (1981) regarding Western trade, slaving, spirits, and witchcraft.

5. "Trade was carried out, with the emphasis no longer being placed on the drying of tears by gifts to console the soul, but rather upon the exchange of furs for the European commodities now so vital to the Indian existence. Consolation was no longer found in the reburial of loved ones, but rather in the receipt of rum and tobacco" (Nekich 1974:14).

6. Similarly, "firearms were most useful in contributing honorific explosions to funeral celebrations, and they could be displayed on graves, as were elephant tusks" (MacGaffey 1986:29 regarding the BaKongo of Zaire).

7. Variety may be favored to allow aristocrats access to new styles or types of goods not yet available to the wider populace. See, for example, Miller (1988:71, 82–83, 125). Concerning abundance, Sahlins notes that "the accumulation of deluxe items outran any possibility of personal consumption. The objective was thesaurization as much as display. The chiefs hoarded up the exotic returns of the sandalwood trade—quite to the point of waste. Fine cloths and Chinese curios were accumulated in unusable quantities; they lay moldering away in the storehouses until perhaps at the chief's death they were ritually set adrift in the ocean. Even if the goods were needed for some current purpose, the ali'i showed a certain disinclination to make any inroads on their stocks-on-hand, as if this could be taken as a sign of failing powers. They preferred in such cases to make additional purchases of the kinds of things they already possessed in superfluity" (Sahlins 1990:49 regarding Hawaii).

8. Concepts of what constitutes crafted or processed versus nonprocessed or natural may vary considerably, particularly from Western perceptions. See Helms (1993: chap. 9).

9. For an interesting variation on this theme consider the Siassi legend that attributes the mythical origins of all the types of wealth objects that the Siassi acquire on trading voyages to a primordial Tree of Wealth and Plenty (Pomponio 1992:46–50). Trees of life, of course, are frequently described as the original sources of plant and animal forms in general.

10. Bones themselves can also be "transformed" into other types of valuable products, as in the beliefs of some Africans that ashes of the bones of people sent off as slaves to the Land of the Dead returned as gunpowder (Miller 1988:86).

11. Ethnography also attests to the quantities of goods that can be produced

by hard-working spouses not only for daily domestic needs but also, and especially, for ceremonial occasions with political-ideological import for the house. To the extent that this work evidences processual, "coming into being" activities (e.g., raising animals or agricultural produce), this spousal labor is another example of the co-opting of the affinal first-principle world in support of the ambitions of the house to "bring into being" its own importance. Regarding access to wealth by trade with nonaffinal Others, this activity has the potential (especially if it is extensive, as in much European trade) to establish outside associations that may open paths to prominence by reducing, subverting, or transcending the preeminence of affinal connections (and of affinal legitimations, too) in pursuit of political goals (Golson 1982:112–113; Thune 1989:158; Rowlands 1985:59, 61–62; Miller 1988:96–97, 101–102).

12. See Helms (1993) for further discussion of artisans and crafting in this context.

13. In cosmologies where the spatial or cosmographical outside realm is defined in terms of the chaos of the uncontrolled (i.e., as wild, untamed, or "subhuman" relative to the house), the characteristics attributed to things derived therefrom may be defined in quite other terms. See, for example, Kent (1989:15) regarding wild versus domesticated animals or Karim (1981: chaps. 1 and 3) regarding why, in the opinion of the Ma'Betisék of Malaysia, plants and animals can be consumed as food.

12. CONCLUDING REMARKS

1. See also Bean (1977) regarding the parallel and complementary importance of concepts regarding supernatural power.

REFERENCES

Allen, Michael
  1981   Innovation, Inversion, and Revolution as Political Tactics in West
          Aoba. In *Vanuatu: Politics, Economics, and Ritual in Island Melane-
          sia,* ed. Michael Allen, 105–134. Sydney: Academic Press Australia.
  1984   Elders, Chiefs, and Big Men: Authority Legitimation and Political
          Evolution in Melanesia. *American Ethnologist* 11:20–41.

Almagor, Uri
  1989   The Dialectic of Generation Moieties in an East African Society. In
          *The Attraction of Opposites: Thought and Society in the Dualistic
          Mode,* ed. David Maybury-Lewis and Uri Almagor, 143–170. Ann
          Arbor: University of Michigan Press.

Alpers, Edward A.
  1969   Trade, State, and Society among the Yao in the Nineteenth Century.
          Journal of African History 10:405–420.
  1975   *Ivory and Slaves.* Berkeley: University of California Press.

Anderson, David G.
  1994a   Factional Competition and the Political Evolution of Mississippian

Chiefdoms in the Southeastern United States. In *Factional Competition and Political Development in the New World,* ed. Elizabeth M. Brumfiel and John W. Fox, 61–76. Cambridge: Cambridge University Press.

1994b *The Savannah River Chiefdoms: Political Change in the Late Prehistoric Southeast.* Tuscaloosa: University of Alabama Press.

Anderson, Martha G., and Christine Mullen Kreamer
1989 *Wild Spirits Strong Medicine: African Art and the Wilderness.* New York: Center for African Art/Seattle: University of Washington Press.

Appadurai, Arjun
1986 Is Homo Hierarchicus? *American Ethnologist* 13:745–761.

Appell, George N.
1976a The Cognitive Tactics of Anthropological Inquiry: Comments on King's Approach to the Concept of the Kindred. In *The Societies of Borneo: Explorations in the Theory of Cognatic Social Structure,* ed. G. N. Appell, 146–151. Washington, D.C.: American Anthropological Association.
1976b The Rungus: Social Structure in a Cognatic Society and Its Ritual Symbolization. In *The Societies of Borneo: Explorations in the Theory of Cognatic Social Structure,* ed. G. N. Appell, 66–86. Washington, D.C.: American Anthropological Association.

Arensberg, Conrad M.
1968 *The Irish Countryman.* New York: Natural History Press.

Århem, Kaj
1992 Dance of the Water People. *Natural History* 101 (no. 1):47–52.

Aristotle
1995 *The Politics,* trans. Ernest Barker. Oxford: Oxford University Press.

Armstrong, Robert G.
1980 The Dynamics and Symbolism of Idoma Kingship. In *West African Culture Dynamics: Archaeological and Historical Perspectives,* ed. B. K. Swartz, Jr., and Raymond E. Dumett, 393–411. The Hague: Mouton.

Bamberger, Joan
1974 Naming and the Transmission of Status in a Central Brazilian Society. *Ethnology* 13:363–378.

Bargatsky, Thomas
1985 Person Acquisition and the Early State in Polynesia. In *Development*

and Decline: The Evolution of Sociopolitical Organization, ed.
Henri J. M. Claessen, Pieter van de Velde, and M. Estellie Smith,
290–310. South Hadley, Mass.: Bergin and Garvey.

Barnard, Alan, and James Woodburn

    1988   Introduction. In *Hunters and Gatherers 2: Property, Power, and
Ideology,* ed. Tim Ingold, David Riches, and James Woodburn, 4–
31. Oxford: Berg.

Barnes, R. H.

    1974   *Kédang: A Study of the Collective Thought of an Eastern Indone-
sian People.* Oxford: Clarendon Press.

    1979   Lord, Ancestor, and Affine: An Austronesian Relationship Name.
NUSA 7:19–34.

    1985   Hierarchy without Caste. In *Contexts and Levels: Anthropological
Essays on Hierarchy,* ed. R. H. Barnes, Daniel de Coppet, and R. J.
Parkin, 8–20. Oxford: Journal of the Anthropological Society of
Oxford.

Barraud, Cécile

    1985   The Sailing-Boat: Circulation and Values in the Kei Islands, Indone-
sia. In *Contexts and Levels: Anthropological Essays on Hierarchy,*
ed. R. H. Barnes, Daniel de Coppet, and R. J. Parkin, 117–130. Oxford: Journal of the Anthropological Society of Oxford.

Battaglia, Debbora

    1990   *On the Bones of the Serpent.* Chicago: University of Chicago Press.

Bean, Lowell John

    1972   *Mukat's People: The Cahuilla Indians of Southern California.*
Berkeley: University of California Press.

    1977   Power and Its Application in Native California. In *The Anthropol-
ogy of Power: Ethnographic Studies from Asia, Oceania, and the
New World,* ed. Raymond D. Fogelson and Richard N. Adams,
117–129. New York: Academic Press.

Beck, Lois

    1990   Tribes and the State in Nineteenth- and Twentieth-Century Iran. In
Tribes and State Formation in the Middle East, ed. Philip S. Khoury
and Joseph Kostiner, 185–225. Berkeley: University of California
Press.

Becker, Ernest

    1975   *Escape from Evil.* New York: Free Press.

Beidelman, Thomas O.

    1971   Nuer Priests and Prophets: Charisma, Authority, and Power among the Nuer. In *The Translation of Culture: Essays to E. E. Evans-Pritchard,* ed. Thomas O. Beidelman, 375–416. London: Tavistock Publications.

Berger, John
  1985   Why Look at Animals? In *The Language of the Birds: Tales, Texts, and Poems of Interspecies Communication,* ed. David M. Guss, 275–287. San Francisco: North Point Press.

Berger, Peter L.
  1967   *The Sacred Canopy: Elements of a Sociological Theory of Religion.* Garden City, N.Y.: Doubleday.

Berger, Peter L., and Thomas Luckmann
  1966   *The Social Construction of Reality.* Garden City, N.Y.: Doubleday.

Berreman, Gerald D.
  1978   Scale and Social Relations. *Current Anthropology* 19:225–245.
  1981   Social Inequality: A Cross-Cultural Analysis. In *Social Inequality: Comparative and Developmental Approaches,* ed. Gerald D. Berreman, 3–40. New York: Academic Press.

Béteille, André
  1977   *Inequality among Men.* Oxford: Basil Blackwell.

Binford, Sally R.
  1968   A Structural Comparison of Disposal of the Dead in the Mousterian and the Upper Paleolithic. *Southwestern Journal of Anthropology* 24:139–154.

Bird-David, Nurit
  1990   The Giving Environment: Another Perspective on the Economic System of Gatherer-Hunters. *Current Anthropology* 31:189–196.
  1992   Beyond "The Original Affluent Society." *Current Anthropology* 33:25–47.

Bishop, Charles A.
  1991   Northern Algonquian Resource Management. Paper presented at the annual meeting of the American Anthropological Association, Chicago.

Blackwood, Peter
  1981   Rank, Exchange, and Leadership in Four Vanuatu Societies. In *Vanuatu: Politics, Economics, and Ritual in Island Melanesia,* ed. Michael Allen, 35–84. New York: Academic Press.

Blau, Peter M.
   1977   *Inequality and Heterogeneity: A Primitive Theory of Social Structure.* New York: Free Press.

Bloch, Maurice
   1971   *Placing the Dead: Tombs, Ancestral Villages, and Kinship Organization in Madagascar.* London: Seminar Press.
   1973   The Long Term and the Short Term: The Economic and Political Significance of the Morality of Kinship. In *The Character of Kinship,* ed. Jack Goody, 75–87. Cambridge: Cambridge University Press.
   1974   Symbols, Song, Dance, and Features of Articulation *or* Is Religion an Extreme Form of Traditional Authority? *Archives Européennes de Sociologie* 15:55–81.
   1982   Death, Women, and Power. In *Death and the Regeneration of Life,* ed. Maurice Bloch and Jonathan Parry, 211–230. Cambridge: Cambridge University Press.
   1989   *Ritual, History, and Power: Selected Papers in Anthropology.* London: Athlone Press.
   1992   *Prey into Hunter: The Politics of Religious Experience.* Cambridge: Cambridge University Press.

Bloch, Maurice, and Jonathan Parry
   1982   Introduction. In *Death and the Regeneration of Life,* ed. Maurice Bloch and Jonathan Parry, 1–44. Cambridge: Cambridge University Press.

Bonte, Pierre
   1981   Kinship and Politics: The Formation of the State among the Pastoralists of the Sahara and the Sahel. In *The Study of the State,* ed. Henri J. M. Claessen and Peter Skalnik, 35–57. The Hague: Mouton.

Bozzoli de Wille, Maria E.
   1975   Birth and Death in the Belief System of the Bribri Indians of Costa Rica. Ph.D. diss., University of Georgia, Athens.

Brain, James L.
   1979   Ancestors as Elders in Africa—Further Thoughts. Reprinted in *Reader in Comparative Religion: An Anthropological Approach,* 4th ed. Ed. William A. Lessa and Evon Z. Vogt, 393–400. New York: Harper & Row.

Brown, James A.
   1985   The Mississippian Period. In *Ancient Art of the American Woodland Indians,* by David S. Brose, James A. Brown, and David W. Penney, 93–146. New York: Harry N. Abrams/Detroit Institute of Arts.

Brown, Michael F.
1991   Beyond Resistance: A Comparative Study of Utopian Renewal in Amazonia. *Ethnohistory* 38:388–413.

Brown, Paula
1964   Enemies and Affines. *Ethnology* 3:335–356.
1970   Chimbu Transactions. *Man* 5:99–117.

Brown, Peter
1981   *The Cult of the Saints.* Chicago: University of Chicago Press.

Brumfiel, Elizabeth M.
1994   Factional Competition and Political Development in the New World: An Introduction. In *Factional Competition and Political Development in the New World,* ed. Elizabeth M. Brumfiel and John W. Fox, 3–13. Cambridge: Cambridge University Press.

Brunton, Ron
1975   Why Do the Trobriands Have Chiefs? *Man* 10:544–558.

Bulmer, Ralph
1967   Why Is the Cassowary Not a Bird? A Problem of Zoological Taxonomy among the Karam of the New Guinea Highlands. *Man* 2:5–25.

Burckhardt, Titus
1987   *Mirror of the Intellect.* Albany: State University of New York Press.

Burton, John W.
1983   Same Time, Same Space: Observations on the Morality of Kinship in Pastoral Nilotic Societies. *Ethnology* 22:109–119.

Campbell, Alan Tormaid
1989   *To Square with Genesis: Causal Statements and Shamanic Ideas in Wayãpí.* Iowa City: University of Iowa Press.

Campbell, Shirley
1989   A Vakutan Mortuary Cycle. In *Death Rituals and Life in the Societies of the Kula Ring,* ed. Frederick H. Damon and Roy Wagner, 46–72. DeKalb: Northern Illinois University Press.

Cannon, Walter B.
1979   "Voodoo" Death. Reprinted in *Reader in Comparative Religion: An Anthropological Approach,* 4th ed. Ed. William A. Lessa and Evon Z. Vogt, 367–373. New York: Harper & Row.

Carlson, Robert G.
1993   Hierarchy and the Haya Divine Kingship: A Structural and Symbolic

Reformulation of Frazer's Thesis. *American Ethnologist* 20:312–335.

Carneiro, Robert L.
  1967 On the Relationship between Size of Population and Complexity of Social Organization. *Southwestern Journal of Anthropology* 23: 234–243.
  1987 Village Splitting as a Function of Population Size. In *Themes in Ethnology and Culture History,* ed. Leland Donald, 94–124. Meerut, India: Archana Publications.

Carsten, Janet, and Stephen Hugh-Jones, eds.
  1995 *About the House: Lévi-Strauss and Beyond.* Cambridge: Cambridge University Press.

Casiño, Eric S.
  1976 The Jama Mapun of Cagayan de Sulu: A Samalan Group of Northwestern Sulu. In *The Societies of Borneo: Explorations in the Theory of Cognatic Social Structure,* ed. G. N. Appell, 16–39. Washington, D.C.: American Anthropological Association.

Chapman, Anne
  1992 *Masters of Animals: Oral Traditions of the Tolupan Indians, Honduras.* Yverdon, Switzerland: Gordon and Breach.

Chernela, Janet M.
  1988 Righting History in the Northwest Amazon: Myth, Structure, and History in an Arapaço Narrative. In *Rethinking History and Myth: Indigenous South American Perspectives on the Past,* ed. Jonathan D. Hill, 35–49. Urbana: University of Illinois Press.
  1993 *The Wanano Indians of the Brazilian Amazon: A Sense of Space.* Austin: University of Texas Press.

Chesser, Barbara
  1975 The Anthropomorphic Personal Guardian Spirit in Aboriginal South America. *Journal of Latin American Lore* 1:107–126.

Chowning, Ann
  1989 Death and Kinship in Molima. In *Death Rituals and Life in the Societies of the Kula Ring,* ed. Frederick H. Damon and Roy Wagner, 97–129. DeKalb: Northern Illinois University Press.

Claessen, Henri J. N.
  1981 Specific Features of the African Early State. In *The Study of the State,* ed. Henry J. M. Claessen and Peter Skalník, 59–86. The Hague: Mouton.

220 | *References*

Claessen, Henri J. M., and Pieter van de Velde
1985 Sociopolitical Evolution as Complex Interaction. In *Development and Decline: The Evolution of Sociopolitical Organization,* ed. Henri J. M. Claessen, Pieter van de Velde, and M. Estellie Smith, 246–263. South Hadley, Mass.: Bergin and Garvey.

Clastres, Pierre
1987 *Society against the State: Essays in Political Anthropology.* New York: Zone Books.

Cohen, Ronald
1976 The Natural History of Hierarchy: A Case Study. In *Power and Control: Social Structures and Their Transformation,* ed. Tom R. Burns and Walter Buckley, 185–214. London: Sage.
1977 Oedipus Rex and Regina: The Queen Mother in Africa. *Africa* 47:14–30.
1981 Evolution, Fission, and the Early State. In *The Study of the State,* ed. Henri J. M. Claessen and Peter Skalník, 87–115. The Hague: Mouton.

Cohen, A. P., and J. L. Comaroff
1976 The Management of Meaning: On the Phenomenology of Political Transactions. In *Transaction and Meaning: Directions in the Anthropology of Exchange and Symbolic Behavior,* ed. Bruce Kapferer, 87–107. Philadelphia: Institute for the Study of Human Issues.

Collier, Jane Fishburne
1988 *Marriage and Inequality in Classless Societies.* Stanford: Stanford University Press.

Colson, Elizabeth
1960 Ancestral Spirits among the Plateau Tonga. In *Cultures and Societies of Africa,* ed. Simon and Phoebe Ottenberg, 372–387. New York: Random House.

Comaroff, John L., and Jean Comaroff
1981 The Management of Marriage in a Tswana Chiefdom. In *Essays on African Marriage in Southern Africa,* ed. Eileen Jensen Krige and John L. Comaroff, 29–49. Capetown: Jula and Co.

Connerton, Paul
1989 *How Societies Remember.* Cambridge: Cambridge University Press.

Counts, Dorothy Ayers, and David R. Counts
1985 Introduction: Linking Concepts Aging and Gender, Aging and Death. In *Aging and Its Transformations: Moving toward Death in*

Pacific Societies, ed. Dorothy Ayers Counts and David R. Counts, 1–24. Lanham, Md.: University Press of America.

Crocker, J. Christopher
1969 Reciprocity and Hierarchy among the Eastern Bororo. *Man* 4: 44–58.
1979 Selves and Alters among the Eastern Bororo. In *Dialectical Societies: The Gê and Bororo of Central Brazil,* ed. David Maybury-Lewis, 249–300. Cambridge, Mass.: Harvard University Press.

Cunningham, Clark E.
1964 Order in the Atoni House. *Bijdragen tot de Taal-, Land-, en Volkenkunde* 120:34–68.

Cunnison, Ian
1957 History and Genealogies in a Conquest State. *American Anthropologist* 59:20–31.

Dalton, Douglas M.
1996 The Aesthetic of the Sublime: An Interpretation of Rawa Shell Valuable Symbolism. *American Ethnologist* 23:393–415.

Damon, Frederick H., and Roy Wagner, eds.
1989 *Death Rituals and Life in the Societies of the Kula Ring.* DeKalb: Northern Illinois University Press.

D'Andrade, Roy
1995 Moral Models in Anthropology. *Current Anthropology* 16:399–408.

Davenport, William H.
1994 *Pi'o: An Enquiry into the Marriage of Brothers and Sisters and Other Close Relatives in Old Hawai'i.* Lanham, Md.: University Press of America.

d'Azevedo, Warren L.
1962 Uses of the Past in Gola Discourse. *Journal of African History* 3:11–34.

de Dampierre, Eric
1971 Elders and Youngers in the Nzakara Kingdom. In *Kinship and Culture,* ed. Francis L. K. Hsu, 246–270. Chicago: Aldine.

Dieterlen, Germaine
1973 The Mande Creation Myth. Reprinted In *Peoples and Cultures of*
[1957] *Africa,* ed. Elliott P. Skinner, 634–653. Garden City, N.Y.: Natural History Press.

Dillehay, Tom D.
　1992　Keeping Outsiders Out: Public Ceremony, Resource Rights, and Hi-
　　　　erarchy in Historic and Contemporary Mapuche Society. In *Wealth
　　　　and Hierarchy in the Intermediate Area,* ed. Frederick W. Lange,
　　　　379–422. Washington, D.C.: Dumbarton Oaks Research Library
　　　　and Collections.

Dillon, Mary, and Thomas Abercrombie
　1988　The Destroying Christ: An Aymara Myth of Conquest. In *Rethink-
　　　　ing History and Myth: Indigenous South American Perspectives on
　　　　the Past,* ed. Jonathan D. Hill, 50–77. Urbana: University of Illinois
　　　　Press.

Douglas, Mary
　1966　*Purity and Danger.* London: Routledge and Kegan Paul.

Dove, Michael R.
　1992　The Dialectical History of "Jungle" in Pakistan: An Examination of
　　　　the Relationship between Nature and Culture. *Journal of Anthro-
　　　　pological Research* 48:231–253.

Driscoll, Stephen T.
　1988　Power and Authority in Early Historic Scotland: Pictish Symbol
　　　　Stones and Other Documents. In *State and Society: The Emergence
　　　　and Development of Social Hierarchy and Political Centralization,*
　　　　ed. John Gledhill, Barbara Bender, and Mogens Trolle Larsen, 215–
　　　　236. London: Unwin Hyman.

Drummond, Lee
　1981　The Serpent's Children: Semiotics of Cultural Genesis in Arawak
　　　　and Trobriand Myth. *American Ethnologist* 8:633–660.

Dumont, Louis
　1982　On Value. *Proceedings of the British Academy* 46(1980):207–241.
　　　　London: Oxford University Press.
　1983　*Affinity as a Value* Chicago: University of Chicago Press.

Earle, Timothy K.
　1987　Chiefdoms in Archaeological and Ethnohistorical Perspective. *An-
　　　　nual Reviews of Anthropology* 16:279–308.
　1991　The Evolution of Chiefdoms. In *Chiefdoms: Power, Economy, and
　　　　Ideology,* ed. Timothy Earle, 1–15. Cambridge: Cambridge Univer-
　　　　sity Press.

Eder, James F.
　1991　The Diversity and Cultural Evolutionary Trajectories of Philippine
　　　　"Negrito" Populations. In *Profiles in Cultural Evolution,* ed. A. Terry

Rambo and Kathleen Gillogly, 247–259. Ann Arbor: Museum of Anthropology, University of Michigan.

Ekholm, Kajsa
    1978   External Exchange and the Transformation of Central African So-
            cial Systems. In *The Evolution of Social Systems,* ed. Jonathan Fried-
            man and Michael J. Rowlands, 115–136. Pittsburgh: University of
            Pittsburgh Press.

Eliade, Mircea
    1959a   *Cosmos and History: The Myth of The Eternal Return.* New York:
            Harper & Brothers.
    1959b   *The Sacred and The Profane: The Nature of Religion* New York:
            Harcourt, Brace and World.

Elmendorf, William W.
    1971   Coast Salish Status Ranking and Intergroup Ties. *Southwestern
            Journal of Anthropology* 27:353–380.

Endicott, Kirk
    1979   *Batek Negrito Religion: The World-View and Rituals of a Hunting
            and Gathering People of Peninsular Malaysia.* Oxford: Clarendon
            Press.

Englebert, Victor
    1973   Somba: In the Presence of the Ancestors, the Time of Harvest. In
            Primitive Worlds: People Lost in Time, ed. Robert L. Breeden, 113–
            139. Washington, D.C.: National Geographic Society.

Erikson, Philippe
    1990   Near Beer of the Amazon. *Natural History* 99 (no. 8):53–60.

Errington, Frederick Karl
    1974   *Karavar: Masks and Power in a Melanesian Ritual.* Ithaca: Cornell
            University Press.

Errington, Frederick, and Deborah Gewertz
    1985   The Chief of the Chambri: Social Change and Cultural Permeability
            among a New Guinea People. *American Ethnologist* 12:442–454.
    1986   The Confluence of Powers: Entropy and Importation among the
            Chambri. *Oceania* 57:99–113.

Errington, Shelly
    1977   Order and Power in Karavar. In *The Anthropology of Power:
            Ethnographic Studies from Asia, Oceania, and the New World,* ed.
            Raymond D. Fogelson and Richard N. Adams, 23–43. New York:
            Academic Press.

1987   Incestuous Twins and the House Societies of Insular Southeast Asia. *Cultural Anthropology* 2:403–444.

Evans-Pritchard, E. E.
1940   *The Nuer.* Oxford: Clarendon Press.

Evens, Terence M. S.
1984   Nuer Hierarchy. In *Différences, Valeurs, Hiérarchie: Textes Offerts à Louis Dumont,* ed. Jean-Claude Galey, 319–334. Paris: Éditions de l'École des Hautes Études en Sciences Sociales.

Fairley, Nancy J.
1989   Ritual Rivalry among the Ben'Ekie. In *Creativity of Power: Cosmology and Action in African Societies,* ed. W. Arens and Ivan Karp, 289–312. Washington, D.C.: Smithsonian Institution Press.

Fardon, Richard
1988   *Raiders and Refugees: Trends in Chamba Political Development, 1750–1950.* Washington, D.C.: Smithsonian Institution Press.
1990   *Between God, the Dead, and the Wild: Chamba Interpretations of Religion and Ritual.* Washington, D.C.: Smithsonian Institution Press.

Feinman, Gary, and Jill Neitzel
1984   Too Many Types: An Overview of Sedentary Prestate Societies in the Americas. In *Advances in Archaeological Method and Theory,* vol. 7. Ed. Michael B. Schiffer, 39–102. Orlando, Fla.: Academic Press.

Flanagan, James G.
1989   Hierarchy in Simple "Egalitarian" Societies. *Annual Review of Anthropology* 18:245–266.

Flanagan, James G., and Steve Rayner
1988   Introduction. In *Rules, Decisions, and Inequality,* ed. James G. Flanagan and Steve Rayner, 1–19. Aldershot, Eng.: Avebury.

Forde, Daryll
1950   Double Descent among the Yakö. In *African Systems of Kinship and Marriage,* ed. A. R. Radcliffe-Brown and Daryll Forde, 285–332. London: Oxford University Press.

Fortes, Meyer
1945   *The Dynamics of Clanship among the Tallensi.* London: Oxford University Press.
1960   Oedipus and Job in West African Religion. Reprinted in *Anthropology of Folk Religion,* ed. Charles Leslie, 5–49. New York: Vintage Books.

1962a Introduction. In *Marriage in Tribal Societies,* ed. Meyer Fortes, 1–13. Cambridge: Cambridge University Press.

1962b Ritual and Office in Tribal Society. In *Essays on the Ritual of Social Relations,* ed. Max Gluckman, 53–88. Manchester: Manchester University Press.

1974 The First Born. *Journal of Child Psychology and Psychiatry* 15:81–104.

1976 An Introductory Commentary. In *Ancestors,* ed. William H. Newell, 1–16. The Hague: Mouton.

1983 *Oedipus and Job in West African Religion.* Cambridge: Cambridge University Press.

Fortune, R. F.

1935 *Manus Religion: An Ethnological Study of the Manus Natives of the Admiralty Islands.* Philadelphia: American Philosophical Society.

Foster, Robert J.

1990 Nurture and Force-Feeding: Mortuary Feasting and the Construction of Collective Individuals in a New Ireland Society. *American Ethnologist* 17:431–448.

Fox, James

1987 The House as a Type of Social Organization on the Island of Roti, Indonesia. In *De la Hutte au Palais: Sociétés "á Maison" en Asie du Sud-Est Insulaire,* ed. Charles Macdonald et al., 171–178. Paris: Editions du Centre National de la Recherche Scientifique.

Friedman, Jonathan

1975 Tribes, States, and Transformation. In *Marxist Analyses and Social Anthropology,* ed. Maurice Bloch, 161–200. New York: John Wiley and Sons.

1992 The Past in the Future: History and the Politics of Identity. *American Anthropologist* 94:837–859.

Fürer-Haimendorf, Christoph von

1969 *The Konyak Nagas: An Indian Frontier Tribe.* New York: Holt, Rinehart and Winston.

Furst, Peter T.

1978 The Art of "Being Huichol." In *Art of the Huichol Indians,* ed. Kathleen Berrin, 18–34. New York: Harry N. Abrams/Fine Arts Museums of San Francisco.

Geertz, Clifford

1966 Religion as a Cultural System. In *Anthropological Approaches to the Study of Religion,* ed. Michael Banton, 1–46. London: Tavistock.

Giddens, Anthony
　1979　*Central Problems in Social Theory: Action, Structure, and Contradiction in Social Analysis.* Berkeley: University of California Press.
　1984　*The Constitution of Society: Outline of the Theory of Structuration.* Berkeley: University of California Press.

Glazier, Jack
　1984　Mbeere Ancestors and the Domestication of Death. *Man,* n.s., 19:133–148.

Gluckman, Max
　1962　Les Rites de Passage. In *Essays on the Ritual of Social Relations,* ed. Max Gluckman, 1–52. Manchester: Manchester University Press.
　1965　*Politics, Law, and Ritual in Tribal Society.* New York: New American Library.

Godelier, Maurice
　1982　Social Hierarchies among the Baruya of New Guinea. In *Inequality in New Guinea Highlands Societies,* ed. Andrew Strathern, 3–34. Cambridge: Cambridge University Press.
　1986　*The Making of Great Men: Male Domination and Power among the New Guinea Baruya.* Cambridge: Cambridge University Press.

Goldman, Irving
　1963　*The Cubeo: Indians of the Northwest Amazon.* Urbana: University of Illinois Press.
　1970　*Ancient Polynesian Society.* Chicago: University of Chicago Press.
　1975　*The Mouth of Heaven.* New York: John Wiley and Sons.

Golson, Jack
　1982　The Ipomoean Revolution Revisited: Society and the Sweet Potato in the Upper Wahgi Valley. In *Inequality in New Guinea Highlands Societies,* ed. Andrew Strathern, 109–136. Cambridge: Cambridge University Press.

González Cháves, Alfredo, and Fernando González Vásquez
　1989　*La casa cósmica Talamanqueña y sus simbolismos.* San José, Costa Rica: Editorial de la Universidad de Costa Rica, Editorial Universidad Estatal a Distancia.

Goodale, Jane C., and Joan D. Koss
　1967　The Cultural Context of Creativity among Tiwi. In *Essays on the Verbal and Visual Arts,* ed. June Helm, 175–191. Seattle: University of Washington Press.

Goodrich, Peter
1990   *Languages of Law: From Logics of Memory to Nomadic Masks.* London: Weidenfeld and Nicol

Goody, Jack
1959   The Mother's Brother and the Sister's Son in West Africa. *Journal of the Royal Anthropological Institute* 89:61–88.
1962   *Death, Property, and the Ancestors: A Study of the Mortuary Customs of the Lodagaa of West Africa.* Stanford: Stanford University Press.

Gossen, Gary H.
1979   Temporal and Spatial Equivalents in Chamula Ritual Symbolism. In *Reader in Comparative Religion: An Anthropological Approach,* 4th ed. Ed. William A. Lessa and Evon Z. Vogt, 116–129. New York: Harper & Row.

Gough, Kathleen
1971   Nuer Kinship, a Re-examination. In *The Translation of Culture: Essays to E. E. Evans-Pritchard,* ed. T. O. Beidelman, 79–122. London: Tavistock.

Gould, Stephen Jay
1991   Fall in the House of Ussher. *Natural History* 100 (no. 11):12–21.
1994   Jove's Thunderbolts. *Natural History* 103 (no. 10):6–12.

Gray, Robert F.
1953   Positional Succession among the Wambugwe. *Africa* 23:233–243.

Gregor, Thomas
1977   *Mehinaku: The Drama of Daily Life in a Brazilian Indian Village.* Chicago:University of Chicago Press.

Grinker, Roy R.
1990   Images of Denigration: Structuring Inequality between Foragers and Farmers in the Ituri Forest, Zaire. *American Ethnologist* 17:111–130.

Guddemi, Phillip
1992   When Horticulturalists Are Like Hunter-Gatherers: The Sawiyano of Papua New Guinea. *Ethnology* 31:303–314.

Gudeman, Stephen
1986   *Economics as Culture: Models and Metaphors of Livelihood.* London: Routledge and Kegan Paul.

Guenther, Mathias
>1988   Animals in Bushman Thought, Myth, and Art. In *Hunters and Gatherers 2: Property, Power, and Ideology,* ed. Tim Ingold, David Riches, and James Woodburn, 192–202. Oxford: Berg.

Gulbrandsen, Ørnulf
>1991   On the Problem of Egalitarianism: The Kalahari San in Transition. In *The Ecology of Choice and Symbol: Essays in Honour of Fredrik Barth,* ed. Reidar Gronhaug, Gunnar Haaland, and Georg Henriksen, 81–110. Bergen: Alma Mater.

Gurevich, A. Ya.
>1969   Space and Time in the Weltmodell of the Old Scandinavian Peoples. *Mediaeval Scandinavia* 2:42–53.

Handler, Richard, and Daniel A. Segal
>1985   Hierarchies of Choice: The Social Construction of Rank in Jane Austen. *American Ethnologist* 12:691–706.

Harkin, Michael
>1992   Person, Time, and Being: Northwest Coast Rebirth in Comparative Perspective. Typescript.

Harms, Robert W.
>1981   *River of Wealth, River of Sorrow.* New Haven: Yale University Press.

Harris, Grace
>1962   Taita Bridewealth and Affinal Relationships. In *Marriage in Tribal Societies,* ed. Meyer Fortes, 55–87. Cambridge: Cambridge University Press.

Harris, Olivia
>1982   The Dead and the Devils among the Bolivian Laymi. In *Death and the Regeneration of Life,* ed. Maurice Bloch and Jonathan Parry, 45–73. Cambridge: Cambridge University Press.

Harrison, Simon
>1985a   Concepts of the Person in Avatip Religious Thought. *Man* (n.s.) 20:115–130.
>1985b   Ritual Hierarchy and Secular Equality in a Sepik River Village. *American Ethnologist* 12:413–426.
>1987   Cultural Efflorescence and Political Evolution on the Sepik River. *American Ethnologist* 14:491–507.
>1990   *Stealing People's Names: History and Politics in a Sepik River Cosmology* Cambridge: Cambridge University Press.

Hastorf, Christine A.
    1990   One Path to the Heights: Negotiating Political Inequality in the Sausa of Peru. In *The Evolution of Political Systems*, ed. Steadman Upham, 146–176. Cambridge: Cambridge University Press.

Hatch, Elvin
    1987   Theories of Social Honor. Paper presented at the annual meeting of the American Anthropological Association, Chicago.

Hayden, Brian
    1995   A New Overview of Domestication. In *Last Hunters — First Farmers*, ed. T. Douglas Price and Anne Birgitte Gebauer, 3–19. Santa Fe: School of American Research Press.

Headley, Stephen C.
    1987   The Idiom of Siblingship: One Definition of "House" Societies in South-East Asia. In *De la Hutte au Palais: Sociétés "à Maison" en Asie du Sud-Est Insulaire*, ed. Charles Macdonald et al., 209–218. Paris: Éditions du Centre National de la Recherche Scientifique.

Helms, Mary W.
    1979   *Ancient Panama: Chiefs in Search of Power*. Austin: University of Texas Press.
    1988   *Ulysses' Sail: An Ethnographic Odyssey of Power, Knowledge, and Geographical Distance*. Princeton: Princeton University Press.
    1993   *Craft and the Kingly Ideal: Art, Trade, and Power*. Austin: University of Texas Press.

Hertz, Robert
    1960a   Contribution to the Study of the Collective Representation of Death. In *Death and the Right Hand*, trans. Rodney and Claudia Needham, 29–86. Glencoe, Ill.: Free Press.
    1960b   The Pre-eminence of the Right Hand: A Study in Religious Polarity. In *Death and The Right Hand*, trans. Rodney and Claudia Needham, 89–113. Glencoe, Ill: Free Press.

Hickerson, Harold
    1960   The Feast of the Dead among the Seventeenth-Century Algonkians of the Upper Great Lakes. *American Anthropologist* 62:81–107.

Hill, Jonathan D.
    1984   Social Equality and Ritual Hierarchy: The Arawakan Wakuénai of Venezuela. *American Ethnologist* 11:528–544.

Hill, Robert M., III
    1991   The Social Uses of Writing among the Colonial Cakchiquel Maya:

Nativism, Resistance, and Innovation. In *Columbian Consequences,* vol. 3: *The Spanish Borderlands in Pan-American Perspective,* ed. David Hurst Thomas, 283–299. Washington, D.C.: Smithsonian Institution Press.

1992   *Colonial Cakchiquels.* Fort Worth: Harcourt, Brace, Jovanovich.

Hinnant, John
1989   Ritual and Inequality in Guji Dual Organization. In *The Attraction of Opposites: Thought and Society in the Dualistic Mode,* ed. David Maybury-Lewis and Uri Almagor, 57–76. Ann Arbor: University of Michigan Press.

Hocart, Arthur M.
1923   The Uterine Nephew. *Man,* o.s., 4:11–13.
1970   *Kings and Councillors: An Essay in the Comparative Anatomy of*
[1936] *Human Society.* Chicago: University of Chicago Press.

Hodder, Ian
1990   *The Domestication of Europe: Structure and Contingency in Neolithic Societies.* Oxford: Basil Blackwell.

Hoopes, John W.
1988   The Complex Tribe in Prehistory: Sociopolitical Organization in the Archaeological Record. Paper presented at the annual meeting of the Society for American Archaeology, Phoenix.

Horton, Robin
1972   Stateless Societies in the History of West Africa. In *History of West Africa,* vol. 1. Ed. J. F. A. Ajayi and Michael Crowder, 78–119. New York; Columbia University Press.
1979   Ritual Man in Africa. In *Reader in Comparative Religion: An Anthropological Approach,* 4th ed. Ed. William A. Lessa and Evon Z. Vogt, 243–254. New York: Harper & Row.
1983   Social Psychologies: African and Western. Appended to *Oedipus and Job in West African Religion,* by Meyer Fortes, 41–82. Cambridge: Cambridge University Press.

Hoskins, Janet
1987   Complementarity in this World and the Next: Gender and Agency in Kodi Mortuary Ceremonies. In *Dealing with Inequality: Analysing Gender Relations in Melanesia and Beyond,* ed. Marilyn Strathern, 174–206. Cambridge: Cambridge University Press.

Howard, Alan
1985   History, Myth, and Polynesian Chiefship: The Case of Rotuman Kings. In *Transformations of Polynesian Culture,* ed. Antony Hooper and Judith Huntsman, 39–78. Auckland: Polynesian Society.

Howard, Catherine V.

1991   Fragments of the Heavens: Feathers as Ornaments among the Wai-wai. In *The Gift of Birds: Featherwork of Native South American Peoples,* ed. Ruben E. Reina and Kenneth M. Kensinger, 50–69. Philadelphia: University Museum of Archaeology and Anthropology, University of Pennsylvania.

Howell, Signe

1991   Access to the Ancestors: Re-constructions of the Past in Non-literate Society. In *The Ecology of Choice and Symbol: Essays in Honour of Fredrik Barth,* ed. Reidar Grønhaug, Gunnar Haaland, and Georg Henriksen, 225–243. Bergen: Alma Mater.

1992   Time Past, Time Present, Time Future: Contrasting Temporal Values in Two Southeast Asian Societies. In *Contemporary Futures: Perspectives from Social Anthropology,* ed. Sandra Wallman, 124–137. London: Routledge.

Hugh-Jones, Christine

1977   Skin and Soul: The Round and the Straight. Social Time and Social Space in Pira-Parana Society. In *Social Time and Social Space in Lowland South American Societies,* comp. Joanna Overing-Kaplan, 185–204. Actes XLII Congrès International des Americanistes, vol. 2. Paris.

Hugh-Jones, Stephen

1979   *The Palm and the Pleiades: Initiation and Cosmology in Northwest Amazonia.* Cambridge: Cambridge University Press.

Huntington, Richard, and Peter Metcalf

1979   *Celebrations of Death: The Anthropology of Mortuary Ritual.* Cambridge: Cambridge University Press.

Huxley, Francis

1995   *Affable Savages.* Salem, Wis.: Sheffield.
[1956]

Ingold, Tim

1982   Comment. *Current Anthropology* 23:531–532.

1987   *The Appropriation of Nature: Essays on Human Ecology and Social Relations.* Iowa City: University of Iowa Press.

Ingold, Tim, ed.

1988   *What Is an Animal?* London: Unwin Hyman.

Iteanu, André

1985   Levels and Convertibility. In *Contexts and Levels: Anthropological*

Essays on Hierarchy, ed. R. H. Barnes, Daniel de Coppet, and R. J. Parkin, 91–102. Oxford: Journal of the Anthropological Society of Oxford.

Jackson, Michael
  1977   The Identity of the Dead. *Cahiers d'Etudes Africaines* 66–67:271–297.

James, Wendy
  1990   Antelope as Self-Image among the Uduk. In *Signifying Animals: Human Meaning in the Natural World,* ed. Roy Willis, 196–203. London: Unwin Hyman.

Johnson, Allen W., and Timothy Earle
  1987   *The Evolution of Human Societies: From Foraging Group to Agrarian State.* Stanford: Stanford University Press.

Johnson, Gregory
  1982   Organizational Structure and Scalar Stress. In *Theory and Explanation in Archaeology,* ed. Colin Renfrew, Michael Rowlands, and B. Segraves, 389–421. New York: Academic Press.

Jonaitis, Aldona, ed.
  1991   Preface to *Chiefly Feasts,* ed. Aldona Jonaitis, 11–14. Seattle: University of Washington Press.

Josephides, Lisette
  1985   *The Production of Inequality: Gender and Exchange among the Kewa* London: Tavistock.

Judkins, Russell A.
  1973   Mortuary Studies in the History of Anthropological Theory. Ph.D. diss., Cornell University, Ithaca, N.Y.

Kahn, Miriam
  1990   Stone-faced Ancestors: The Spatial Anchoring of Myth in Wamira, Papua New Guinea. *Ethnology* 29:51–66.

Kammeyer, Kenneth C. W.
  1976   The Dynamics of Population. In *Irish History and Culture,* ed. Harold Orel, 189–223. Lawrence: University Press of Kansas.

Kan, Sergei
  1986   The 19th-century Tlingit Potlatch: A New Perspective. *American Ethnologist* 13:191–212.
  1989   *Symbolic Immortality: The Tlingit Potlatch of the Nineteenth Century.* Washington, D.C.: Smithsonian Institution Press.

Kanowski, Maxwell
  1987   *Old Bones: Unlocking Archaeological Secrets.* Melburne, Australia: Longman Cheshire.

Karim, Wazir-Jahan Begum
  1981   *Ma' Betisék Concepts of Living Things.* New Jersey: Athlone Press and Humanities Press.

Karsten, Rafael
  1968   *The Civilization of the South American Indians.* Chicago:
  [1926]   Argonaut.

Keesing, Roger M.
  1968   Step Kin, In-Laws, and Ethnoscience. *Ethnology* 7:59–70.
  1971   Shrines, Ancestors, and Cognatic Descent: The Kwaio and Tallensi. In *Melanesia: Readings on a Culture Area,* ed. L. L. Langness and John C. Weschler, 142–169. Scranton, Pa.: Chandler.
  1975   *Kin Groups and Social Structure* New York: Holt, Rinehart and Winston.
  1982   *Kwaio Religion: The Living and the Dead in a Solomon Island Society.* New York: Columbia University Press.

Kelly, Raymond C.
  1985   *The Nuer Conquest: The Structure and Development of an Expansionist System.* Ann Arbor: University of Michigan Press.
  1993   *Constructing Inequality: The Fabrication of a Hierarchy of Virtue among the Etoro.* Ann Arbor: University of Michigan Press.

Kelly, Robert L.
  1992   Mobility/Sedentism: Concepts, Archaeological Measures, and Effects. *Annual Review of Anthropology* 21:43–66.

Kemp, Jeremy H.
  1978   Cognatic Descent and the Generation of Social Stratification in South-East Asia. *Bijdragen tot de Taal-, Land- en Volkenkunde* 134:63–83.

Kent, Susan
  1989   Cross-Cultural Perceptions of Farmers as Hunters and the Value of Meat. In *Farmers as Hunters: The Implications of Sedentism,* ed. Susan Kent, 1–17. Cambridge: Cambridge University Press.

Kerner, Karen
  1976   The Malevolent Ancestor: Ancestral Influence in a Japanese Religious Sect. In *Ancestors,* ed. William H. Newell, 205–218. The Hague: Mouton.

Kopytoff, Igor
    1987   Introduction. In *The African Frontier: The Reproduction of Traditional African Societies,* ed. Igor Kopytoff, 3–86. Bloomington: Indiana University Press.

Krige, E. Jensen, and J. D. Krige
    1943   *The Realm of a Rain-Queen: A Study of the Pattern of Lovedu Society.* London: Oxford University Press.

Labbé, Armand J.
    1986   *Colombia before Columbus: The People, Culture, and Ceramic Art of Prehispanic Colombia.* New York: Rizzoli.

Labby, David
    1976   *The Demystification of Yap: Dialectics of Culture on a Micronesian Island.* Chicago: University of Chicago.

La Fontaine, Jean
    1962   Gisu Marriage and Affinal Relations. In *Marriage in Tribal Societies,* ed. Meyer Fortes, 88–120. Cambridge: Cambridge University Press.
    1975   The Mother's Brother as Patron. *Archives Européennes de Sociologie* 16:76–92.

Lambek, Michael
    1990   Taboo as Cultural Practice in Mayotte. Paper presented at the annual meeting of the American Ethnological Society, Atlanta.

Landes, Ruth
    1986   Dakota Warfare. *Journal of Anthropological Research* 42:239–
    [1959] 248.

Lapidus, Ira M.
    1990   Tribes and State Formation in Islamic History. In *Tribes and State Formation in the Middle East,* ed. Philip S. Khoury and Joseph Kostiner, 25–47. Berkeley: University of California Press.

Lave, Jean
    1979   Cycles and Trends in Krĩkatí Naming Practices. In *Dialectical Societies: The Gê and Bororo of Central Brazil,* ed. David Maybury-Lewis, 16–45. Cambridge, Mass.: Harvard University Press.

Leach, Edmund R.
    1961   *Rethinking Anthropology.* London: Athlone Press.
    1965   *Political Systems of Highland Burma: A Study of Kachin Social Structure.* Boston: Beacon Press.
    1979a   Anthropological Aspects of Language: Animal Categories and Verbal Abuse. In *Reader in Comparative Religion: An Anthropological*
    [1964]

Approach, 4th ed. Ed. William A. Lessa and Evon Z. Vogt, 153–166. New York: Harper & Row.

1979b Two Essays Concerning the Symbolic Representation of Time. In
[1961] *Reader in Comparative Religion: An Anthropological Approach,* 4th ed. Ed. William A. Lessa and Evon Z. Vogt, 221–229. New York: Harper & Row.

1979c Ritualization in Man in Relation to Conceptual and Social Devel-
[1966] opment. In *Reader in Comparative Religion: An Anthropological Approach,* 4th ed. Ed. William A. Lessa and Evon Z. Vogt, 229–233. New York: Harper & Row.

Lee, Richard B.
1981 Politics, Sexual and Nonsexual, in an Egalitarian Society: The !Kung San. In *Social Inequality: Comparative and Developmental Approaches,* ed. Gerald D. Berreman, 83–102. New York: Academic Press.

Lepowsky, Maria
1989 Death and Exchange: Mortuary Ritual on Vanatinai (Sudest Island). In *Death Rituals and Life in the Societies of the Kula Ring,* ed. Frederick Damon and Roy Wagner, 199–229. DeKalb: Northern Illinois University Press.

Lévi-Strauss, Claude
1964 *Tristes Tropiques.* New York: Atheneum.
1966 *The Savage Mind.* Chicago: University of Chicago Press.
1969a *The Elementary Structures of Kinship.* Boston: Beacon Press.
1969b *The Raw and The Cooked.* New York: Harper & Row.
1982 *The Way of the Masks.* Seattle: University of Washington Press.
1987 *Anthropology and Myth: Lectures 1951–1982.* Oxford: Basil Blackwell.
1993 Father Christmas Executed. In *Unwrapping Christmas,* ed. Daniel
[1952] Miller, 38–51. Oxford: Clarendon Press.

Levy, Jerrold E.
1992 *Orayvi Revisited: Social Stratification in an "Egalitarian" Society.* Santa Fe: School of American Research Press.

Lienhardt, Godfrey
1955 Nilotic Kings and Their Mothers' Kin. *Africa* 25:29–42.
1961 *Divinity and Experience: The Religion of the Dinka.* Oxford: Clarendon Press.

Liep, John
1989 The Day of Reckoning on Rossell Island. In *Death Rituals and Life in the Societies of the Kula Ring,* ed. Frederick H. Damon and Roy Wagner, 230–253. DeKalb: Northern Illinois Press.

Lifton, Robert Jay
 1979   *The Broken Connection: On Death and the Continuity of Life.* New York: Simon and Schuster.

Lindholm, Charles
 1986   Kinship Structure and Political Authority: The Middle East and Central Asia. *Comparative Studies in Society and History* 28:334–355.

Lindstrom, Lamont
 1990   Big Men as Ancestors: Inspiration and Copyrights on Tanna (Vanuatu). *Ethnology* 29:313–324.

Lloyd, Peter C.
 1965   The Political Structure of African Kingdoms: An Exploratory Model. In *Political Systems and the Distribution of Power,* ed. Michael Banton, 63–112. London: Tavistock.

Lopes da Silva, Aracy
 1989   Social Practice and Ontology in Akwe-Xavante Naming and Myth. *Ethnology* 28:331–341.

Lovejoy, A. O.
 1942   *The Great Chain of Being.* Cambridge, Mass.: Harvard University Press.

Lowenthal, David
 1985   *The Past Is a Foreign Country.* Cambridge: Cambridge University Press.

Lowie, Robert H.
 1979   The Vision Quest among the North American Indians. In *Reader in*
 [1954]   *Comparative Religion: An Anthropological Approach,* 4th ed. Ed. William A. Lessa and Evon Z. Vogt, 285–288. New York: Harper & Row.

MacGaffey, Wyatt
 1986   *Religion and Society in Central Africa: The BaKongo of Lower Zaire.* Chicago: University of Chicago Press.

Macintyre, Martha
 1989   The Triumph of the *Susu*: Mortuary Exchanges on Tubetube. In *Death Rituals and Life in the Societies of the Kula Ring,* ed. Frederick Damon and Roy Wagner, 133–152. DeKalb: Northern Illinois University Press.

Maddock, Kenneth

    1989   The Complexity of Dual Organization in Aboriginal Australia. In *The Attraction of Opposites: Thought and Society in the Dualistic Mode,* ed. David Maybury-Lewis and Uri Almagor, 77–96. Ann Arbor: University of Michigan Press.

McAnany, Patricia A.

    1995   *Living with the Ancestors.* Austin: University of Texas Press.

McKellin, William H.

    1985   Passing Away and Loss of Life: Aging and Death among the Managalase of Papua New Guinea. In *Aging and Its Transformations: Moving toward Death in Pacific Societies,* ed. Dorothy Ayers Counts and David R. Counts, 181–201. Lanham, Md.: University Press of America.

McKinley, Robert

    1976   Human and Proud of It! A Structural Treatment of Headhunting Rites and the Social Definition of Enemies. In *Studies in Borneo Societies: Social Process and Anthropological Explanation,* ed. G. N. Appell, 92–145. DeKalb: Center for Southeast Asian Studies, Northern Illinois University.

McKinnon, Susan

    1991   *From a Shattered Sun: Hierarchy, Gender, and Alliance in the Tanimbar Islands.* Madison: University of Wisconsin Press.

Mair, Lucy

    1965   *An Introduction to Social Anthropology.* Oxford: Clarendon Press.

Malinowsky, Bronislaw

    1935   *Coral Gardens and Their Magic.* New York: American Book Co.

Maquet, Jacques J.

    1961   *The Premise of Inequality in Ruanda.* London: Oxford University Press.

Maranda, Elli Köngäs

    1967   The Cattle of the Forest and the Harvest of Water: The Cosmology of Finnish Magic. In *Essays on the Verbal and Visual Arts,* ed. June Helm, 84–95. Proceedings of the 1966 Annual Meeting of the American Ethnological Society. Seattle: University of Washington Press.

Marcus, George E.

    1992   The Concern with Elites in Archaeological Reconstructions: Mesoamerican Materials. In *Mesoamerican Elites: An Archaeological*

Assessment, ed. Diane Chase and Arlen Chase, 292–302. Norman: University of Oklahoma Press.

Marcus, George, ed.
1983   *Elites: Ethnographic Issues.* Albuquerque: University of New Mexico Press.

Maybury-Lewis, David
1974   *Akwe-Shavante Society.* New York: Oxford University Press.
1979   Cultural Categories of the Central Gê. In *Dialectical Societies: The Gê and Bororo of Central Brazil,* ed. David Maybury-Lewis, 218–248. Cambridge, Mass.: Harvard University Press.
1989a   The Quest for Harmony. In *The Attraction of Opposites: Thought and Society in the Dualistic Mode,* ed. David Maybury-Lewis and Uri Almagor, 1–18. Ann Arbor: University of Michigan Press.
1989b   Social Theory and Social Practice: Binary Systems in Central Brazil. In *The Attraction of Opposites: Thought and Society in the Dualistic Mode,* ed. David Maybury-Lewis and Uri Almagor, 97–116. Ann Arbor: University of Michigan Press.

Mbiti, John S.
1969   *African Religions and Philosophy.* New York: Praeger.

Mead, Margaret
1938   *The Mountain Arapesh. 1. An Importing Culture.* Anthropological Papers of the American Museum of Natural History, vol. 36, pt. 3. New York: American Museum of Natural History.
1940   *The Mountain Arapesh. 2. Supernaturalism.* Anthropological Papers of the American Museum of Natural History, vol. 37, pt. 3. New York: American Museum of Natural History.

Meggett, M. J.
1972   Understanding Australian Aboriginal Society: Kinship Systems or Cultural Categories? In *Kinship Studies in the Morgan Centennial Year,* ed. Priscilla Reining, 64–87. Washington, D.C.: Anthropological Society of Washington.

Melatti, Julio Cezar
1979   The Relationship System of the Krahó. In *Dialectical Societies: The Gê and Bororo of Central Brazil,* ed. David Maybury-Lewis, 46–82. Cambridge, Mass.: Harvard University Press.

Metcalf, Peter
1976   The Berawan Afterlife: A Critique of Hertz. In *Studies in Borneo Societies: Social Process and Anthropological Explanation,* ed. G. N. Appell, 72–91. DeKalb: Center for Southeast Asian Studies, Northern Illinois University.

1982   *A Borneo Journey into Death: Berawan Eschatology from Its Rituals.* Philadelphia: University of Pennsylvania Press.

Metraux, Rhoda
    1978   Aristocracy and Meritocracy: Leadership among the Eastern Iatmul. *Anthropological Quarterly* 5:47–58.

Middleton, John
    1977   Ritual and Ambiguity in Lugbara Society. In *Secular Ritual,* ed. Sally F. Moore and Barbara G. Myerhoff, 73–90. Amsterdam: Van Gorcum, Assen.
    1982   Lugbara Death. In *Death and the Regeneration of Life,* ed. Maurice Bloch and Jonathan Parry, 134–154. Cambridge: Cambridge University Press.

Miller, Daniel
    1989   The Limits of Dominance. In *Domination and Resistance,* ed. Daniel Miller, Michael Rowlands, and Christopher Tilley, 63–82. London: Unwin Hyman.

Miller, Joseph C.
    1976   *Kings and Kinsmen: Early Mbundu States in Angola.* Oxford: Clarendon Press.
    1981   Lineages, Ideology, and the History of Slavery in Western Central Africa. In *The Ideology of Slavery in Africa,* ed. Paul E. Lovejoy, 41–71. Beverly Hills: Sage.
    1988   *Way of Death: Merchant Capitalism and the Angolan Slave Trade 1730–1830.* Madison: University of Wisconsin Press.

Miller, Walter B.
    1955   Two Concepts of Authority. *American Anthropologist* 57:271–289.

Mitchell, J. Clyde
    1956   *The Yao Village.* Manchester: Manchester University Press.

Mitchell, William E.
    1978   On Keeping Equal: Polity and Reciprocity among the New Guinea Wape. *Anthropological Quarterly* 51:5–15.
    1988   The Defeat of Hierarchy: Gambling as Exchange in a Sepik Society. *American Ethnologist* 15:638–657.

Modjeska, Nicholas
    1982   Production and Inequality: Perspectives from Central New Guinea. In *Inequality in New Guinea Highlands Societies,* ed. Andrew Strathern, 50–108. Cambridge: Cambridge University Press.

Morphy, Howard
   1991   *Ancestral Connections: Art and an Aboriginal System of Knowl-edge.* Chicago: University of Chicago Press.

Moss, Madonna L.
   1993   Shellfish, Gender, and Status on the Northwest Coast: Reconciling Archaeological, Ethnographic, and Ethnohistorical Records of the Tlingit. *American Anthropologist* 95:631–652.

Muller, Jean-Claude
   1981   "Divine Kingship" in Chiefdoms and States: A Single Ideological Model. In *The Study of the State,* ed. Henri J. M. Claessen and Peter Skalník, 239–250. The Hague: Mouton.
   1985   Political Systems as Transformation. In *Development and Decline: The Evolution of Sociopolitical Organization,* ed. Henri J. M. Claessen, Pieter van de Velde, and M. Estelli Smith, 62–81. South Hadley, Mass.: Bergin and Garvey.

Mundkur, Balaji
   1988   Human Animality, the Mental Imagery of Fear, and Religiosity. In *What Is an Animal?,* ed. Tim Ingold, 141–184. London: Unwin Hyman.

Munn, Nancy D.
   1986   *The Fame of Gawa: A Symbolic Study of Value Transformation in a Massim (Papua New Guinea) Society.* Cambridge: Cambridge University Press.

Murdock, George Peter
   1934   *Our Primitive Contemporaries.* New York: Macmillan.

Murphy, William P., and Caroline H. Bledsoe
   1987   Kinship and Territory in the History of a Kpelle Chiefdom (Liberia). In *The African Frontier: The Reproduction of Traditional African Societies,* ed. Igor Kopytoff, 123–147. Bloomington: Indiana University Press.

Myerhoff, Barbara G.
   1979   The Deer-Maize-Peyote Symbol Complex among the Huichol Indians of Mexico. In *Reader in Comparative Religion: An Anthropological Approach,* 4th ed. Ed. William A. Lessa and Evon Z. Vogt, 105–111. New York: Harper & Row.

Myers, Fred R.
   1986   *Pintupi Country, Pintupi Self: Sentiment, Place, and Politics among Western Desert Aborigines.* Washington, D.C.: Smithsonian Institution Press.

Nadel, S. F.
  1947   *The Nuba: An Anthropological Study of the Hill Tribes of Kordo-
         fan.* London: Oxford University Press.

Nekich, Sandra
  1974   The Feast of the Dead: The Origin of Indian-White Trade Cere-
         monies in the West. *Western Canadian Journal of Anthropology*
         4:1–28.

Netting, Robert McC.
  1990   Population, Permanent Agriculture, and Polities: Unpacking the
         Evolutionary Portmanteau. In *The Evolution of Political Systems,*
         ed. Steadman Upham, 21–61. Cambridge: Cambridge University
         Press.

Ngubane, Harriet Sibisi
  1981   Marriage, Affinity, and the Ancestral Realm: Zulu Marriage in Fe-
         male Perspective. In *Essays on African Marriage in Southern Africa,*
         ed. Eileen Jensen Krige and John L. Comaroff, 84–95. Capetown:
         Juta and Co.

Nutini, Hugo G.
  1995   *The Wages of Conquest.* Ann Arbor: University of Michigan Press.

Nzimiro, Ikenna
  1965   A Study of Mobility among the Ibos of Southern Nigeria. In *Kin-
         ship and Geographical Mobility,* ed. Ralph Piddington, 117–130.
         Leiden: E. J. Brill.

O'Connor, Richard A.
  1989   Cultural Notes on Trade and the Tai. In *Ritual, Power, and Econ-
         omy: Upland-Lowland Contrasts in Mainland Southeast Asia,* ed.
         Susan D. Russell, 27–66. DeKalb: Northern Illinois University, Cen-
         ter for Southeast Asian Studies.

Parkin, David
  1991   *Sacred Void: Spatial Images of Work and Ritual among the Giriama
         of Kenya.* Cambridge: Cambridge University Press.

Parmentier, Richard J.
  1984   House Affiliation Systems in Belau. *American Ethnologist* 11:656–
         676.
  1987   *The Sacred Remains: Myth, History, and Polity in Belau.* Chicago:
         University of Chicago Press.

Patterson, Mary
  1981   Slings and Arrows: Rituals of Status Acquisition in North Ambryn.

In *Vanuatu: Politics, Economics, and Ritual in Island Melanesia,* ed. Michael Allen, 189–236. New York: Academic Press.

Pauwels, Simonne
  1985   Some Important Implications of Marriage Alliance: Tanimbar, Indonesia. In *Contexts and Levels: Anthropological Essays on Hierarchy,* ed. R. H. Barnes, Daniel de Coppet, and R. J. Parkin, 131–138. Oxford: Journal of the Anthropological Society of Oxford.

Pearce, Susan M.
  1987   Ivory, Antler, Feather, and Wood: Material Culture and the Cosmology of the Cumberland Sound Inuit, Baffin Island, Canada. *Canadian Journal of Native Studies* (Special Issue, Amerindian Cosmology) 7:307–322.

Peebles, Christopher S., and Susan M. Kus
  1977   Some Archaeological Correlates of Ranked Societies. *American Antiquity* 42:421–447.

Peoples, James G.
  1993   Political Evolution in Micronesia. *Ethnology* 32:1–17.

Peregrine, Peter
  1991   Some Political Aspects of Craft Specialization. *World Archaeology* 23:1–9.

Peters, Emrys
  1960   The Proliferation of Segments in the Lineage of the Bedouin of Cyrenaica. *Journal of the Royal Anthropological Institute* 90:29–53.

Petersen, Glenn
  1993   "On Cross-Cutting and Contradictory Hierarchies." Paper presented at the Thirteenth International Congress of Anthropological and Ethnological Sciences, Mexico City, July 29–August 5.

Philippi, Donald L.
  1985   Inter-Species Communication and the Ainu Way of Life. In *The Language of the Birds: Tales, Texts, and Poems of Interspecies Communication,* ed. David M. Guss, 186–201. San Francisco: North Point Press.

Pitt-Rivers, Julian
  1973   The Kith and the Kin. In *The Character of Kinship,* ed. Jack Goody, 89–105. Cambridge: Cambridge University Press.

Plog, Stephen
  1990   Agriculture, Sedentism, and Environment in the Evolution of Politi-

cal Systems. In *The Evolution of Political Systems: Socio-politics in Small-Scale Sedentary Societies,* ed. Steadman Upham, 177–202. Cambridge: Cambridge University Press.

Pomponio, Alice
1992   *Seagulls Don't Fly into the Bush: Cultural Identity and Development in Melanesia.* Belmont, Calif.: Wadsworth.

Poole, Fitz John Porter
1982   The Ritual Forging of Identity: Aspects of Person and Self in Bimin-Kuskusmin Male Initiation. In *Rituals of Manhood,* ed. Gilbert Herdt, 99–154. Berkeley: University of California Press.

Powell, H. A.
1960   Competitive Leadership in Trobriand Political Organization. *Journal of the Royal Anthropological Institute* 90:118–145.

Poyer, Lin
1993   Egalitarianism in the Face of Hierarchy. *Journal of Anthropological Research* 49:111–133.

Price, T. Douglas
1995   Social Inequality at the Origins of Agriculture. In *Foundations of Social Inequality,* ed. T. Douglas Price and Gary M. Feinman, 129–154. New York: Plenum Press.

Price, T. Douglas, and Anne Birgitte Gebauer
1995   New Perspectives on the Transition to Agriculture. In *Last Hunters—First Farmers,* ed. T. Douglas Price and Anne Birgitte Gebauer, 3–19. Santa Fe: School of American Research Press.

Radcliffe-Brown, Alfred R.
1952   *Structure and Function in Primitive Society.* New York: Free Press.
1965   The Mother's Brother in South Africa. In *Structure and Function in Primitive Society,* ed. A. R. Radcliffe-Brown, 15–31. New York: Free Press.

Reichel-Dolmatoff, Gerardo
1985   Tapir Avoidance in the Colombian Northwest Amazon. In *Animal Myths and Metaphors in South America,* ed. Gary Urton, 107–143. Salt Lake City: University of Utah Press.
1986   A Hunter's Tale from the Colombian Northwest Amazon. *Journal of Latin American Lore* 12:65–74.
1987   *Shamanism and Art of the Eastern Tukanoan Indians: Colombian Northwest Amazon.* Leiden: E. J. Brill.

Richards, Audrey I.
  1950   Some Types of Family Structure amongst the Central Bantu. In *African Systems of Kinship and Marriage,* ed. A. R. Radcliffe-Brown and Daryll Forde, 207–251. London: Oxford University Press.
  1961   African Kings and Their Royal Relatives. *Journal of the Royal Anthropological Institute* 91:135–150.

Robinson, Marguerite S.
  1962   Complementary Filiation and Marriage in the Trobriand Islands: A Re-examination of Malinowski's Material. In *Marriage in Tribal Societies,* ed. Meyer Fortes, 121–155. Cambridge: Cambridge University Press.

Rodman, Margaret
  1992   Empowering Place: Multilocality and Multivocality. *American Anthropologist* 94:640–656.

Rosaldo, Renato I., Jr.
  1979   Metaphors of Hierarchy in a Mayan Ritual. Reprinted in *Reader in Comparative Religion: An Anthropological Approach,* 4th ed. Ed. William A. Lessa and Evon Z. Vogt, 266–276. New York: Harper & Row.

Rosenberg, Michael
  1990   The Mother of Invention: Evolutionary Theory, Territoriality, and the Origins of Agriculture. *American Anthropologist* 92:399–415.

Rosenblatt, Paul C., R. Patricia Walsh, and Douglas A. Jackson
  1976   *Grief and Mourning in Cross-Cultural Perspective.* New Haven, Conn.: Human Relations Area Files Press.

Rosman, Abraham, and Paula G. Rubel
  1989   Dual Organization and Its Developmental Potential in Two Contrasting Environments. In *The Attraction of Opposites: Thought and Society in the Dualistic Mode,* ed. David Maybury-Lewis and Uri Almagor, 209–234. Ann Arbor: University of Michigan Press.

Rousseau, Jérôme
  1979   Kayan Stratification. *Man* 14:215–236.
  1985   The Ideological Prerequisites of Inequality. In *Development and Decline: The Evolution of Sociopolitical Organization,* ed. Henri J. M. Claessen, Pieter van de Velde, and M. Estellie Smith, 36–45. South Hadley, Mass.: Bergin and Garvey.

Rowlands, Michael
  1985   Exclusionary Tactics in the Logic of Collective Dynamics. *Critique of Anthropology* 5:47–69.

Rubel, Paula, and Abraham Rosman
    1994   The Past and the Future of Anthropology. *Journal of Anthropological Research* 50:335–343.

Rubinstein, Robert L.
    1981   Knowledge and Political Process on Malo. In *Vanuatu: Politics, Economics, and Ritual in Island Melanesia,* ed. Michael Allen, 135–172. New York: Academic Press.

Sahlins, Marshall D.
    1962   *Moala: Culture and Nature on a Fijian Island.* Ann Arbor: University of Michigan Press.
    1965   On the Ideology and Composition of Descent Groups. *Man,* o.s., 65 (no. 97):104–107.
    1976   *Culture and Practical Reason.* Chicago: University of Chicago Press.
    1983   Distinguished Lecture: Other Times, Other Customs: The Anthropology of History. *American Anthropologist* 85:517–547.
    1990   The Political Economy of Grandeur in Hawaii from 1810 to 1830. In *Culture through Time: Anthropological Approaches,* ed. Emiko Ohnuki-Tierney, 26–56. Stanford: Stanford University Press.

Sanday, Peggy Reeves
    1986   *Divine Hunger: Cannibalism as a Cultural System.* Cambridge: Cambridge University Press.

Schapera, I.
    1950   Kinship and Marriage among the Tswana. In *African Systems of Kinship and Marriage,* ed. A. R. Radcliffe-Brown and Daryll Forde, 140–165. London: Oxford University Press.

Scheffler, Harold W.
    1965   *Choiseul Island Social Structure.* Berkeley: University of California Press.

Schele, Linda, and David Freidel
    1990   *A Forest of Kings.* New York: William Morrow.

Schlegel, Alice
    1992   African Political Models in the American Southwest: Hopi as an Internal Frontier Society. *American Anthropologist* 94:376–397.

Schoenwetter, James
    1991   Cultivation Activity and Hunter-Gatherer Prehistory. Paper presented at the 90th annual meeting of the American Anthropological Association, Chicago, November 20.

Schrimpff, Marianne Cardale
1989   The Snake and the Fabulous Beast: Themes from the Pottery of the Ilama Culture. In *Animals into Art,* ed. Howard Morphy, 75–108. London: Unwin Hyman.

Seeger, Anthony
1981   *Nature and Society in Central Brazil: The Suyá Indians of Mato Grosso.* Cambridge, Mass.: Harvard University Press.
1987   *Why Suyá Sing.* Cambridge: Cambridge University Press.

Seguin, Margaret
1986a   The Northwest Coast—A Regional Overview. In *Native Peoples: The Canadian Experience,* ed. R. Bruce Morrison and C. Roderick Wilson, 467–472. Toronto: McClelland and Stewart.
1986b   Understanding Tsimshian Potlatch. In *Native Peoples: The Canadian Experience,* ed. R. Bruce Morrison and C. Roderick Wilson, 473–500. Toronto: McClelland and Stewart.

Service, Elman R.
1978   *Profiles in Ethnology,* 3rd. ed. New York: Harper & Row.

Sharp, Henry S.
1988   *The Transformation of Bigfoot: Maleness, Power, and Belief among the Chipewyan.* Washington, D.C.: Smithsonian Institution Press.

Sider, Karen Blu
1967   Affinity and the Role of the Father in the Trobriands. *Southwestern Journal of Anthropology* 23:90–109.

Spencer, Charles S.
1987   Rethinking the Chiefdom. In *Chiefdoms in the Americas,* ed. Robert D. Drennan and Carlos A. Uribe, 369–390. Lanham, Md.: University Press of America.
1994   Factional Ascendance, Dimensions of Leadership, and the Development of Centralized Authority. In *Factional Competition and Political Development in the New World,* ed. Elizabeth M. Brumfiel and John W. Fox, 31–43. Cambridge: Cambridge University Press.

Stone, Andrea
1989   Disconnection, Foreign Insignia, and Political Expansion: Teotihuacan and the Warrior Stelae of Piedras Negras. In *Mesoamerica after the Decline of Teotihuacan a.d. 700–900,* ed. Richard A. Diehl and Janet Catherine Berlo, 153–172. Washington, D.C.: Dumbarton Oaks Research Library and Collection.

Strathern, Andrew
1982   Two Waves of African Models in the New Guinea Highlands. In

Inequality in New Guinea Highlands Society, ed. Andrew Strathern, 35–49. Cambridge: Cambridge University Press.

Sutlive, Vinson H., Jr.
  1978   *The Iban of Sarawak.* Arlington Heights, Ill.: AHM Publishing.

Suttles, Wayne
  1991   The Traditional Kwakiutl Potlatch. In *Chiefly Feasts,* ed. Aldona Jonaitis, 71–134. Seattle: University of Washington Press.

Sutton, Douglas G.
  1990   Organisation and Ontology: The Origins of the Northern Maori Chiefdom, New Zealand. *Man* 25:667–692.

Szemiński, Jan
  1993   The Last Time the Inca Came Back: Messianism and Nationalism in the Great Rebellion of 1780–1783. In *South and Meso-American Native Spirituality: From the Cult of the Feathered Serpent to the Theology of Liberation,* ed. Gary H. Gossen in collaboration with Miguel León-Portilla, 279–299. New York: Crossroad.

Szynkiewicz, Slawoj
  1990   Sheep Bone as a Sign of Human Descent: Tibial Symbolism among the Mongols. In *Signifying Animals: Human Meaning in the Natural World,* ed. Roy Willis, 74–84. London: Unwin Hyman.

Tambiah, Stanley J.
  1979   The Form and Meaning of Magical Acts: A Point of View. In *Reader in Comparative Religion: An Anthropological Approach,* 4th ed. Ed. William A. Lessa and Evon Z. Vogt, 352–362. New York: Harper & Row.

Tapper, Richard L.
  1988   Animality, Humanity, Morality, Society. In *What Is an Animal?,* ed. Tim Ingold, 47–62. London: Unwin Hyman.

Taylor, Luke
  1989   Seeing the 'Inside': Kunwinjku Painting and the Symbol of the Divided Body. In *Animals into Art,* ed. Howard Morphy, 371–389. London: Unwin Hyman.

Taylor, Paul Michael, and Lorraine V. Aragon
  1991   *Beyond the Java Sea: Art of Indonesia's Outer Islands.* Washington, D.C.: National Museum of Natural History, Smithsonian Institution/Harry N. Abrams.

Thune, Carl
    1989   Death and Matrilineal Reincorporation on Normanby Island. In *Death Rituals and Life in the Societies of the Kula Ring,* ed. Frederick H. Damon and Roy Wagner, 153–178. DeKalb: Northern Illinois University.

Tonkinson, Robert
    1988   'Ideology and Domination' in Aboriginal Australia: A Western Desert Test Case. In *Hunters and Gatherers,* vol. 2: *Property, Power, and Ideology,* ed. Tim Ingold, David Riches, and James Woodburn, 150–164. Oxford: Berg.

Townsend, Joan B.
    1985   The Autonomous Village and the Development of Chiefdoms. In *Development and Decline: The Evolution of Sociopolitical Organization,* ed. Henri J. M. Claessen, Pieter van de Velde, and M. Estellie Smith, 141–155. South Hadley, Mass.: Bergin and Garvey.

Traube, Elizabeth G.
    1980   Affines and the Dead: Mambai Rituals of Alliance. *Bijdragen tot de Taal-, Land- en Volkenkunde* 136:90–115.
    1989   Obligations to the Source: Complementarity and Hierarchy in an Eastern Indonesian Society. In *The Attraction of Opposites: Thought and Society in the Dualistic Mode,* ed. David Maybury-Lewis and Uri Almagor, 321–344. Ann Arbor: University of Michigan Press.

Trigger, Bruce
    1990   Maintaining Economic Equality in Opposition to Complexity: An Iroquoian Case Study. In *The Evolution of Political Systems,* ed. Steadman Upham, 119–145. Cambridge: Cambridge University Press.

Trouwborst, Albert
    1965   Kinship and Geographical Mobility in Burundi. In *Kinship and Geographical Mobility,* ed. Ralph Piddington, 166–182. Leiden: E. J. Brill.

Turnbull, Colin M.
    1961   *The Forest People.* New York: Doubleday.

Turner, James West
    1988   A Sense of Place: Locus and Identity in Matailobau, Fiji. *Anthropos* 83:421–431.

Turner, Terence S.
    1971   Cosmetics: The Language of Bodily Adornment. In *Conformity and*

Conflict, ed. James P. Spradley and David W. McCurdy, 96–105. Boston: Little, Brown.

1977   Transformation, Hierarchy, and Transcendence: A Reformulation of Van Gennep's Model of the Structure of Rites de Passage. In *Secular Ritual,* ed. Sally F. Moore and Barbara G. Myerhoff, 53–70. Amsterdam: Van Gorcum, Assen.

1979   The Gê and Bororo Societies as Dialectical Systems: A General Model. In *Dialectical Societies: The Gê and Bororo of Central Brazil,* ed. David Maybury-Lewis, 147–178. Cambridge, Mass.: Harvard University Press.

1984   Dual Opposition, Hierarchy, and Value. Moiety Structure and Symbolic Polarity in Central Brazil and Elsewhere. In *Différences, Valeurs, Hièrarchie: Textes offerts à Louis Dumont,* ed. Jean-Claude Galez, 335–370. Paris: L'École des Hautes Études en Sciences Sociales.

Turner, Victor W.
1969   *The Ritual Process: Structure and Anti-Structure.* Chicago: Aldine.

1977   Variations on a Theme of Liminality. In *Secular Ritual,* ed. Sally F. Moore and Barbara G. Myerhoff, 36–52. Amsterdam: Van Gorcum, Assen.

1979   Betwixt and Between: The Liminal Period in *Rites de Passage.* Reprinted in *Reader in Comparative Religion: An Anthropological Approach,* 4th ed. Ed. William A. Lessa and Evon Z. Vogt, 234–243. New York: Harper & Row.

Tuzin, Donald F.
1972   Yam Symbolism in the Sepik: An Interpretative Account. *Southwestern Journal of Anthropology* 28:230–254.

Uchendu, Victor C.
1976   Ancestorcide! Are African Ancestors Dead? In *Ancestors,* ed. William H. Newell, 283–296. The Hague: Mouton.

Valeri, Valerio
1994   Buying Women But Not Selling Them: Gift and Commodity Exchange in Huaulu Alliance. *Man* 29:1–26.

1990   Constitutive History: Genealogy and Narrative in the Legitimation of Hawaiian Kingship. In *Culture through Time: Anthropological Approaches,* ed. Emiko Ohnuki-Tierney, 154–192. Stanford: Stanford University Press.

1985   The Conqueror Becomes King: A Political Analysis of the Hawaiian Legend of 'Umi. In *Transformations of Polynesian Culture,* ed. Antony Hooper and Judith Huntsman, 79–104. Auckland: Polynesian Society.

Van der Kroef, Justus M.
1954　Dualism and Symbolic Antithesis in Indonesian Society. *American Anthropologist* 56:847–862.

van Gennep, Arnold
1960　*The Rites of Passage.* Chicago: University of Chicago Press.

Vansina, Jan
1985　*Oral Tradition as History.* Madison: University of Wisconsin Press.
1990　*Paths in the Rainforests: Toward a History of Political Tradition in Equatorial Africa.* Madison: University of Wisconsin Press.

Vitebsky, Piers
1993　*Dialogues with the Dead: The Discussion of Mortality among the Sora of Eastern India.* Cambridge: Cambridge University Press.

Viveiros de Castro, Eduardo
1986　*From the Enemy's Point of View: Humanity and Divinity in an Amazonian Society.* Chicago: University of Chicago Press.

Walens, Stanley
1982　The Weight of My Name Is a Mountain of Blankets: Potlatch Ceremonies. In *Celebration,* ed. Victor Turner, 178–189. Washington, D.C.: Smithsonian Institution Press.

Wallman, Sandra
1992　Introduction: Contemporary Futures. In *Contemporary Futures: Perspectives from Social Anthropology,* ed. Sandra Wallman, 1–20. London: Routledge.

Watson, James L.
1982　Of Flesh and Bones: The Management of Death Pollution in Cantonese Society. In *Death and the Regeneration of Life,* ed. Maurice Bloch and Jonathan Parry, 155–186. Cambridge: Cambridge University Press.

Watson, William
1958　*Tribal Cohesion in a Money Economy: A Study of the Mambwe People of Northern Rhodesia.* Manchester, Eng.: Manchester University Press.

Weeks, Kent R.
1979　Art, Word, and the Egyptian World View. In *Egyptology and the Social Sciences,* ed. Kent Weeks, 57–81. Cairo: American University in Cairo Press.

Weiner, Annette B.
  1976   *Women of Value, Men of Renown: New Perspectives in Trobriand Exchange*. Austin: University of Texas Press.
  1982   Sexuality among the Anthropologists, Reproduction among the Informants. *Social Analysis* 12:52–65.
  1992   *Inalienable Possessions: The Paradox of Keeping-While-Giving*. Berkeley: University of California Press.

Weiner, James F.
  1987   Diseases of the Soul: Sickness, Agency, and the Men's Cult among the Foi of New Guinea. In *Dealing with Inequality: Analysing Gender Relations in Melanesia and Beyond*, ed. Marilyn Strathern, 255–277. Cambridge: Cambridge University Press.

Weissleder, Wolfgang
  1978   Aristotle's Concept of Political Structure and the State. In *Origins of the State*, ed. Ronald Cohen and Elman R. Service, 187–203. Philadelphia: Institute for the Study of Human Issues.

Wike, Joyce
  1967   The Role of the Dead in North-West Coast Culture. In *Indian Tribes of Aboriginal America*, ed. Sol Tax, 97–103. New York: Cooper Square Publishers.

Willis, Roy
  1990   Introduction. In *Signifying Animals: Human Meaning in the Natural World*, ed. Roy Willis, 1–24. London: Unwin Hyman.

Wilson, Richard
  1995   *Maya Resurgence in Guatemala: Q'eqchi' Experiences*. Norman: University of Oklahoma Press.

Winter, Edward H.
  1956   *Bwamba: A Structural-Functional Analysis of a Patrilineal Society*. Cambridge, Eng.: W. Heffer & Sons.

Woodburn, James
  1982a   Egalitarian Societies. *Man* 17:431–451.
  1982b   Social Dimensions of Death in Four African Hunting and Gathering Societies. In *Death and the Regeneration of Life*, ed. Maurice Bloch and Jonathan Parry, 187–210. Cambridge: Cambridge University Press.
  1988   African Hunter-gatherer Social Organization: Is It Best Understood as a Product of Encapsulation? In *Hunters and Gatherers*, vol. 1: *History, Evolution, and Social Change*, ed. Tim Ingold, David Riches, and James Woodburn, 31–64. Oxford: Berg.

Woodward, Mark R.
    1989   Economy, Polity, and Cosmology in the Ao Naga Mithan Feast. In *Ritual, Power, and Economy: Upland-Lowland Contrasts in Mainland Southeast Asia,* ed. Susan D. Russell, 121–142. DeKalb: Northern Illinois University, Center for Southeast Asian Studies.

Woodward, Mark R., and Susan D. Russell
    1989   Introduction: Transformations in Ritual and Economy in Upland and Lowland Southeast Asia. In *Ritual, Power, and Economy: Upland-Lowland Contrasts in Mainland Southeast Asia,* ed. Susan D. Russell, 1–26. DeKalb: Northern Illinois University, Center for Southeast Asian Studies.

Yamba, C. Bawa
    1992   Going There and Getting There: The Future as a Legitimating Charter for Life in the Present. In *Contemporary Futures: Perspectives from Social Anthropology,* ed. Sandra Wallman, 109–123. London: Routledge.

Zarur, Elizabeth Netto Calil
    1991   Social and Spiritual Languages of Feather Art: The Bororo of Central Brazil. In *The Gift of Birds: Featherwork of Native South American Peoples,* ed. Ruben E. Reina and Kenneth M. Kensinger, 26–39. Philadelphia: University Museum of Archaeology and Anthropology, University of Pennsylvania.

Zuidema, R. Tom
    1989   The Moieties of Cuzco. In *The Attraction of Opposites: Thought and Society in the Dualistic Mode,* ed. David Maybury-Lewis and Uri Almagor, 255–276. Ann Arbor: University of Michigan Press.

INDEX

Abundance: and aristocracy, 169, 211n7

Affines: and ancestors, 35, 40–41, 47, 52–53, 62, 69, 85, 88–90; and animals, 40, 42; as artisans, 87, 171–172; categories of, 55–56; defined, 8–9, 57–59; and communitas 66–70, 89–90; and cosmogony, 47, 52–53, 59–60, 69, 79, 82–90, 100–101, 107–108; and the dead, 30–33, 35, 52, 64–66, 68–69, 83–85, 189n18; as foreigners, 58–59; and hierarchy, 9, 70, 98, 99–108; and the house, 59–72, 76; as liminal status, 66, 67, 69; and mortuary rites, 43, 82–85 (*see also* Mortuary rites); and political legitimation, 11, 52–53, 70–72, 88–90, 126; qualities of, 43, 57, 59–72,

88, 100, 110; and ritual knowledge, 63–64; and wealth, 171, 211n11

Affinity: and aristocracy, 9, 120, 122–144; in dialectical societies, 64

Amba, 37

Ancestors: and affines, 35, 40–41, 47, 52–53, 62, 69, 88–90; and animals, 41, 42, 52; and aristocrats, 6, 117–120; and bones, 50–52; categories of, 37–39, 43–44, 75, 77; and cosmogony 38, 75, 77; creation of, 36–37, 49–51, 65, 85; and foreigners, 40–41; and the house, 39–40, 43–44, 51; personifications of, 40, 46, 47, 69; qualities of, 35–39, 42–43, 110; as source of wealth, 168

Animals: and affines, 40, 42; and

ancestors, 40, 41, 42, 52, 191n7; and cosmology, 44–46, 191n7, 192n22, 206n5; and the dead, 35; and personness, 41–42, 44–46, 189nn14–15; qualities of bones, 29; as transformed humans, 29–30

Ao Naga, 98, 103, 119

Arapesh, 28

Araweté, 32–33, 99, 194n26

Aristocracy: and affinity, 9, 120, 122–144, 205n21, 208n21; and cosmogony, 100–101, 114–115, 118, 119, 150; and death, 204n17; defined, 185n2; development of, 12; and foreign contacts, 159–161, 163; and hierarchy, 9, 98–101; history 115, 155; and rank endogamy, 138–139

Aristocrats: and ancestor, 6; as living ancestors, 117–120, 124, 133–134, 143–144, 169–170, 205n20; qualities of, 5, 6, 95–96, 100, 110–120, 123–124, 143, 144, 165–166; and skilled crafting, 114; and sumptuary laws, 116–117; ties with commoners, 142–143 (*see also* Wife-takers; Wife-givers); and wealth, 168–169

Aristotle, 15

Artisan: affines as, 171–172

Ashanti, 67

Avatip, 62

BaKongo, 43, 61–62, 63, 83

Bamileke, 206n10

Barasana, 172

Barnard, Alan, 59, 80

Barnes, R. H., 70, 102

Batak, 60–61

Belau, 155, 169

Bemba, 118

Benares, 77

Berawan, 18

Bledsoe, Caroline, 126–128

Bloch, Maurice, 68, 103, 193n25

Bones, 165, 166, 169, 170–171, 188nn8–11, 211n2, 211n10; and ancestors, 52; as regalia, 166; and relics, 50–51; as source of life, 27–29, 32

Borno, 152

Bororo, 26, 29–30, 64, 84, 97, 105, 168, 201n11

Bribri, 86

Bridewealth, 104, 132–133, 171, 202n17, 206n10; related to death payment, 207n13

Bwamba, 76

Cahuilla, 64

California tribes, 99

Cameroon grassfields chiefdoms, 157–158

Chamba, 43

Chambri, 40–41

Chernela, Janet, 97

Chiefdom: defined, 4; development of, 129–130, 148–163, 178–179; and hierarchy, 96, 98; marriage patterns, 125–144. *See also* Hierarchy; Political centralization

Chiefship: and foreign contacts, 159–161, 163

Clastres, Pierre, 121–122

Coast Salish, 141

Cohen, Ronald, 140

Commoners: and access to origins, 128, 134, 135, 137; as affines for aristocracy, 126–138 (*see also* Wife-givers; Wife-takers); attitudes toward aristocrats, 123, 124, 142–143; and lack of wealth, 168–169; qualities of, 111, 112–113, 115, 118, 204n11

Communitas: and affines, 66–70, 87, 89–90; and aristocracy, 111–112, 114, 126, 129–130, 203n5; and bridewealth, 104; and chiefship, 157; historical development of, 197n21; and origins, 81

Connerton, Paul, 115

Conquest: and aristocracy, 159–160

Cosmogony, 73–74; and affines, 47, 52–53, 59–60, 69, 82–90, 107–108, 139; and ancestors, 38; and animals, 42, 44–46; and archetypes, 74; and aristocracy, 114–115, 118, 119; categories of, and hierarchy, 100–101; and commoners, 128, 134, 135, 137; contexts of, 7, 103–104, 198n4, 201n12; and the house, 55; and legitimacy, 10–11; and origins, 74–79, 87–88; and political activities, 74–75, 80–82, 91; and wealth 172–173. *See also* Founders

Cosmography, xi–xii; and aristocracy, 114, 150; and hunter-gatherer societies, 44–46; and origins, 75–77

Cosmology: and animals, 34–35, 206n5; and aristocrats, 6, 123–124, 126, 129–130; and the dead, 24–25, 34–35; developmental stages of, 44–49; and first settlers, 106; and hierarchy, 9; and the house, 34–35, 46–48; models of and models for living, 7–8, 174–175; and social-political activities, 53–54, 101–102, 121–122, 149; and tangible goods, 104. *See also* Cosmogony

Cosmos: means of contacting, 8

Crafting: and aristocracy, 114

Crocker, J. Christopher, 84, 97

Crow, 63

Dahomey, 188n6

Dakota, 83

Dead, The, 187n1; and affines, 30–33, 35, 52, 64–66, 68–69, 83–85, 189n18; and ancestors, 35, 49–50, 204n17; and animals, 35, 206n5; bones of, 27–29, 32; fate of, 23–24, 35–36, 190n1, 191n9, 193n22; and the house, 24–25, 47–48; personification of, 24–25; and plants, 30; related to the living, 23–24, 25–26, 27; and types of societies, 45, 47–48

Death: degrees of, 25–27; imagery of, 50

Dialectical societies: and affinity, 64, 84; and hierarchy, 105, 201n11

Dinka, 106

Dobu, 31, 38, 61

Dumont, Louis, 57

Easter Islanders, 117

East Flores Islanders, 105

Ekie, 161–163

Eliade, Mircea, 5

Elite, 185n2. *See also* Aristocracy; Aristocrats

Ethnography: use of analogies, 192n17

Etoro, 99

Europeans: and the dead, 199n13

Evans-Pritchard, E. E., 129

Evens, Terence, 198n11

Firstborn, 8, 48, 78–79, 179, 198n11

First settlers: and ceremonial roles, 158–159, 162; as legitimizers, 155, 158, 162; and political centralization, 150–151, 156. *See also* Founders

Fission: reduction of community, 151, 152, 154; and seniority, 209n6

Foreigners: as affines, 58–59; as ancestors, 40–41; and hierarchy, 105–106; and moral order, 159, 210n17

Fortes, Meyer, 142

Founders, 106, 127, 128, 150; and political centralization, 151, 152, 153–155, 161. *See also* First settlers

Fox Islanders, 152

Friedman, Jonathan, 91, 129

Gender: and hierarchy, 105–106, 130–131

Generations: and hierarchy, 105
Giddens, Anthony, 14–15
Gisu, 61, 103
Gola, 43–44, 153–154
Goldman, Irving, 109–111
Goody, Jack, 142
Gough, Kathleen, 128–129
Gould, Stephen Jay, 13
Gurevich, A., 5

Hawaii, 115
Haya, 119
Headhunting, 199n14
Heirlooms, 165, 169, 173
Hierarchy: and affinity, 9, 70, 98–
 108, 127–144; and aristocracy,
 98–101, 124, 206n10; categories
 of, 97–99; in cosmos, 9, 96–99,
 176, 178–179, 200n7; and dialectical societies, 105, 201n11;
 and foreigners, 105–106; and
 gender, 105–106, 130–131,
 200n10; and generations, 105;
 and political economy, 12; and
 social structure, 107, 151–152,
 154–155, 178, 202n21. *See also*
 Political centralization
History: and aristocracy, 115, 155
Hocart, Arthur, 121
Hodder, Ian, 16, 17, 45
Hopi, 70–71, 97–98
Horton, Robin, 195n8
House, 15–19, 46, 59, 64, 75–77;
 and affines, 55–72, 85–87, 107–
 108; and ancestors, 37–40, 43–
 44, 50–51; and animals, 41–42;
 and cosmology, 34–35, 46–47,
 55, 73–74, 100–102; and the
 dead, 47–48; and senior persons,
 48
Hua, 59
Huaulu, 58
Hugh-Jones, Stephen, 172
Hunter-gatherer societies: and cos-
 mology, 44–46
Huron, 167

Iban, 86–87
Inca, 139
Inequality, 178. *See also* Hierarchy
Ingold, Tim, 29
In-laws. *See* Affines; Affinity
Ireland, 26, 188n6

Jama Mapun, 114

Kachin, 129–130
Kan, Sergei, 88–90, 171–172
Karavar, 62–63
Kayan, 113, 135
Kayapó, 71
Kédang, 60, 86, 102
Kei Archipelago, 106
Kinship: and political agency, 122,
 205n1
Kogi, 30
Kopytoff, Igor, 82, 158
Kpelle, 126–128
Krahó, 83
!Kung, 41, 72
Kwaio, 25, 36, 43
Kwakiutl, 17, 19, 112, 118

Leach, Edmund R., 47
Lee, Richard, 72
Legitimacy: and cosmogony, 10–11.
 See also Political legitimation
Lévi-Strauss, Claude, 15, 84
Liminality, 196n16; and affines, 66,
 67, 69 (*see also* Living Ances-
 tors); and aristocracy, 111, 118,
 203n4. *See also* Communitas
Lio, 86, 152
Living ancestors: aristocrats and
 affines as, 6, 8–9, 88–90, 117–
 120, 124, 133–134, 143–144,
 165–166, 176 (*see also* Affines;
 Ancestors); and need for symbols,
 169–170: in noncentralized soci-
 ety, 205n20
LoDagaba, 142–143
Lovedu, 103, 137–138
Luapula, 115

Luba, 161–163
Lugbara, 17, 76, 81
Luwu, 112

Mambai, 18
Mambwe, 137
Managalase, 25
Manambu, 41, 46–47, 63, 99
Mandok, 78
Mangareva, 117
Maori, 117
Marriage. *See* Affines; Affinity; Wife-givers; Wife-takers
Maya, 115, 118–119
Mbeere, 80
Mbundu, 154–155
McKinnon, Susan, 130–132
Mehinaku, 61
Mesoamerica, 18
Migration: and chiefship, 155–159
Miller, Daniel, 101
Miller, Joseph, 154–155
Moieties. *See* Dialectical societies
Mortuary rites, 38, 45, 48, 50, 64–66, 67–69, 172; and affines, 43, 82–83, 84–85, 88–90; importance of guests at, 35; and wealth, 70
Murphy, William, 126–128

Naga, 30
Nootka, 27–28
Normanby Islanders, 84
Nuba, 63, 80, 116
Nuer, 67, 70, 106, 128–129

Origins: multiple means of contacting, 8, 10–11, 74, 81–82, 114, 175. *See also* Cosmogony

Pabir, 114, 140, 152–153
Parkin, David, 58
Parmentier, Richard, 155
Pintupi, 81, 98
Plants, 30; and cosmology, 192n11.
See also Sacred groves

Political activities: related to cosmological origins, 8, 10–11, 74, 80–82, 101, 102, 114, 175
Political authority: and affines, 70–72, 87–89; and aristocratic marriages, 126; aristocratic monopoly of, 125; and cosmology, 74–75, 99–101, 122
Political centralization: development of, 91, 148–163, 209n8 (*see also* Conquest; Migration); presaged in precentralized societies, 149. *See also* Chiefdoms
Political decentralization, 156
Political economy: and hierarchy, 12
Political legitimation: and cosmology, 63–64, 91, 139 (*see also* Legitimacy); and queen mother, 139–140
Political organization, 121–122; legitimized by affines, 52–53
Positional succession, 199n15, 203n10
Potlatch, 88–90, 199n19
Primacy, 198n9. *See also* Firstborn
Pygmies, 25

Queen mother: as legitimizing affine, 139–140

Rain-making: and chiefship, 137–138, 153–155, 157, 207n15
Rawa, 60, 61
Regalia, 165–166, 171–173
Relics, 154. *See also* Bones
Resources: material, 186n7
Rosaldo, Renato, 97
Rousseau, Jérôme, 114, 135

Sabarl Islanders, 36
Sacred groves, 198n3
Sacrificed retainers, 204n17
Sahlins, Marshall, 57, 193n25, 211n7
Samoa, 117
Seniority, 167, 168, 198n11; as cosmological concept, 75–76; and fission, 209n6

Shilluk, 141–142
Society Islanders, 117
Sora, 25
South Indian hunter-gatherers, 40, 42, 43
Stabilization: cosmic, 164–166
Stone, Andrea, 209n8
Sudest Island, 171
Sumbanese, 189n18
Sumptuary laws, 116–117
Suya, 187n1

Taita, 88
Tallensi, 67, 142
Tanebar-Evav Islanders, 197
Tanimbar, 75, 85, 103, 105, 113, 114, 115, 130–132, 138, 144, 169
Tlingit, 88–90, 116–117, 171–172, 190n1
Tolupan, 99
Townsend, Joan, 152
Trade: and avoidance of affinal ties, 211n11; and access to origins, 166–167, 170–171; and chief-ship, 153, 155, 157
Trobriand Islanders, 62, 119, 136
Tshidi, 62, 138–139
Tsimshian, 18, 19, 113, 144
Tswana, 58
Tuareg, 115
Tubetube, 31–32, 172

Tukano, 29, 81
Turner, Terence, 196n16
Turner, Victor, 66–67, 70, 169
Tutsi, 116

Vanatinai, 28
Viveiros de Castro, Eduardo, 99

Waiwai, 59, 200n10
Wanano, 97, 112
Wape, 61
Wealth: and access to origins, 166, 168–173; and affines, 171, 211n11; and ancestors, 168; and ceremony, 170; chiefly, 166, 168–169; worth of, 172–173. *See also* Bones
Weeks, Kent, 190n2
Wife-givers: aristocracy as, for com-moners, 126–132; and wife-receivers, 102–103, 105–108
Wife-takers: aristocrats as, for com-moners, 132–138; and wife-providers, 103–104, 106
Woodburn, James, 59, 80

Yao, 156–157, 167
Yap, 113, 114

Zinacantan, 97
Zulu, 86